New Proclamation

NEW PROCLAMATION

YEAR B, 1999–2000

ADVENT THROUGH HOLY WEEK

ADVENT/CHRISTMAS

DAVID L. BARTLETT

EPIPHANY

NANCY KOESTER

LENT

K. C. HANSON

HOLY WEEK

GERARD S. SLOYAN

FORTRESS PRESS

MINNEAPOLIS

NEW PROCLAMATION
Year B, 1999–2000
Advent through Holy Week

Scripture quotations, unless otherwise noted, are from the New Revised Standard Version Bible and are copyright © 1989 by the Division of Christian Education of the National Council of Churches in the United States of America and are used by permission.

Cover and book design: Joseph Bonyata
Illustrations: Tanja Butler, *Graphics for Worship,* copyright © 1996 Augsburg Fortress.

ISBN 0-8006-4241-4

The paper used in this publication meets the minimum requirements of American National Standard for Information Sciences—Permanence of Paper for Printed Library Materials, ANSI Z329.48-1984.

Manufactured in the U.S.A.   AF 1-4241

03   02   01   00   99   1   2   3   4   5   6   7   8   9   10

Contents

The Season of Epiphany
Nancy Koester

THE SEASON OF LENT
K. C. HANSON

HOLY WEEK
GERARD S. SLOYAN

PUBLISHER'S FOREWORD

Twenty-five years ago Fortress Press embarked on an ambitious project to produce a lectionary preaching resource that would provide the best in biblical exegetical aids for a variety of lectionary traditions. This resource, *Proclamation,* became both a pioneer and a standard-bearer in its field, sparking a host of similar products from other publishers. Few, however, have become as widely used and well known as *Proclamation.*

Thoroughly ecumenical and built around the three-year lectionary cycle, *Proclamation's* focus has always been on the biblical text first and foremost. Where other resources often have offered canned sermons or illustrations for the preacher to use or adapt, *Proclamation's* authors have always asserted the best resource for the preacher is the biblical text itself. *Proclamation* has always been premised on the idea that those who are well equipped to understand a pericope in both its historical and liturgical context will also be well equipped to compose meaningful and engaging sermons. For that reason, *Proclamation* consistently has invited the cream of North American biblical scholars and homileticians to offer their comments because of their commitments to the text.

New Proclamation represents a significant change in Fortress Press's approach to the lectionary resource, but it still retains the best of the hallmarks that have made it so widely used and appreciated. Long-time users of the series will immediately notice the most major change, that is, the switch from eight to two volumes per year. The volume you are holding covers the lectionary texts for approximately the first half of the church year, from Advent through Holy Week, which culminates with the Great Vigil of Easter. By going to this two-volume format, we are able to offer you a larger, workbook-style page size with a lay-flat binding and plenty of white space for taking notes.

Because the Evangelical Lutheran Church in America adopted the Revised Common Lectionary as its recommended lectionary source several years ago, the lectionary from the Lutheran Book of Worship no longer appears in *New Proclamation*. This allows our authors to write more expansively on each of the texts for each of the three lectionary traditions addressed here. When a text appears in less than all three of these lectionaries or is offered as an alternative text, these are clearly marked as follows: RC (Roman Catholic); RCL (Revised Common Lectionary); and BCP (Episcopal, for Book of Common Prayer).

Although they are not usually used as preaching texts, *New Proclamation* offers brief commentary on each assigned psalm (or, as they are listed, the Responsive Reading) for each preaching day so that the preacher can incorporate reflections on these readings as well in a sermon. Call-out quotes in the margins help signal significant themes in the texts for the day.

New Proclamation retains *Proclamation's* emphasis on the biblical text but offers a new focus on how the preacher may apply those texts to contemporary situations. Exegetical work is more concise, and thoughts on how the text addresses today's world and our personal situations take a more prominent role. Throughout most of the book, exegetical comments are addressed under the heading "Interpreting the Text," and the homiletical materials come under the heading "Responding to the Text." Readers will note, however, that sometimes there is not an easy division between exegesis and application.

Each section of this book is prefaced by a brief introduction that helps situate the liturgical season and its texts within the context of the church year. Unlike *Proclamation,* which was not dated according to its year of publication, this volume of *New Proclamation* is dated specifically for the years 1999–2000 when the texts for Series B next appear. Although preachers may have to work a bit harder to reuse these books in three years' time, they will also find that the books should coordinate better with other dated lectionary materials that they may be using at the same time. When feast or saint's days land on a Sunday (such as the Feast of St. Stephen) in 1999 and 2000, the texts for those days are commented on so that preachers have the option of celebrating those days appropriately. Those traditions that follow the numbering of propers or days in Ordinary Time will find those listed as well.

Other conveniences also appear in *New Proclamation*. Preachers who conduct services at different times on Christmas Eve and Christmas Day will find David L. Bartlett has commented on three different sets of texts that are appropriate for each of those times. Bibliographies and notes accompany most of the sections as well.

For all its changes, *New Proclamation* does not claim to reinvent the preaching lectionary resource. It is, in many ways, a work in progress and readers will see even more helpful changes in future volumes. One thing that has not changed, however, is the commitment to offer preachers access to the ideas of the best biblical scholars and homileticians in North America. David L. Bartlett, Nancy Koester, K. C. Hanson, and Gerard S. Sloyan have each risen to the occasion to address these texts in fresh ways and to make *New Proclamation* truly new. We are grateful to them for their contributions to this new effort.

Appreciation also goes to the panel of preachers and homileticians who served as a focus group for producing *New Proclamation:* Reverend Mary Halvorson (Grace University Lutheran Church, Minneapolis), Reverend Susan Moss (St. James Episcopal, Minneapolis), Father Jim Motl (St. Paul Seminary, St. Paul), Reverend Rob Englund (Lebanon Lutheran Church, Minneapolis), and Dr. Michael Rogness (Luther Seminary, St. Paul). Finally, we wish to express a heartfelt thanks to Julie Odland, whose keen editorial eye and unrelenting dedication have brought this volume to fruition.

THE SEASONS
OF ADVENT
AND
CHRISTMAS

DAVID L. BARTLETT

T HE EXPECTATIONS ADVENT BRINGS ARE TWOFOLD: we await the child in the manger and we await the glorious Son of God returning at the end of time. The first advent foreshadows the second, and the second consummates the first. We probably do well to be as chaste as the Gospels and look toward to the second coming with modest humility: we do not know for certain the signs, or what the gift will look like when it comes. We certainly do well to be as hopeful as the Gospels and proclaim that the first gift we wait for is the gift of God's great reconciliation of humankind—in the one man, Jesus Christ.

The Sundays of Christmas are Sundays of celebration. The familiar narratives and songs are strange and astonishing still. They point us to the mystery of incarnation: above all, the Word incarnate in the flesh, but in a smaller way the Word incarnate in these stories, with their continued power to astonish us and bring us joy.

Preaching is always pastoral. Wise preaching will know that in the season when church declares "Joy," the world declares "Happiness," and the whole culture shouts "Family!" Some will be joyless, some will be sad, and some—not necessarily the same people—will be alone.

Incarnation does not depend on the Christmas buzz for its power. Joy to the world is sometimes joy despite the world. Our preaching will acknowledge that.

We will also attend to the calendar without playing make-believe. We will not pretend that we do not know that for Christians the expectations of the prophets were fulfilled in the manger. Quite properly we may choose not to sing Christmas carols, but we won't pretend we don't know that the day for their singing is just around the corner. We wait and know what we wait for simultaneously, yet are perpetually surprised, perpetually relieved. In our house we have the Advent rituals by which we await God's Son, but we also have the rituals by which we await our sons—coming home from college. Among those rituals, for each son there is the trip to the airport. We know how the ritual will end. The door from the jetway will open, and—always it seems toward the very end of the line of travelers—our son arrives. Yet the certainty of the outcome does not diminish the excitement of the expectation or the joy at its conclusion. This is real waiting and ends with real joy.

So our Advent preaching will not pretend that we do not know how Advent ends. We will not beat our homiletical breasts wondering if the Messiah will ever come. But we will acknowledge that this is always a real wait. However certainly we know that Christmas is the end of that wait, we always greet Christmas—greet Christ—with amazement and delight.

We know (as if our texts did not warn us often enough) that the manger is the beginning of the story, not the end. We welcome him, with guidance from all those chapters of the Gospel (and of the Epistles, and of Acts, and of the life of the church ever since) that help us understand whom we welcome: tiny child, strong teacher, Satan's foe, broken servant, risen Lord. That is whom we welcome, and we will not pretend we don't know that, either.

Without the rest of the story of Jesus' life, this is only a nice birthday tale. With the rest of the story, it is redemption, joy to the world.

> WE KNOW (AS IF OUR TEXTS DID NOT WARN US OFTEN ENOUGH) THAT THE MANGER IS THE BEGINNING OF THE STORY, NOT THE END. ... WITHOUT THE REST OF THE STORY, THIS IS ONLY A NICE BIRTHDAY TALE. WITH THE REST OF THE STORY, IT IS REDEMPTION, JOY TO THE WORLD.

FIRST SUNDAY IN ADVENT

NOVEMBER 28, 1999

REVISED COMMON	EPISCOPAL (BCP)	ROMAN CATHOLIC
Isa. 64:1-9	Isa. 64:1-9a	Isa. 63:16-17, 19; 64:2-7
Ps. 80:1-7, 17-19	Ps. 80 or 80:1-7	Ps. 80:2-4, 15-16, 18-19
1 Cor. 1:3-9	1 Cor. 1:1-9	1 Cor. 1:3-9
Mark 13:24-37	Mark 13:(24-32), 33-37	Mark 13:33-37

A YALE DIVINITY SCHOOL STUDENT preached a splendid sermon remembering the Advent anticipation of his childhood. One way that he and his sister would get themselves ready (I think "psyched up" was the phrase he used) for Christmas was to remember the events of Christmas past: "Remember what you got last year? Remember what we ate last Christmas Eve?"

Remembrance feeds hope. We remember the story in order to celebrate the story anew. More than that, we remember the first Advent to anticipate the second. We remember the prophets because they pointed ahead to the story which is now past but which is always, also, yet to come. We light the candles; we open the windows on the calendars; we open our hearts.

GOSPEL
MARK 13:24-37

The Gospel lesson reminds us that at Advent we await both the coming of the incarnate God in the child of Bethlehem and the glorious Son of Man who will return at the end of time. Although Mark's Gospel lacks infancy narratives, in its own way it declares both the coming of God's Son in history and the return of God's Son at the end of history. As we shall see on the second Sunday in Advent, Mark's Gospel begins with John the Baptist's proclamation that Jesus, the Stronger One, has now begun his ministry—he has entered the realm of human affairs. Jesus' own preaching begins with words that stress the presence and immediacy of God's activity: "The time is filled up, the Kingdom of God is at hand, repent and believe in the Gospel" (Mark 1:14).

Yet throughout the Gospel, and especially in Mark 13, there is the clear reminder that what begins in Galilee will end with the cosmic triumph of Jesus, Messiah, Son of God.

Our passage carries with it all the power and all the promises of apocalyptic literature. The Jesus whom Mark presents predicts the signs that will accompany the end of human history—the woes from which the faithful should flee, the return which the faithful should welcome. Such apocalyptic discourse permeates both Jewish literature of the early centuries of our era and early Christian literature. Works like the extracanonical books of Enoch as well as Revelation are full of apocalyptic tradition—but so are the Gospels and the letters of Paul, perhaps especially 1 Thessalonians.

Apocalyptic literature is subject to abuse. All of us have heard predictions of the end of the world, readings of signs that turn this nation or that into the ancient enemy, promises that this or that historical event is clear evidence that the end is at hand. As we move toward the shift in the millennia, the number of books and pamphlets grows from more to still more, conflicting hermeneutics of astonishing certainty.

Notice how carefully Mark's Gospel cautions us about this kind of cryptographic reading of history. In the first place, Jesus himself warns that no one knows the exact day and hour of the end of time—not the angels and not Jesus himself (Mark 13:32-33).

In the second place, the language of apocalyptic is presented throughout in poetry, in metaphor. We are well aware that in Mark's Gospel when Jesus delivers his first great speech about the Kingdom (chapter four) he speaks in parables. We need to note that in this second great speech about the Kingdom (chapter thirteen) he speaks in parables as well. The fig tree is every bit as much a metaphor for the Kingdom as the mustard seed. The man who goes on the journey is as symbolic a figure as the Sower. (See Mark 13:28 with Mark 4:32; Mark 13:34 with Mark 4:3.)

These images symbolize the clear confidence that God is in charge of history. The worst of circumstances or the most villainous of tyrants cannot outdo or undo God's hand in history. What the images symbolize is the confidence that the shape of history can be discerned in the shape of Jesus Christ. The promise to which history moves is the promise of Jesus Christ, Messiah, Son of God. Whether or not we await him to appear literally on the clouds (an image itself borrowed from Daniel 7), what we are invited to believe at Advent is that history moves toward him. What we find in our lives and in human history is not "a tale told by an idiot, full of sound and fury, signifying nothing" (Shakespeare, *Macbeth,* Act V, scene 5) but a tale told by God, a narrative whose hero is Jesus—a divine comedy that is bound to end in rejoicing.

The whole apocalyptic discourse ends with a parable, again a reminder that to try to read this material as if it presented literal and measurable signs of the end is to misread it. The parable stresses the ethical implications of the life lived in eschatological hope. Notice the power of "as if." It is as if a householder goes away (though God has not gone away). It is as if he leaves his slave in charge (though we are not really in charge). But, we are responsible: "the earth is the Lord's and the fullness thereof," but we are stewards of the earth and servants of the Lord. Apocalyptic hope should not inspire us to slough off, nor to mumble, "What does it matter? It will all end anyway." Apocalyptic hope should inspire us to work and to declare that the glory of Christ is the hope of the world, and that the duty of believers is to live out that hope, wide-awake.

Of course it is not easy to preach this hope at Advent or at any other time. At the celebration of the eucharist or Lord's Supper, Christians make three affirmations: "Christ has died; Christ is risen; Christ will come again." For most congregations today, I suspect, the certainty of the affirmation diminishes as the list continues. Of crucifixion there is no doubt; of resurrection, some; of return, considerable. What can we say to this?

We can affirm that history is in God's hands, and that the shape of history is outlined in the story of Jesus Christ. We can affirm that we all live in expectation, first of our little ends, and finally of the great end when our story and all of history are caught up into the triumph of God. Poetry, music, visual art—all can capture something of that majestic finality. Exposition fails and prediction is time and again disconfirmed. When St. Paul speaks of the apocalyptic conclusion to history he says, "I tell you a mystery." And nothing, not even careful readings of Mark 13, makes it any less mysterious.

We can affirm that we live responsibly. In the light of the end that God writes to each of our lives and the end that God will write to human history, we are to be careful, watchful, and loving. We are to wake up, lest our lives pass us by and we miss them—miss the story, miss our role. We are to wake up, lest history become something that simply happens to us, not the drama we ourselves can help to shape. However modest our stewardship of our own story and of human history, we are called to be alert, be on the watch, take charge.

This Advent season comes at the end of a millennium (whether this December 31 or December 31, 2000 is of course debated). Anticipation always heats up at the turning points of the ages or the centuries. What we as Christians can anticipate is this: In the year 2000, as in every year before, God will be God,

ANTICIPATION ALWAYS HEATS UP AT THE TURNING POINTS OF THE AGES OR THE CENTURIES. WHAT WE AS CHRISTIANS CAN ANTICIPATE IS THIS: . . . IN THE YEAR 2000, AS IN EVERY YEAR BEFORE, WE WILL BE CALLED TO LIVE IN HOPE— RESPONSIBLE FOR OUR RELATIONSHIPS TO ONE ANOTHER, TO GOD, AND TO GOD'S CREATION.

working out his purpose, leading history in the direction of God's Christ. In the year 2000, as in every year before, we will be called to live in hope—responsible for our relationships to one another, to God, and to God's creation.

FIRST READING
ISAIAH 64:1-9

Isaiah 64 lays hold of God's past in order to lay claim on God's future. Many scholars now believe that Isaiah consists of at least two main portions: first Isaiah, the oracles of the eighth-century prophet in Isaiah 1-39, and a later exilic prophet in Isaiah 40-55. The material in Isaiah 56-66 may represent yet a further reflection on God's judgment and mercy during some post-exilic crisis for the people of Judah. It needs to be said that even this division is not always firm: material that seems appropriate to one of the "three" Isaiahs sometimes appears in one of the other Isaiah's sections.

Here, in this section, as is often the case in the later chapters of Isaiah, the prophet or the hymnodist thinks back on the traditions of Israel. The prophet remembers the way in which God used to appear to God's people: "When you did awesome deeds that we did not expect, you came down, the mountains quaked at your presence." Though we cannot be sure, I suspect that the prophet here recalls the great events of the Exodus and Sinai, the mountain where God visited Israel.

The prophet prays that those days might be repeated—that the mountains would quake again, the heavens be opened. In many ways, the prophet prays for the kind of radical divine action that Jesus predicts in Mark 13. The signs and portents of apocalyptic are not for Isaiah primarily signs of threat: they are signs of hope. At least God has not forgotten; at least God is not silent.

Isaiah is quite sure why God has been silent, why in the long period since Sinai and the earlier prophets Israel has been short on signs and portents. It is sin that has turned God from God's people. Because Israel has not called on God, God has not looked on Israel. Israel is silent; God turns away.

The end of the passage is a prayer of hope (again, it moves from past to future). To paraphrase: Remember who you are, O God, the potter and we the clay. Our creator and we your creations. Our sovereign and we your people. Remember your *self*, O God. When you remember yourself you will no longer remember our iniquity.

It is the child pleading to the parent: Remember me. Who I am. Whose I am. It is repentance, but more than that it is longing that we hear in this prophetic word.

The passage helps us better read Mark 13. All these signs and portents are not just the spectacular special effects for a divine show; they are the startling reminders that God still cares. Is there judgment? Of course. Danger? To be sure. But how much better the judgment and danger of God's return than these long years of abysmal silence.

For Mark, Jesus is the end of history's silence (Dorothy Day called her waiting for God *The Long Loneliness*). Through Jesus' ministry in Galilee, the Creator returns to claim the creation, the potter owns the vessels God has made. The promise and terror of the second coming are inseparable from the love that does not let us go, does not let our history go, but returns time and time again to claim us—and will one day once again claim the whole creation.

ISAIAH 63:16-17, 19 (RC)

This, too, is a petition for God's mercy, written out of the context of 2 Isaiah where the people in exile wait and hope for return. The petition really begins with verse 15: "Look down from heaven and see." In a sense, the prophet calls to God behind God. The visible God, the evident God has hardened the hearts of the people. What God did to Pharaoh in Egypt God has now done to God's own people—turned them from faith and penitence. But the prophet calls for the hidden God to remember the covenant, to be a true Father to these people.

The petition includes confession: "We have long been like those whom you do not rule, like those not called by your name." The "like" is important. It is as if Israel is no longer God's people, but the prophet hopes and prays and trusts that this is "as if" only—that in the heart of God the people still belong and that God will indeed remember God's own glory and God's favor to the people.

The oracle provides an astonishingly powerful prayer for Advent. Advent is not only God's new gift, it is the confirmation of the gifts promised of old. In this reading it is not so much that God becomes the Father of God's people in Jesus Christ but that this fatherhood is reestablished, confirmed. We sin (Paul would say this, too) when we do not remember who we are or whose we are. Our true selves are faithful and live under the rule of God; our false selves pretend to be orphans, strangers to God's parenthood and rule. Though it may seem that God has deserted us, we pray to the true God who is ever ready to turn to us.

DAVID L.
BARTLETT

SECOND READING

1 CORINTHIANS 1:1-9 (BCP), 1:3-9 (RCL/RC)

This is one of Paul's great "in the meantime" texts. Mark 13, Isaiah 64, 1 Corinthians 15—all point to the great day coming when God claims for his own history at its consummation. But in the meantime, the church lives out its life. How? In faithfulness and in expectation.

It is these "thanksgiving" sections of the Pauline Epistles where Paul spells out the major themes of the letter to follow. Two themes evident here are crucial to Paul's whole discussion in 1 Corinthians. The first is that faithful people are still waiting for the consummation of history in Christ. We do not yet have all the gifts we shall receive, and if we act as if we have it all, we misunderstand the way in which Christians still live as part of the "not yet"—hoping for a promise not yet fulfilled. The second theme is precisely the stress on the diversity of gifts within the community of faith: the way in which each of us is called to use the gifts that God has given, not in boasting but in mutual service. A single phrase of the thanksgiving sums up the great themes of this letter: "so that you are not lacking in any spiritual gift as you wait for the revealing of our Lord Jesus Christ" (1 Cor. 1:7).

The reading from 1 Corinthians is a healthy reminder that Advent life consists not only in hope and prayer, but also in getting along with each other, trusting in God, building up the fellowship of the faithful, living responsibly—all the gifts and obligation that 1 Corinthians enjoins. The historian Alfred Loisy once said that what Jesus preached was the kingdom and what he got was the church. Loisy thought that was a great falling off, but Paul would not have had a clue what he meant. For Paul, the church was the faithful band of those who live in the kingdom and wait for the kingdom. Living responsibly as the church, as community, is the best possible way to live faithfully in the time of Advent, when we live in expectation but don't get so bogged down in expectation that we forget the gifts of the present.

> THE HISTORIAN ALFRED LOISY ONCE SAID THAT WHAT JESUS PREACHED WAS THE KINGDOM AND WHAT HE GOT WAS THE CHURCH. LOISY THOUGHT THAT WAS A GREAT FALLING OFF, BUT . . . FOR PAUL, THE CHURCH WAS THE FAITHFUL BAND OF THOSE WHO LIVE IN THE KINGDOM AND WAIT FOR THE KINGDOM.

Furthermore, the promise in 1 Corinthians is absolutely clear: though we wait for God we do not wait without God. The one who strengthens us until the final revelation is the same one who is indeed revealed to us in the gifts of every day: worship, service, love of thy neighbor, answer to prayer. The one for whom we wait strengthens us in the waiting; the one to whom we journey accompanies us on the way.

RESPONSIVE READING
PSALM 80

This psalm follows a pattern that will become familiar to us as we look at the psalms assigned for Advent. The psalmist remembers a better time when God showed mercy on God's people. The psalmist bemoans the present age as a time when God seems absent. The psalmist prays for God to show mercy once again. The prayer for God's help recurs time and again in a kind of refrain, in variations (vv. 3, 7, 19).

The better time was the time of the exodus and the planting in Canaan, with the image of the vine used as a symbol of Israel itself (see Isaiah 5; Jeremiah 12; Matthew 20; Mark 12; Luke 20). The present time is marked not only by God's absence but by the slings and arrows of marauding nations, and by the sad fact that Israel has become a laughing stock: "You make us the scorn of our neighbors; our enemies laugh among themselves."

God will provide, we hope and pray, but now God has provided tears for bread and drink. God will redeem them from surrounding peoples, hopes Israel, but now God makes them a laughingstock to their neighbors.

The psalmist prays both for God to look to the divine reputation and to remember the better days of yore. The psalmist beseeches God in prayers fit for Advent:

- Restore us, O God. (vv. 3, 7, 19)
- Let your face shine that we may be saved. (vv. 7, 19)
- Turn again. (v. 14)

Look after your own, O God, the psalmist prays. Planter of vines, look after the vine you have planted. Shepherd of Israel, look to your flock.

These are Advent prayers, prayers fulfilled in the ministry of Jesus that Mark announces. God claiming God's own, the shepherd coming to lead the sheep (see Mark 14:28). Prayers to be fulfilled in the second coming of the Son of Man: when the fig tree sends forth buds, pray God, the vineyard will bear fruit again. God's light shine in the darkness. God's face turn to God's people. Advent.

PRAYER

Because you have already come among us, we wait for you, O Christ, in confidence and hope. We wait for your coming at Christmas, confident that the promise of old will be made new—of peace on earth and goodwill among humankind. We wait for your coming at the end of the ages, knowing that in you

DAVID L.
BARTLETT

God moves history toward its consummation. Yet sometimes the signs of your coming are obscure and hope grows dim. Strengthen us, we pray, by your Spirit and illuminate our minds and hearts that we may await you eagerly and preach your word with gladness. In your holy name, Amen.

SECOND SUNDAY IN ADVENT

DECEMBER 5, 1999

REVISED COMMON	EPISCOPAL (BCP)	ROMAN CATHOLIC
Isa. 40:1-11	Isa. 40:1-11	Isa. 40:1-5, 9-11
Ps. 85:1-2, 8-13	Ps. 85 or 85:7-13	Ps. 85:8-14
2 Peter 3:8-15a	2 Peter 3:8-15a, 18	2 Peter 3:8-14
Mark 1:1-8	Mark 1:1-8	Mark 1:1-8

THE PASSAGES FOR THE DAY ALL HELP US TO LOOK AHEAD. The Old Testament prophets as well as the New Testament prophet, John the Baptist, keep us focused on what God does and intends to do. Christians believe that this intention is acted out in Jesus Christ. There is an ongoing host of witnesses: Isaiah points to John who points to Jesus. The Psalm and 2 Peter, in their own quite different ways, remind believers not to lose heart, not to lose hope. God is faithful; we can count on that.

GOSPEL
MARK 1:1-8

Having pointed us to Christ's second Advent, the Gospel reading for this Sunday brings us back to the first Advent as Mark presents it to us. It is commonplace that Mark's Gospel lacks any of the birth narratives we associate with the beginning of Jesus' story. Mark begins at the beginning of Jesus' ministry—more exactly, Mark begins with the necessary preparation for Jesus' ministry.

The opening line, the title, gives us the information the entire Gospel will interpret for us: This Jesus is Messiah (Christ); this Jesus is Son of God. This Jesus is Messiah, and therefore the heir to all the promises of Israel. This Jesus is Son of God, and therefore God's chosen one, not for Israel alone but for all people. (Some early manuscripts lack the phrase "Son of God," but the best evidence suggests that we should include it.) We wonder what the first readers or hearers of this Gospel thought when they heard those two titles for Jesus. We know how easy it is for us to miss the oddity of Mark's claim. In Mark we have a Messiah who is most notable for his humility (Mark 11:1-11) and we have a Son of God who shows his sonship most when he confesses that he feels abandoned by his Father (Mark 15:33-39). Perhaps in Advent it is too soon (in the church year, in Mark's Gospel) to begin to spell out these claims—but it is hard to read Mark without knowing that the shadow of the cross falls even on the first verses of the story.

When Mark says that this is "the beginning of the good news of Jesus Christ," does he mean that this verse is the beginning of the good news, or that his entire book, 1—16:7, is the beginning? If the latter, then the whole book is the first chapter of a Gospel that lived on in the lives of first-century "followers of the Way" and continues to live on in the lives of twenty-first-century Christians, too. The second Sunday in Advent is a way of marking the beginning of that beginning. (Mark 16:8 is the end of the beginning but a new beginning as well.)

The good news of Jesus Christ is both the good news about Jesus Christ (of which Mark's Gospel is full) and the good news that Jesus Christ preaches, first in Mark 1:14, but again in the parables of chapter 4 and the apocalypse of chapter 13—indeed throughout the book.

Mark provides two guides to Jesus' ministry, or two doors that believers need to pass through before they can find the Son of God. We come to Jesus only through the Old Testament, and we come to Jesus only through John the Baptist. Mark begins with a quotation claimed to be from Isaiah, but which in fact includes a bit from Exodus and a bit from Malachi as well. Mark is not unduly scrupulous about citing his exact sources—but it is clear that he believes that prophecy points to Jesus. The fact that this earliest Gospel can only begin with the Old Testament is a strong reminder to us Christians that there is no way to Jesus that does not lead through the Torah and the Prophets. Even Paul, who has the most complicated understanding of the relationship of Hebrew Scripture to the Christian story, can describe that understanding only by quoting that Scripture. One of the earliest Christian heresies was that of Marcion who thought you could simply scrap the Old Testament (and much of the New) to get Jesus unencumbered by the past. Mark will have none of it; the past is not encumbrance, it is prologue, overture, opening.

The little snatch that the late Marvin Pope once cited in a sermon sums up the tension and the promise nicely: "How odd of God to choose the Jews" (not that Jews are especially odd; just that it's odd for God to choose). He added (as Mark would have understood): "It was because his Son was one." There is no way to Jesus apart from the prophets and Moses and the people of Israel.

And there is no way to approach Jesus except through John the Baptist. We may think that as Advent arrives we can turn to gentle Jesus meek and mild (though that Messiah is hard to find anywhere in Mark's Gospel), but the fact that John the Baptist points the way, and leads the way, makes it hard for us to ignore the harshness, the toughness of the message. John begins with the baptism of repentance for the forgiveness of sins and reminds us that Advent, like Lent, is a time of preparation. We prepare by letting go of what holds us down—above all those sins and transgressions we carry like old luggage. Only when we lay it down by the real or figurative river side of repentance and hope are we freed at last.

John is clothed like and acts like Elijah, and it is clear throughout Mark's Gospel that John is really Elijah returned to prepare the way for the Messiah (as some Jewish speculation thought he would). Elijah is the one who prepares for the end of time, so the beginning of Advent (and the beginning of this Gospel) is not just the beginning of the beginning; it is the beginning of the end. Mark 1 points to Mark 13. The Son who comes is the Son who will come as well. Baptism in water will be baptism with fire.

Karl Barth suggested that the role of the preacher is that of John the Baptist: never to point to ourselves, always to point to him. We are called to be witnesses, and pray to be as faithful and humble as John.

First Reading
ISAIAH 40:1-11

The material is almost certainly from second Isaiah, from the time of exile. The promise of a way through the wilderness is a promise of its own kind of reversal. Those who came out of Zion into bondage will return to Zion in joy. Gospel is always news of return—whether Isaiah preaches it, or John, or Jesus. Advent is always the time when we look toward home.

When Mark quotes Isaiah 40:3 we notice that he punctuates the text differently than the NRSV does (and almost certainly differently than the intentions of the first texts of Isaiah). Mark says: "A voice cries in the wilderness, 'Prepare the way of the Lord.'" Isaiah probably meant: "A voice cries, 'In the wilderness, prepare the way of the Lord.'"

> ADVENT, LIKE LENT, IS A TIME OF PREPARATION. WE PREPARE BY LETTING GO OF WHAT HOLDS US DOWN—ABOVE ALL THOSE SINS AND TRANSGRESSIONS WE CARRY LIKE OLD LUGGAGE. ONLY WHEN WE LAY IT DOWN BY THE REAL OR FIGURATIVE RIVER SIDE OF REPENTANCE AND HOPE ARE WE FREED AT LAST.

Though Mark may confuse Isaiah's understanding of wilderness, his Gospel confirms Isaiah's understanding of the message. What Isaiah calls "comfort" Mark calls "good news—gospel," and from first to last Mark's Gospel provides the good news of the comfort of God. (In Isaiah 40:9 it is Zion who proclaims the Gospel.)

The comfort of God is that the world will be turned upside down. Valleys lifted up and mountains brought low. The afflicted comforted and the comforted afflicted. Anonymous little people saved through faith while important big people (both Pharisees and disciples) are caught in terrible muddles.

The comfort of God is that God's word will abide forever. The word that God speaks to and through the prophet abides forever. But also, the word that God speaks through John the Baptizer, and especially the word that God speaks through Jesus, will abide forever. Parables, promises, hard injunctions outlast human flesh. Mark says that what he writes is the beginning of the gospel (Mark 1:1). Therefore the words that Mark records and passes on outlast Mark's generation and the generations to come, and as we move toward the third millennium (grass withering and flower fading), God's breath still moves across the creation and across the church, and God's word not only endures, it prevails.

The comfort of God is that God is both king and shepherd, sovereign and guide. In Mark's Gospel the king is Jesus the Crucified One, who is also God's own son. In Mark's Gospel the shepherd is Jesus, the one who gathers the lost and the sinners to himself (see Mark 6:34; 14:27).

When we read the Gospel and the prophet together, the prophet provides a commentary on the Gospel's good news: Here is what God has promised; here is what comfort looks like; here is where comfort comes, in Jesus Christ.

Second Reading
2 PETER 3:8-18

Second Peter 3:8-10 indicates that the problem of the delay of Christ's return is hardly a recent development. Already by the time of this letter, Peter, or more likely someone writing in Peter's name, finds a way to demythologize apocalyptic expectation. On the one hand, it looks a little like an evasion, to say that words do not mean what words mean and that God's language is a code. "One day = a thousand years." By this standard we are just coming up on the end of the second day after Christ, so no wonder the return is delayed. More accurately, and helpful, the epistle reminds us that the language of return is metaphorical and that God deals in mystery, not obfuscation but wonder and amazement, and we should not wonder or be amazed that the time has not yet come.

My own guess is that the earliest generation of Christians thought that Christ would come again very soon—and they believed that quite literally. By the time this letter is written it is impossible to believe literally what the first generation believed. So 2 Peter has to do what we have to do: find a meaning subtler and deeper behind the particular predictions. When I preach apocalyptic I do what 2 Peter does not; I say that early Christian expectations were wrong in important respects and right in more important ones. How you will preach such texts depends, of course, on your theology, your doctrine of biblical inspiration, and your congregation. All of us can agree that the timeline was not the main motif of apocalyptic, though it was important enough that 2 Peter's audience has been grumbling its disappointment.

What 2 Peter urges is his own version of the apocalyptic responsibility we saw last week at the end of Mark 13. Steadfast hope for this epistle issues in holiness, godliness, stability. Not, perhaps, the most exciting of virtues, but in our fragmented and fractious age not to be despised. As in all those sermons where we heap praise on the prodigal son and then in the announcements that follow ask all the holy, godly, and stable elder brothers and sisters in the congregation to help us meet our goals for the pledge campaign—or take their turn at the soup kitchen. Second Peter is an epistle for elder brothers and sisters, praising the virtues of those who stay at home. The hope that all will repent is the appropriate hope of the faithful for the wayward who are as yet outside the community of faith.

RESPONSIVE READING
PSALM 85:1-13

Here is the pattern we saw in Psalm 80 (and in Isaiah 64) but with an important addition. Again the psalmist (like the prophet) remembers with gratitude God's former mercies. My guess here is that this is a remembrance of the return from the Babylonian exile, so in a sense the claim is even stronger than that of Psalm 85. Not just "Remember when you loved us in our innocence," but remember how previously you forgave us of our sins. It is a pattern appropriate for the twofold hope of Advent. We look forward to Christ but we also remember him, that mercy we knew in his ministry, death, and resurrection. We have wandered far astray from that hope with which we began: may we not be forgiven and restored again? Is that not part of the hope of second Advent?

> WE HAVE WANDERED FAR ASTRAY FROM THAT HOPE WITH WHICH WE BEGAN: MAY WE NOT BE FORGIVEN AND RESTORED AGAIN? IS THAT NOT PART OF THE HOPE OF SECOND ADVENT?

Restoration has apparently not been all that the people had hoped. Again the psalmist notes God's apparent absence, or at least the signs of God's wrath: "Will you be angry with us forever?" (85:5).

Again there is the prayer for restoration. "Will you not revive us again? Show us your steadfast love. . . . Grant us your salvation" (vv. 6, 7).

Artur Weiser, the Old Testament scholar, notes that the tension between joy in God's past actions and sorrow at the present state of the people is a tension and not a contradiction:

If man's eyes are entirely focused on the reality of God, as in verses 1–3, then he is confronted with the abundant riches of the divine grace on the ground of a faith that possesses that grace . . . but if his eyes are fixed on the actual state of affairs in the world that surrounds him, then he perceives the distance that separates human reality from divine reality and his faith becomes one that is waiting for God's grace. . . . The New Testament saying, "I believe; help my unbelief" testifies to the same tension (Weiser, 573).

What is different here from either Psalm 80 or Isaiah 64 is the assurance, the promise that God will indeed "speak peace to his people." Not only the Advent prayer but the Advent promise is foreshadowed. The psalmist says that *chesed* (that great Hebrew word that comes close to Paul's Greek word for "grace") and faithfulness or truthfulness will greet each other; righteousness and peace, *shalom,* will kiss each other. *Shalom* brings the greeting of "Shalom!" God's attributes are active and they interact. So, also, in Jesus Christ God's attributes come together and come among us—in the astonishing attributes of Jesus, whom we await at this season.

The psalm reminds us of our liturgies; perhaps it is liturgical. Begin with an invocation of the goodness and majesty of God. Confess your sins in the light of that majesty. Pray God's forgiveness for your sins. Rejoice in the words of assurance.

The shape of the liturgy reflects the shape of our Advent hope. Remembering the goodness of God we await the goodness of God—in penitence and confidence. "Show us your steadfast love, O God, and grant us your salvation."

Kenneth Scott Latourette, the great historian of missions, used to recall the darkest days of his life when he nearly lost all faith in God and in himself. What saved him was the memory of his father, a man in whom God's goodness and steadfastness had been evident. Remembering the goodness of the past, he was able at last to trust in God's goodness for the future. That is Advent hope, too.

PRAYER

Gracious God, it is not always easy to come into the presence of your Son. We know the mercy that we find in him, but we know the demands as well—the call to repent, to reform, to shape our lives anew in the light of his harsh goodness. Grant us not to grow too complacent or too lazy to follow in his way. And when we preach, let us not be so quick to please that we fail to speak the truth of Christ's demand, as well as the fullness of his grace. In his name we pray. Amen.

THIRD SUNDAY IN ADVENT

DECEMBER 12, 1999

REVISED COMMON	EPISCOPAL (BCP)	ROMAN CATHOLIC
Isa. 61:1-4, 8-11	Isa. 65:17-25	Isa. 61:1-2, 10-11
Psalm 126	Psalm 126	Luke 1:46-50, 53-54
or Luke 1:47-55		
1 Thess. 5:16-24	1 Thess. 5:(12-15), 16-28	1 Thess. 5:16-24
John 1:6-8, 19-28	John 1:6-8, 19-28	John 1:6-8, 19-28
	or 3:23-30	

"WITNESS" IS A GOOD WORD FOR MUCH OF THE Christian life. Witnesses see or hear, and witnesses bear testimony, and witnesses finally stake their lives on what they see and what they say. In Luke's Gospel, Mary becomes a witness to the mercy of God in her son, and in all the Gospels, John the Baptist is a witness to the one who comes after him and is greater than he. The Psalms bear witness, not just the witness of an individual writer, but the witness of the people who could sing of joy even in the time of tears. Paul became a great witness, speaking out of his faith to the faith of brand-new Christians, encouraging them, urging them not to lose heart.

Do not lose heart. That is a strong and good message for Advent. All the trappings in the stores and in our homes do not guarantee joy. We cannot even promise Christmas cheer. We can promise Christ, God's courage and God's joy (despite all sorrow). We do not lose heart.

DO NOT LOSE HEART. THAT IS A STRONG AND GOOD MESSAGE FOR ADVENT. ALL THE TRAPPINGS IN THE STORES AND IN OUR HOMES DO NOT GUARANTEE JOY. WE CANNOT EVEN PROMISE CHRISTMAS CHEER. WE CAN PROMISE CHRIST, GOD'S COURAGE AND GOD'S JOY (DESPITE ALL SORROW).

RESPONSIVE READING
LUKE 1:47-55 (RC)

The RCL provides portraits of two witnesses to the coming of Jesus, Messiah—the portrait of Mary and the portrait of John the Baptizer.

It is a little odd that the reading from Luke begins with Luke 1:47 and ends with verse 55. We get the speech without the speaker, or the song without the singer, and the song itself is displaced from its narrative context. There is some textual confusion about whether in the earliest versions of Luke the person who sang the Magnificat was Elizabeth or Mary, but the best evidence points to Mary—as do centuries of tradition. The verse that closes the paragraph, "And Mary remained with [Elizabeth] three months and then returned to her home," reminds us that the song is part of a story, the story of promise and fulfillment. We will get more of the story as Christmas approaches, but there is no harm in reminding the congregation of the context of the song even now. The God who fills the hungry with good things has filled the barren Elizabeth with the child of her hopes and the virgin Mary with the child of everyone's hope.

This is a God who turns the world upside down, but in this narrative the upside-down world begins with our expectations about childbirth. One woman conceives a child too late and the other too soon. Except, of course, that our "too lates" and "too soons" are just the right time for God.

The use of the past tense in Mary's song seems odd at first until we see that this, too, is a matter of God's own timetable. Our "too lates" and "too soons" vanish before the promise of what is bound to happen because in the determination of God it has already happened. Traditional values and commonplace powers are turned upside down because God has promised it. Traditional values and commonplace powers are also turned upside down in a revolution that Mary herself embodies. Notice that it is a woman bearing an illegitimate child who first proclaims or sings the good news in Luke's Gospel.

A seminary student from Ghana, also named Mary, preached on the Magnificat and caught something of its meaning: "Think of it," she said, "I who am poor am given money to study for ministry. I who am African am invited to come to America. I who am a woman am called to be a minister of Jesus Christ. My soul doth magnify the Lord."

Our version of time is challenged and corrected by Advent promise. To us (as to first-century hearers) Abraham seems long ago and social justice seems far away. Mary sees the whole history with a God's-eye view: Abraham and the baby to be born, and our present and the world's future are caught in the great scope of a hymn.

It is a hymn; the rhythms and the rhetoric are that of the Psalms. Not only the content but the form reminds us. The prayers that the people of Israel have prayed for all these years are being fulfilled: the Mighty One has done great things.

No wonder all generations (Protestant and Catholic and Orthodox alike) rightly call Mary blessed. She is blessed as all the heroines and heroes of the faith are blessed, because God has chosen her and named her and commissioned her.

JOHN 1:6-8, 19-28

God has also chosen and named and commissioned John the Baptizer. In John's Gospel, as in the synoptic Gospels, John helps point to Jesus. Only here that part of his mission is the whole of his mission. Who is John the Baptizer? He is the one who points to Jesus. John the Baptizer is not primarily baptizer in the Fourth Gospel. He is witness.

Scholars rightly suspect, I think, that at the time John's Gospel was written there were still Baptists active in the communities for which John wrote. Not Christian Baptists but real Baptists, followers of John the Baptizer, who must have thought that Jesus was a kind of Jesus-come-lately. And they remembered that their hero had baptized Jesus after all and not vice-versa; that is why John's Gospel never mentions Jesus being baptized at all. It might imply Jesus' subordination to the one who baptized him. That's why John's affirmation sounds oddly like a negation. When the priests and Levites ask, "Who are you?" what he says is, "Here's who I'm not. I'm not the Messiah." Note, too, that for John's Gospel, John the Baptizer is not Elijah, as he surely is for Mark. The whole sense of apocalyptic expectation shifts in John's Gospel, and perhaps John does not sense the need for the forerunner, Elijah, to appear at the last of days.

Though John does not pick up on the synoptic theme of John's baptizing Jesus, he does, like Mark, remind us that John points to one who is greater than he: "I am not worthy to untie the thong of his sandal." In the verse that succeeds our section, John the witness makes clear the greatness of the one who comes after him. It is not (as in Mark) that Jesus baptizes with the Holy Spirit, but that he is the Lamb of God who takes away the sins of the world. Does the Fourth Gospel remember that John claimed the baptism of repentance for the forgiveness of sins—and claim that it is not baptism that takes away our sins, but the Lamb lifted up upon the cross?

The witnesses point to him: the baby who will come in the manger yet throw kings and dominions from their thrones. The Nazarene who is greater than John the Baptizer and who will bear the sins of the whole world on the cross: take them up and take them away as well.

Here it is Advent and we keep wanting to rush to the baby in Bethlehem, as well we should; but we are not allowed to forget that the baby at Bethlehem has come to turn the world upside down and to bear the world's sins on the cross. The old medieval lyric about Christ's nativity began: "Who is this

> HERE IT IS ADVENT AND WE KEEP WANTING TO RUSH TO THE BABY IN BETHLEHEM, BUT WE ARE NOT ALLOWED TO FORGET THAT THE BABY AT BETHLEHEM HAS COME TO TURN THE WORLD UPSIDE DOWN AND TO BEAR THE WORLD'S SINS ON THE CROSS.

stupendous stranger?" The Advent texts remind us that he is strange, different, surprising—and stupendous, too.

JOHN 3:23-30 (BCP)

Here is another image for John the Baptist as the one who prepares the way for Jesus. Not only is he "not-Messiah," he is "not-bridegroom." At the great celebratory wedding where God marries God's people, John is not the groom but the best man. He raises a toast to the happy couple. More than that (shifting the imagery somewhat), the one who until now has proclaimed listens, the one who has borne witness becomes a witness.

The passage provides a rich picture of the meaning of Christ's coming: it fulfills the ancient prophecies that God will claim his people as a groom claims a bride (see Isa. 62:5; Jer. 2:2; Hosea 2:16-20). It may also point ahead to chapter 2 in John's Gospel where Jesus is the host at a wedding where new wine fills the old jars. What we see in Jesus is new, but not brand new. The old vision comes to completion: the celebration of the wedding feast begins.

First Reading
ISAIAH 61:1-4, 8-11 (RCL),
61:1-2, 10-11 (RC)

The first verses are the passage that Luke has Jesus read in the synagogue at the beginning of his ministry—Luke 4:16-21. In its original context, the passage almost certainly pointed to the return of the people from exile and the restoration of a blessed community in the homeland. Yet it is not only the promise that those who return will be blessed, there is also the promise that the nations will see in their return a sign of the enduring promises of God—the covenant that cannot be broken.

It is the Spirit of the Lord that confirms this proclamation of good news—perhaps for the prophet, perhaps for an anonymous servant to whom the prophet points. In the Greek translation of the passage, what the servant does is precisely to "preach good news," to "evangelize."

In one sense, this is always God's promise, to bring those who are in exile to their homes and to recompense them against oppressors. For some modern Jews, much of this promise is on its way to being fulfilled in the land of Israel. For Christians (who are bound to read the text with Luke's Gospel in mind), God has sent a servant whose gifts are more astonishing even than those the prophet dreamed. In Jesus (as we have seen time and again) the standards of the world are reversed: the oppressed are liberated and the captives freed and the downtrodden lifted up. The final image is like that in John 3 (though denominationally most of us do not get both John 3 and Isaiah 61 this week). Israel is both bride and groom; God weds the people to Godself.

ISAIAH 65:17-25 (BCP)

Here is another prophecy of promise, if anything, even more fulsome than the promise of Isaiah 61. When the people return there will be a new city, a city of economic justice where people do not labor for the sake of foreign absentee landlords. But there will also be a new heaven and a new earth, long lives for humankind, harmony within the created world. The vision is one of absolute peace, *shalom,* beyond anything the world could give or take away. If we read the passage in conjunction with the passages assigned from John, we can suggest that the fulfillment to which John points, the fulfillment that comes in Jesus, will one day claim the whole world that the Word created. Christ's peace will fill the cosmos.

SECOND READING
1 THESSALONIANS 5:12-28

Paul writes the first letter to the Thessalonians to provide guidance and comfort in the light of a particular situation. Members of the Thessalonian community have been dying, and this surprises their fellow believers who have been confident that Christ would return quickly, probably even before any of these first believers will have died. The Thessalonians may have heard some assurance such as Mark 13:30: "Truly I tell you, this generation will not pass away until these things have taken place." Now "this generation" is beginning to pass away, and the Thessalonians do not know what to believe. Some of them are losing heart. In chapter 4 and the first part of chapter 5, Paul assures the Thessalonians that those who have died will not be left out of the great day of Christ's return. On the contrary, they will first be raised from the dead and taken to Christ. Only after that will living believers be gathered into Christ's heavenly reign.

Whatever we believe about the literal scenario (a cry, an archangel, a trumpet, Christ on the clouds), the comfort here is really an Advent comfort. It is a dramatization of what Paul says more poetically in Romans 8: "Neither death nor life will be able to separate us from the love of God in Christ Jesus our Lord." For Paul and for the early church this is an eschatological promise, a promise about the last act of God's drama with humankind. At Advent we anticipate that last act, and 1 Thessalonians helps us wait with hope.

Yet, like Jesus in Mark 13, Paul insists that hope carries with it responsibility. The verses assigned by the lectionary for this week are the reminders of what faithful life looks like in the light of Advent hope. The relationship between responsibility and hope is made explicit in 1 Thessalonians 5:23b: "and may your spirit and soul and body be kept sound and blameless at the coming of our Lord Jesus Christ."

Paul suggests several marks of the obedience of Advent faith. There is concern for what we can call roughly church order. The Thessalonians are to respect those who are appointed as leaders. They are to listen carefully to those who claim to be inspired to speak Christian prophecy, but they are not to be gullible. Every spirit should be tested. Is this congruent with our faith? Will this add to the increase of charity and compassion? Those who are doing their share of work in the community should encourage, maybe even nag, the lazy into taking fuller responsibility. Maybe the reason for this laziness has been the faith that Jesus will return soon, so there's no point in working hard. Maybe that has been the rationalization. In any case, for Paul, as for the Gospels, the imminent return of Christ is not the reason for laziness but all the more reason for arduous labor.

Another set of injunctions has to do with the life of the spirit, with piety. Rejoicing, praying, giving thanks. The life of prayer is not separate from the life of action. Like Brother Lawrence (1605–91), these earliest communities of faith are to pray when they sweep the house and bake the bread and make decisions for the life of the church. All is prayer; all is thanks. This is obviously a good word for our Advent hope. What is life like as we await Christmas? All is prayer. All is thanks.

Further, there is a set of injunctions that has to do with getting along with the neighbor, both the neighbor in the church and the neighbor outside the church. We are reminded of the Sermon on the Mount, the Sermon on the Plain, Paul himself in the more familiar exhortations of Romans 12 and 13. Do not repay evil with evil, but seek the good of everyone—even of those outside the church who threaten you, even of those inside the church who annoy you. Put negatively, Christians are to abstain from every evil—including the evil that seeks to revenge wrongs against the faithful themselves.

Second coming or no second coming, this seems too much to ask. As always with Paul, along with the directions comes the promise, the prayer. He prays that the God of peace will make these saints what they are: holy. All the injunctions are framed within the profound hope of the Gospel. Christ has come; Christ will come again. In the time between, the God of peace strengthens us, enables us. At Advent we are able to hope for the one who is to come only because He is also already here, present in our praying, present in our hoping.

The final benediction is not only a formula, it is the profound promise which drives all of Paul's ministry: "The grace of our Lord Jesus Christ be with you." Christ who has come; Christ who is to come; Christ who is present even now.

RESPONSIVE READING

PSALM 126

Here it is again, the threefold movement of the Advent Psalms: God did great things for us in the past. God has turned from us. Pray God, turn to us again. And here is the assurance—God will turn to us again.

In its context in the Psalter, this is one of the Psalms of Ascent, and it may indeed have been written or at least been used as part of the liturgy of pilgrims on their way to Jerusalem for one of the great festivals.

The dating of these psalms is notoriously difficult, but the first verses suggest that this psalm was written some time after the return from the exile of the Babylonian captivity as part of some other crisis in the life of the people. As in the other psalms, part of the issue is God's reputation. In the old days when God had restored God's people, everybody knew it; everybody paid attention. Implicit is the plea: All right, God, honor your own name. Gain back your glory.

> THE FINAL BENEDICTION IS NOT ONLY A FORMULA, IT IS THE PROFOUND PROMISE WHICH DRIVES ALL OF PAUL'S MINISTRY: "THE GRACE OF OUR LORD JESUS CHRIST BE WITH YOU." CHRIST WHO HAS COME; CHRIST WHO IS TO COME; CHRIST WHO IS PRESENT EVEN NOW.

In keeping with the hopes of the Advent season, it is also clear that the glory God will gain will be for the sake not only of Israel but of the nations as well; the gentiles, too, will be amazed at the greatness of the Lord.

Two stunning images describe the dilemma and suggest the hope. The psalm is almost parabolic in its use of description. The Negeb is that dry part of the desert that remains lifeless and barren month after month, till the waters come suddenly, and then, streams and rivers! The psalmist writes out of the dryness and prays for God's rain, God's reign. And then the striking contrast between sowing and reaping, weeping and shouting for joy. Implicit is the claim that, as sowing and reaping go together, so do weeping and shouting. No reaping without sowing; no joy without lament. But now, the psalmist prays and hopes, now is the great turning point. The harvest is on the way; rejoicing is just around the corner. It is a hope appropriate to any Advent, but especially to those Advents when, as St. Augustine says, we have become to ourselves "as a barren land."

> "Those who go out weeping, bearing the seed for sowing,
> shall come home with shouts of joy!" (*The Confessions*)

They come home with shouts of joy because the harvest has come, full, rich, bountiful, overflowing. Like the gift of the manger; like the gift of history's ending in the joy of God. The gifts for which Advent hopes and prays.

James Luther Mays suggests that the contrast between sowing and reaping, and tears and shouts of joy may relate to the Near Eastern fertility myths where harvest included both the death of a fertility god and his revival. Israel, of course, reshapes the myth as an affirmation of hope in the one God. In Advent we may hear the psalm in yet another context where, as Mays suggests, "those who move toward Christmas . . . with the 'tears of repentance and need' may enter into the joy" of the season (Mays, 400).

In his imaginative life of the real saint, Godric, Frederick Buechner suggests that Godric's cry of faith sustained him as it can sustain us: "All's lost; all's found."

PRAYER

Most of the time, O God, we are comfortable with the way the world is. We are among your comfortable people, and the thought of a world turned upside down upsets us, too. Open us to your surprises, even the uncomfortable surprises. May we be ready for the demands that are also mercies, and for the gift that gives new life, to us and to your creation. Through Christ our Lord, Amen.

FOURTH SUNDAY IN ADVENT

DECEMBER 19, 1999

REVISED COMMON	EPISCOPAL (BCP)	ROMAN CATHOLIC
2 Sam. 7:1-11, 16	2 Sam. 7:4, 8-16	2 Sam. 7:1-5, 8-11, 16
Luke 1:47-55	Ps. 132 or 132:8-15	Ps. 89:2-5, 27, 29
or Ps. 89:1-4, 19-26		
Rom. 16:25-27	Rom. 16:25-27	Rom. 16:25-27
Luke 1:26-38	Luke 1:26-38	Luke 1:26-38

SERVANTHOOD, OBEDIENCE, AND FAITHFULNESS are the themes for this Sunday. Appropriately we focus not only on the promises of Advent but on our response to those promises. Mary acts faithfully and trusts in the word of the Lord. David receives the covenant and (we hope) struggles toward obedience. Paul tells the Romans that faith—the gift he loves to preach—requires obedience, too.

These are great servants of the Lord—Mary, David, Paul. But we, too, are called into service, and as the time of Christmas draws near we appropriately ask not just, "What does the Lord give to us?" but also "What does the Lord require of us?"

GOSPEL
LUKE 1:26-38

Our lectionary text moves the story backward. Last week in the RCL we heard Mary's song the Magnificat. Now we get the saying that inspires her song, the Annunciation.

Begin with the end of the passage, Mary's faith: "Here I am, the servant of the Lord, let it be with me according to your word." "Here I am"—the words of Abraham to the God who calls him to the mountain (Gen. 22:1); the words of Moses to the voice that calls him from the burning bush; the words that Samuel speaks when the Lord calls him (1 Sam. 3:4); the words of Isaiah the prophet sent forth by the vision (Isa. 6:8).

Mary has faith in the giver, of course, in the promise that God provides through the angel. Angels, TV notwithstanding, are messengers; their job is to deliver a message, and their role is always strictly subservient to the One who sends the message. People in the Bible aren't touched by angels, they are addressed by angels—a way of being addressed by God without having to confront God's glory head-on. "Let it be with me according to your word" is a statement of absolute faith that what God wills is right and that the business of the faithful is to accede and obey.

Implicitly, of course, Mary also has faith in the gift—in this child who will be her child. She receives a twofold promise. Jesus is a King who will inhabit the throne of his ancestor David (though the Davidic ancestry is traced through Joseph)—that is, Jesus is the fulfillment of God's promises to Israel. But Jesus is also the Son of the Most High of whose kingdom there will be no end. That means that Jesus' rule extends not only forever but infinitely in all directions. That is to say it is not the kingdom of Israel only but the re-invention of the whole creation, God's kingdom on earth as in heaven.

Presumably Mary does not fully understand the scope of the promise. After all these years, we do not fully understand the scope of the promise. But she hears the word, knows that it is a word about her, and says, "So be it."

That Mary is a virgin fulfills early Christian reading of the prophecy of Isaiah 7 (though the Christian reading may depend on the Septuagint translation of the Hebrew, which probably refers to a young maiden rather than a virgin). Here, in this birth, only the unpredictable can be predicted. A woman bears a child without having intercourse with a man. So, too, the reference to Elizabeth reminds us that God is acting surprisingly—Elizabeth should be too old to conceive, yet she too will bear a son. The natural order is turned upside down. In the Magnificat which will follow (and which was read in many of our churches on the third Sunday in Advent), the social order is turned upside down. Rulers topple from their thrones and people of low degree are lifted up.

So this maiden who has no claim to fame except a visitation dares name herself a servant of the Lord—like Abraham (Gen. 26:24), like Moses (Exod. 3:7), like Samuel (1 Sam. 3:9), like Isaiah (Isa. 20:3). And the church on this fourth Sunday in Advent honors her, the Lord's true servant, and honors the Lord she serves: The God who gives and the Son who is given.

2 SAMUEL 7:1-16

David receives his own annunciation, only now the messenger is not an angel but a prophet. The function is the same. The prophet, like the angel, declares a direct word from God. Here, as is so often the case with prophetic announcements, both in the Old Testament and the New, God's promise is gracious but not exactly what David expected. David's hope clearly was that he might build a temple for the Ark of the Covenant, a building as splendid as his own palace.

The prophet hints at the divine ambivalence. Is the God that David worships really a God who can be tied down to a holy place? Isn't this a God always on the move? Perhaps Nathan foresees something of the vision that drives Luke's whole story of the spread of the gospel—God's promise moving from Jerusalem to Rome, the temple on its way to destruction, God the God of all creation and not of any particular place.

Nonetheless, Nathan (or God) overcomes the ambivalence about temples. (Scholars tell us that perhaps an editor shapes the material to make it more congenial to the later history of Judah.) Yet even now God does not promise exactly what David had hoped. There will be a temple, but David will not build it.

Walter Brueggemann points out how crucial this passage has been to Israel's messianic hopes:

> The promise made to David is for time to come. It explicitly concerns David's son Solomon, but there are always sons to come, generations of David's yet unborn, each of whom is the carrier of this unconditional gospel. By this announcement, the line of David is no longer simply a historical accident but a constitutive factor in God's shaping of the historical process. Out of this oracle there emerges the hope held by Israel in every season that there is a coming David who will right wrong and establish good government. That coming one may be hidden in the vagaries of history, may experience resistance from the recalcitrance of injustice and unrighteousness, but nevertheless there is one coming who will make things right. (Brueggemann, 257)

Brueggemann points to two other features of this promise. First, in the promise theological hope is tied to political propaganda. The word of the Lord is a word that is highly convenient for the Davidic house as it seeks to establish its authority. This is not surprising, since the word of God is always mixed with human words, and the deepest promises are colored by our sometimes selfish longings. Second, this promise to David is a sign of unconditional grace. With Saul there was no doubt that the kingship was conditional upon his behavior; here the kingship is sheer gift, not to be re-evaluated and not to be rescinded. In its own way it foreshadows the grace that we celebrate in the unconditional gift of Jesus Christ (see Brueggemann, 256–57).

There may be a further tie to themes of Advent (and second Advent) here, too. God is a God of promises, but God does not always promise according to what we ask. God may fulfill our expectations, but not just as we had expected. Who would have expected a maiden from Nazareth to be mother to the Messiah? Or David's son by the woman he stole from Uriah to build the temple? Or a Messiah to be crucified? Or a prosecutor of the church to become a missionary for the church? God is continually making and fulfilling promises, but almost never just the promise we had expected or even desired. Better promises; better fulfillments, but surprising all the same.

One wonders even as we hope for the second Advent whether that may not surprise us, too. Perhaps it will not be trumpets and angels but a birth barely noticed at the margins of official history that turns out to be the consummation of the story.

Of course, the other promise in this passage is one that the early church and the Gospel writers clung to faithfully, hopefully. The kingdom of David's son will be established forever. Taken in the usual way, this promise, too, will fail. At the time of Jesus, no Davidic king sat on the throne in Jerusalem, and Judea was ruled by gentiles. Yet Christians heard in the promise to Solomon a promise that would be fulfilled in the strange king, Jesus of Nazareth—descendant of David and of Solomon.

When Nathan tells David that God will be a Father to Solomon and Solomon a son to him, early church heard the promise of another Son. If to Solomon, how much more will God be a Father to Solomon's descendant David? In the promise that the virgin Mary will bear a son we get one image of what it means for God to be Father of Jesus Christ. In the reminder of the oracle of Nathan to David we remember, too, that God promises to be father of the one anointed. The fatherhood of begetting and the fatherhood of choosing. The images pile upon one another; not doctrine yet, not formulas yet. A picture from Isaiah (probably misread), a picture from 1 Samuel—loosely interpreted. We call it Christology, but it is really poetry drawing the portrait of promise. Advent.

> THERE MAY BE A FURTHER TIE TO THEMES OF ADVENT (AND SECOND ADVENT) HERE, TOO. GOD IS A GOD OF PROMISES, BUT GOD DOES NOT ALWAYS PROMISE ACCORDING TO WHAT WE ASK. GOD MAY FULFILL OUR EXPECTATIONS, BUT NOT JUST AS WE HAD EXPECTED.

ROMANS 16:25-27

A look at the margins of the NRSV will suggest the complicated textual history of these verses. Nonetheless, they fit beautifully as they are printed in that text—as the conclusion to Paul's letter to the Romans.

In many ways the whole book of Romans is about the "obedience of faith" (Rom. 16:26). Romans 1–11 stresses the centrality of the gift of faith. Romans 12–16 shows how faith is lived out in obedience. (For elaboration see Bartlett, 19, 109.)

In our Gospel lesson for today, in the story of Mary, we see faith and obedience joined. "Here am I; the servant of the Lord. Let it be to me according to your word." "Trust and obey," says the old Gospel hymn, and that is precisely what Mary does. She trusts that the word from God is a word from God. She obeys that Word. It is the trusting and obeying that makes her a servant.

> TRUST AND OBEY, SAYS THE OLD GOSPEL HYMN, AND THAT IS PRECISELY WHAT MARY DOES. SHE TRUSTS THAT THE WORD FROM GOD IS A WORD FROM GOD. SHE OBEYS THAT WORD. IT IS THE TRUSTING AND OBEYING THAT MAKES HER A SERVANT.

Throughout Romans Paul has argued that what brings Jews and gentiles alike (all humankind) into a right relationship with God is faith. Neither obedience to the law nor a wise understanding of nature can in themselves commend us to God. What commends us to God is the gift given to those outside the law and to those who aren't too perceptive both—faith, faith in Jesus Christ, and faith in the God who sent him. Trust. We live out that trust by turning to our neighbors in love and by living as good citizens of the larger world. We live out that trust by being a church where all are welcome (Rom. 15:7). Paul's own story, of course, also combines faith and obedience. Like Mary, he receives the last word he would have expected (see Acts 9; Gal. 1). Like Mary, he has to trust the word and then obey the word by becoming an apostle to the gentiles. Like Mary, he is rightly designated a "servant of the Lord."

This is an Advent passage not only because (like the Gospel) it combines faith and obedience; it is an Advent passage because it speaks of expectation and fulfillment. The hidden mystery is now disclosed. The old prophecies are now fulfilled. Expectations are shattered (as in the Magnificat), because it turns out that the prophecies of Israel point beyond Israel to God's intention to include the gentiles in God's family. What is as old as time (the mystery kept secret for long ages, the command of the eternal God) is as new as a manger, as fresh and surprising as these little bands of Christians gathering in Rome to hear and proclaim the gospel. (In less than three hundred years, Rome will be a center of a

Christian faith that reaches out to include churches all across the empire. Who would have believed?)

"To God be the glory forever" (Rom. 16:27).

RESPONSIVE READING

PSALM 89:1-4, 19-26 (RCL), 89:2-5, 27, 29 (RC)

The psalm picks up the affirmation of the oracle in 2 Samuel. Now in ways that are only implicit in the Nathan story, the promise of God to David and his descendants is a promise of "steadfast love," of unconditional grace. Of course, what for Israel was a promise that would extend across generations and rulers for Christians at Advent comes together, finds its focus, and points in the one offspring of David, Jesus of Nazareth. In some ways this embodies the wholeness of Christian hope: that God continues to exercise sovereignty over all of history, that that sovereignty comes to its focus and fullness in this one man.

Yet again we need to deal with the honest difficulties besetting such a promise. By the time that Jesus was born, the promise to David seems to have been broken; David's seed does not rule in power. Or the promise has become eschatological—moved from the midst of history to its end. If Jesus is the fulfillment of that messianic promise, he does not reign in the ways that the psalm might have predicted. At some points his foes crush him, and even the victory of resurrection does not undo the stunning surprise of a suffering Messiah. This, of course, is precisely what the extended psalm, not included in our reading, contemplates or foreshadows: "Lord, where is your steadfast love of old, which by your faithfulness, you swore to David? Remember, O Lord, how your servant is taunted; how I bear in my bosom the insults of the peoples . . ." (vv. 49–50).

The whole psalm calls us to honest advent: we rejoice in the coming of the king who is not the kind of king we might have expected; the joy of Advent is shadowed, necessarily, by the journey toward Good Friday.

PSALM 132 (BCP)

This psalm, perhaps sung on the way to Jerusalem for a festival, affirms in hymn form the promises of the passage from 2 Samuel. The presupposition of the psalm is David's introduction of the Ark to Jerusalem in 1 Samuel 7 and 2 Samuel 6 (see Mays, 409). God's favor rests on David and his offspring. God's favor rests on Jerusalem. This is an appropriate Advent hymn because we believe that Jesus is the fulfillment of the Davidic promise, the offspring on whom the promises of God have come to rest. It may be, too, as James Mays suggests, that the "hardships" David endures in verse 1 point for Christians to the "hardships" the Messiah will undergo as he seeks to reclaim Jerusalem (Mays, 412). But again we have to admit that in Jesus' time (and perhaps in our time) the exact historical, political elements of the promise were not fulfilled. Zion was in thrall to Caesar. How do we welcome the true king when false kings have power everywhere? How do we wait in hope when disappointment is our daily bread? The psalm recalls Israel to God's covenant with David. It recalls us to God's covenant with David and with Jesus, David's son. It reminds us of past mercies so that we can now hold fast to the promises of God.

PRAYER

We would be faithful, O God. We would trust in your promises. We would be open to surprising promises we had not expected. Help us to hear your messengers, in whatever accent they speak, however odd their garb, however familiar or unfamiliar their features. When you speak to us, help us to obey. And by your grace, may we be messengers to your people. Through Christ our Lord, Amen.

NATIVITY OF OUR LORD 1
CHRISTMAS EVE

<small>DECEMBER 24, 1999</small>

REVISED COMMON	EPISCOPAL (BCP)	ROMAN CATHOLIC
Isa. 9:2-7	Isa. 9:2-4, 6-7	Isa. 9:2-7
Ps. 96	Ps. 96 or 96:1-4, 11-12	Ps. 96:1-3, 11-13
Titus 2:11-14	Titus 2:11-14	Titus 2:11-14
Luke 2:1-14, (15-20)	Luke 2:1-14, (15-20)	Luke 2:1-14

O HOLY NIGHT. The blessed story to which the stories of Advent point. The vision shaped by prophecy; the vision that shapes the way we read the prophets. It is not just tradition or sentiment that brings us back to this story every Christmas Eve. Here is the heart of Christmas faith: Advent leads up to it—the journey of faith leads from it to the cross and the resurrection and the church and us. Our journey's end and its beginning.

It is a matter of signs, signs of who God is and what God does. For Luke and for Isaiah, too, there are a number of hints and a number of signals, but only one sign. The child. We read the story because it is his story, and through him it becomes our story and the story of the world. What God does and what God expects.

GOSPEL
LUKE 2:1-14

Luke is the only true "historian" of the Gospel writers. He writes two volumes, Luke and Acts, because he not only has a gospel to preach, he has a history to relate. Therefore, he sets this narrative of the birth of Jesus within the patterns of world history. The emperor is Augustus; the governor is Quirinius. We can say that the sacred story is set within secular history, but if "secular" just means the history of the worlds or of the ages, then secular history is also God's history (who created the world and to whom all ages belong). At the beginning of the story, Caesar's decree goes out to all the world; at the end of the story, Jesus' Gospel will have spread through all the world. A decree goes out from Rome to Judea; the Gospel will spread from Judea to Rome. In a way, the important thing is that

Jesus' story will be more important than Augustus's story; but in a larger way, the important thing is that Augustus's story is included in Jesus' story. Nothing—not politics, nor economics, nor the arts, nor philosophy, nor wisdom—stands outside the realm that God claims in Jesus Christ.

But Luke also reminds us that this is a moment in the story of Israel and Judah. The promise we have seen reiterated in so many of our Advent passages is that God's promise to Israel and Judah is a promise to the house of David, enacted through the house of David. Now David's offspring, Joseph, returns to David's town, Bethlehem. This kingship will not look like David's kingship; Jesus will weep over David's city. But it is a kingship all the same, and without understanding David and the promises to David we cannot understand Jesus and the promises fulfilled in him. And Mary, who has become already a paradigm of faith because she heard God's word, knew that it was a word to her and accepted it in trust. David's offspring, Joseph, and God's servant, Mary, journey to Bethlehem, at Caesar's command—as if Caesar were in charge, as if this were really to fulfill Caesar's decree and not God's.

Sharon Ringe reminds us that the "inn" was probably not really an inn. The family in a Bethlehem home would live in one room, that outside the room was a manger area, and above the manger area would have been the "upper room," where, says Ringe, "visiting relatives or acquaintances, or persons linked to the family by political or economic ties, could be given hospitality. Joseph, having returned with his pregnant wife to his ancestral village, would have anticipated such accommodation. The fact that none was available meant that others from a higher rung on the social ladder . . . had already claimed the space" (Ringe, 42).

The explanation only enriches the connotations of the familiar image. No room in the upper room, or no room in the inn. This is a metaphor for so much of the story. Who makes room for the baby and who does not? God's great gift is now outside the inn, and at the end outside the city wall.

We are the shepherds in this story. The commentators differ on whether they are people of relatively low or relatively high degree in the economy of the time. What we know for sure is that they are going about their own business. They are doing just what they usually do. They have not gone to church, or lit the Advent candles, or prayed through the night. This is a divine interruption (Gabriel to Mary, God's voice to the boy Samuel). Perhaps a nice contrast to that other story from the other gospel which we conflate with this one in our Christmas pageants. The Wise Men seeking signs and finding the right one. The shepherds not seeking for anything at all are suddenly confronted by a word from on high—like a bolt out of the blue. We recall the two parables in Matthew 13:44-46—the merchant searching for a pearl and the landholder stumbling on a treasure. Total fulfillment or complete surprise; the ways of God with humankind.

Here is the sign the shepherds get. The angels are not the sign. The lights are not the sign. The song is not the sign. There is nothing wrong with angels or lights, but they are prelude. The sign is the baby. That he is in a manger is part of the sign. That he is humble and lowly is part of the sign. But *he* is the sign. If they scurry, they will find him. Christmas Eve—that is the only real sign we get. The only one to whom we ought to rush. The only place to kneel. The only hope to count on. How nice that the family has gathered, how lovely the music in church, how warm the light of candles; these are not the sign—comprehended by the sign, hallowed by the sign, but not the sign. The baby is the sign.

One of my favorite Christian women, a dedicated student of the New Testament, grumbled every Christmas about the baby. Sentimentality taking us away from the strong and demanding Jesus who called us to follow him. Sweat and blood, not swaddling clothes and talcum powder. Yes and no. There will be time for the demand and the obedience and the cross. But here is the surprise: God comes this human, this meek, this lowly, this vulnerable. All the strength (like every human strength) can only begin with this weakness. Unto us a child is born.

What the angels sing is presented somewhat differently, even in the earliest manuscripts. They give glory to God in highest heaven, as well they should. But in some versions they declare, "Peace on earth to those whom God favors," and in some versions, "Peace on earth, good will to humankind." Much of Christian theology since has divided along these lines. Is this peace for those who are the chosen, the elect, the members of Christ's body, the church? Or is what is enacted here peace for all the earth, God's loving kindness for all of humankind (whether all of humankind knows it or not)? Much of Luke's Gospel and the book of Acts sounds as though it's all the world that is claimed. Not the Pax Romana anymore but the Pax Christiania. Church lives out the promise for the whole creation. I hope that's right.

First Reading
ISAIAH 9:2-7

This passage is one of the many Old Testament passages that calls forth from us a kind of two-level vision. At the first level, the eighth-century prophet Isaiah hopes for and predicts a king who will redeem Isaiah's people from the oppression of the Assyrian conqueror. His hope may well have focused on a particular king whose promise was a gift to a people threatened by the powers that had already taken over their northern neighbor, Israel. Yet he draws the picture of this king in such exalted language that one can almost say that the hope from the beginning is messianic. This is hope not just for a king, but for *the* King.

At the other level, there is no way for Christians to read this passage without seeing it point to the hope we believe is fulfilled in Jesus of Nazareth. We do not know how much this passage figured in the messianic expectations of the first years of this era, how much its expectations shaped what people hoped for and saw in the ministry of Jesus, how much its language shaped their understanding of Jesus after his death and resurrection. We do know that, in the years since, Isaiah 9 has become one of the great passages delineating Christian confidence and illuminating Christian hope. It is almost impossible for contemporary Christians to hear Isaiah 9:6-7 without hearing it to the music of Handel's *Messiah*. In that context there is no question that these are not words just about a king but about an ideal king, and there is no question who that king is.

What ties our passage to the passage from the Gospel is that the "sign" of Isaiah is very like the "sign" to which the angels point the shepherds. A child is born. The child, like every child, tiny and dependent, is the beginning of God's astonishing reclaiming of the world and our lives—that is true for Isaiah and it's true for Luke as well.

Yet we also have to admit that the promise Isaiah puts forth—that the boots of trampling warriors and garments rolled in blood will all be burned, that peace and justice will reign forever—was not fulfilled absolutely in the arrival of the baby in Bethlehem. The history from that day until now has far too many trampling warriors and far too many bloody garments for us to fool ourselves.

A Jewish friend once said, "If the Messiah has come, where is the messianic age?" The answer for Christians is that it is here and not yet here, sometimes more like a mustard seed than a full-fledged plant. In many ways Jews and Christians alike await the time of fulfillment. Many Jews wait for the Messiah; many Christians wait for the Messiah to come again. Both hope for a justice and peace that are not yet worked out in the world or its history. Christians see that justice and peace begun and foreshadowed, shaped, and guaranteed in the ministry, death, and resurrection of Jesus.

> IN MANY WAYS JEWS AND CHRISTIANS ALIKE AWAIT THE TIME OF FULFILLMENT. MANY JEWS WAIT FOR THE MESSIAH; MANY CHRISTIANS WAIT FOR THE MESSIAH TO COME AGAIN. BOTH HOPE FOR A JUSTICE AND PEACE THAT ARE NOT YET WORKED OUT IN THE WORLD OR ITS HISTORY.

Therefore there is no point pretending we see what we do not see. This is not the best of all possible worlds. This is the world in which we have seen Jesus in his humility and wait to see him in his glory. We do not altogether know what that will mean, but we pray and serve a vision where God rules the world in justice and righteousness.

Taken together, the passage from Luke and the passage from Isaiah remind us of the twofold focus of our Advent hope. We wait for the child in the manger, born for us and our salvation. We wait for the fulfillment of the promise that begins there when God consummates history. For Christians the name of both gifts, both promises, is Jesus Christ.

SECOND READING
TITUS 2:11-14

The Epistle lessons for these Advent and Christmas services stress the responsibilities that faithful people take on in the light of God's great gift in Jesus Christ. In 1 Corinthians, Paul speaks of the right use of spiritual gifts. In Romans he writes of the obedience of faith. In 1 Thessalonians he talks of the life of responsible service in the church in the light of the expectation of Christ's return. The Second Letter of Peter, probably written some time after Paul's epistles, notes that the second coming of Christ has apparently been slower than Christians would have anticipated and urges upon the readers the gifts of holiness and uprightness.

It may be that the letter to Titus was written by a disciple of Paul's in Paul's name, written sometime closer to the writing of 2 Peter than to the writing of 1 Thessalonians. The picture of responsible Christian life in Titus is rather like that of responsible Christian life in 2 Peter: Christians are to be "self-controlled, upright, and godly" (Titus 1:12) and to perform "good deeds" (Titus 2:14).

It is an important mark of the Christian life that faithful people should distinguish themselves from the mores and standards of the world around them. Christians are a peculiar people; if they look just like everybody else they haven't understood their calling and their responsibility.

The framework for these injunctions is precisely the twofold assurance we celebrate at Advent and Christmas. Christ has appeared; Christ will appear. In the first appearance Christ provides the training we need to live piously and in distinction from the standards of the world. In his final glory we can assume that Christ will provide the crown of blessedness to those who have stood firm against the world's blandishments.

The injunctions in Titus are not always easy to follow. On the one hand, there is the strong supplication not to live as the world lives; on the other hand, the picture of Christian life sometimes looks profoundly respectable, straightforward, not particularly risky. Yet for most of us most days, the issue is not heroism; it's integrity. Once in a while we are asked to risk everything bravely for the gospel. Most days we are asked to be honest with our fellow workers, fair and loving with our family, loyal to our church. These days, living in this straightforward and undramatic way may itself be a dramatic commitment to God's Advent gifts.

Responsive Reading
PSALM 96

The psalm fits the celebratory feast of Christmas. It celebrates what the Lord has done, what the Lord is doing, what the Lord will do.

God's power and might are established first of all through the creation. He made the heavens (v. 5) and he made the earth (v. 10). God is still the sovereign Lord over all that God has made: "Say among the nations, 'The Lord reigns'!" God will come at the end of the story to judge all the people and all the nations according to God's own truth.

In its way, the psalm sings the Christmas story. The creator and sustainer of the world now participates in the world and the history God has created. The same God will fulfill all of God's promises at the conclusion of the story, the consummation of the creation. For Christians the pattern through which God creates, the Figure through whom he is present, and the Judge through whom he shall conclude the story are all Jesus Christ. In Christmas past, present, and future come together, in a manger, in a song, in hope.

No wonder the people are called to sing a new song in the light of this new thing that God has done.

PRAYER

O Holy Child of Bethlehem, descend to us, we pray. After all this waiting, after all this hoping, be present among us and be present to us. In this season we preach peace and are the worst examples of frenzy—hyperactive servants of your word. We have chased after the wrong signs and placed our hopes in the false messiahs: but we long for truth, and we kneel before the sign, before the manger, before the lowly, before you. Amen.

NATIVITY OF OUR LORD 2
CHRISTMAS DAWN

REVISED COMMON	EPISCOPAL (BCP)	ROMAN CATHOLIC
Isa. 62:6-12	Isa. 62:6-7, 10-12	Isa. 62:11-12
Ps. 97	Ps. 97 or 97:1-4, 11-12	Ps. 97:1, 6, 11-12
Titus 3:4-7	Titus 3:4-7	Titus 3:4-7
Luke 2:(1-7), 8-20	Luke 2:(1-14), 15-20	Luke 2:15-20

CHRISTMAS CHANGES THINGS. The shepherds leave their sheepherding and then return to their sheepherding, but they are not the same. They have seen the sign and they are changed. The author of the Pastorals reminds Titus how life is lived differently because of what God has done in Jesus Christ. Once our lives looked one way; now they look quite another. And Isaiah showing how God's mercy changes life for Judah helps us think about how God's mercy changes life for Christian believers on this new day. "Holy People"; "Redeemed"; "Sought Out"; "Not Forsaken."

GOSPEL
LUKE 2:1-20 (RCL/BCP), 2:15-20 (RC)

We are the shepherds in this story. They are going about their own business. They are doing what they usually do when suddenly they experience a divine interruption. (We can hardly start the story with verse 15. We need to remind people what the angels have told the shepherds about this boy.)

Luke's story will begin and move toward the end with songs to God in highest heaven. Here the angels sing God's glory; in the last chapters of Luke's Gospel, the multitude and the disciples shout of glory and peace in heaven (Luke 19:38). Is that because, whether they know it or not, earth's peace is about to be shattered by a trial and execution? Here at the beginning there is glory for heaven and peace for earth. And surely from beginning to end peace on earth is part of the promise, too. *Shalom* has become almost a cliché. Tossed off as easily in English as "hello" and "goodbye." But we know that for the people of Israel, from early times until now, it is a word of enormous hope. Peace, wholeness, well-being;

right relationship between humankind and God, a right relationship among people. That is what the angel promises, as we suggested or hoped, for all the world. There are good early manuscript readings both for "on earth peace among those whom God favors" and "on earth peace, good will to humankind"—the difference is in the ending of a noun.

In their own way, the shepherds do what Mary did: they listen to the word and they obey. "Let it happen to me according to your word," she says. "Let us go according to the word," they say. They trust the word; believing will become seeing. The Lord has made it known; now let's go look. So often that is the right order of faith: "If you come, here's what you'll see." Then let us go and see.

And then, like so many other people at the beginning of Luke's Gospel (and again at the beginning of Acts), the shepherds preach the Gospel. They connect the divine word to the divine act. Here's what we heard; here's what we see. Here was the promise; here is the fulfillment. Preaching. People are amazed, as they will be amazed at the words and deeds of God and of God's Christ for the rest of this Gospel (Luke 2:47; 4:32, 36; 5:26; 8:56; 9:43).

> IN THEIR OWN WAY, THE SHEPHERDS DO WHAT MARY DID: THEY LISTEN TO THE WORD AND THEY OBEY. THEY TRUST THE WORD; BELIEVING WILL BECOME SEEING.

Mary has yet other mysteries to ponder. The angel, the conception, the birth, the report of the shepherds. Her soul magnifies the Lord; she has not yet heard from Zechariah the first hint of what it will cost her to be who she will be, both the servant and the mother of the Lord (see Luke 2:35).

The shepherds do not stay to build the Church of the Nativity, any more than Jesus will let the disciples stay and build tents on the Mount of Transfiguration, or let the healed demoniac leave family and friends to follow him. Sometimes faithfulness means "leave everything." Sometimes faithfulness means "go home." But of course they do not return the same people who left those short hours before. They return as those who have heard the Word and seen the vision. T. S. Eliot says it: "The end of all our exploring / Will be to arrive where we started / And know the place for the first time" (Four Quartets, "Little Gidding," V, 27–29). The shepherds now know that the world they live in has been invaded by the glory of God, by the peace that God wills among humankind—and that the sign of this is not Caesar in his palace (remember, this part of the story began with Caesar) or Cyrene in his governor's mansion. The sign of this is now a manger; the sign of this will be a cross.

He has put down the mighty from their thrones and exalted those of low degree (Luke 1:52). For now, by this word, this light, this visit to the stable, God has exalted the shepherds, too.

We are the shepherds in this story. Christmas will end, the lights be extinguished. The week begin again with work to be done, the children to be fed, the presents to be sorted and stored, the papers and ribbons thrown away. As a resource for your sermon look at W. H. Auden's long poem, "For the Time Being," especially the section called "The Flight into Egypt."

FIRST READING
ISAIAH 62:6-12

Here is a song of promise fulfilled. The city that had been overthrown is now built up. The oppressed are freed. God reclaims Zion, the home of God's own heart. It is a promise full of practicality: economic self-determination. The promise is that Judah will no longer be vassal to a foreign power. The promise is that Judah will be able to raise crops for the benefit of its own people and grapes to make wine for its own tables. Those who have been exiled are returning home. God does what we do at times of celebration (baptisms, weddings); God gives new names. The people of Judah are now not just Judeans but "Holy People." "Redeemed." "Sought Out." "Not Forsaken."

One of my closest college friends decided one year to change his vocational plans. At about the same time, he ended a difficult relationship and shortly thereafter started dating the woman to whom he has now been married for thirty years. That year he also started using his middle name as his first name; it was a sign. Things have changed, it said. I have changed.

It is a promise for Christmas morning when we can be sure that many who worship with us will feel unholy, lost, ignored and forsaken. God's promise to Judah was fulfilled for a time; at the time of Jesus' birth it appears to be broken again. Jesus' people do labor to increase the wealth of far away Rome. When Jesus came, Zion would soon again be overthrown; when Luke wrote, Zion had been overthrown already.

What would the psalm have meant to a Jew at the beginning of this era? To a Jew or a Christian toward the end of the first century? Is it a hope or a mockery, a reminder of promises once fulfilled but now gone? The psalm might have sounded the way some of the Christmas carols sound to people who worship with us: full of a hope that they personally do not feel.

We have to preach the promise even when the signs do not seem very promising. We have to remember that the main sign was not the upraised right hand of the Lord or multitudes of people returning triumphant to the city. The main sign (though, of course, Isaiah did not know this) was the sign the shepherds got: the baby, the manger. For Christians he becomes the temple where we worship and the city that is our one true home. But Isaiah helps us to keep from spiritualizing that claim, as does the Magnificat: the Christ who claims us still claims us for justice. The poor should not labor for the benefit of the rich, whether the rich are foreigners or fellow citizens. We do pray and work for the time when fewer of our cities might as well have signs: "Welcome to Ignored; Welcome to Forsaken." Ignored by the government; forsaken by the affluent; abandoned by God? At the end of Luke's story, Jesus will weep over Jerusalem. God loves cities; we desert them. The prophecy becomes a prayer: "You shall be called, 'Sought Out,' and 'A City Not Forsaken.' "

SECOND READING
TITUS 3:4-7

The Pastoral Epistles, as you well know, are 1 and 2 Timothy and Titus. They are pastoral because they deal with pastoral office but also because the author takes on a kind of role of pastoral director. Some people think they were written by Paul late in his life as the churches were getting established and needed some practical wisdom. Other people think they were written by one of Paul's disciples after Paul had died, as the churches were getting established and needed some practical wisdom. I am in the latter group, but I do not think this greatly affects the way we preach on Titus—certainly not on Christmas morning (when one doubts that Titus ought to be at the heart of what we have to say).

We really need verse 3. This is one of those great contrasts that fill the New Testament epistles: Once we were this / now we are that. Once we were minding our own business, minding our sheep / now we have seen the child, now we have borne witness to the Gospel.

What a list of things we once were: "foolish, disobedient, led astray, slaves to various passions and pleasures, passing our days in malice and envy, despicable, hating one another."

What changes, of course, is not what we did but what God did for us (as God acted for Joseph, Mary, the shepherds, Zion). Though the language sounds a little like the original (or earlier) letters of Paul, there is enough of a shift to make us think that this is a different voice, Paul's disciple trying to discern the faith for a somewhat-later generation.

As in Luke (and in Romans and throughout the New Testament), God appears through Jesus Christ, and his appearance makes all the difference. But notice here that what appears in him are just those virtues that the author wants to instill in his readers: "goodness and loving kindness" (quite possibly a translation of the goodness and mercy that follow us at the end of Psalm 23). The Holy One has come to make us holy.

Yet it is clear here (as in the earlier Pauline letters) that the appearance of Jesus is sheer gift: It is mercy. It is grace. It is only by a gift that we are "justified" that we enter into a right relationship with God. Christ saves us to works of righteousness, but our works of righteousness do not save us. In the light of his righteousness we receive two gifts:

- We lead more righteous lives now. (vv. 3-5)
- We are heirs through hope of eternal life. (vv. 6-7)

The passage is trinitarian without explicating a full doctrine of the Trinity. God is savior and Christ is Savior, too. Through Christ God pours out the Holy Spirit. The spirit is the sign of God's justification.

The passage is sacramental without explicating a full doctrine of sacraments. Baptism includes water and regeneration; baptism includes the gift of the Holy Spirit and the promise of eternal life. Is there a hint here of the claims of Galatians that in baptism Christians cry out "Abba!"—Father—and thereby show their adoption into God's family?

> THE APPEARANCE OF JESUS IS SHEER GIFT: IT IS MERCY. IT IS GRACE. IT IS ONLY BY A GIFT THAT WE ARE "JUSTIFIED," THAT WE ENTER INTO A RIGHT RELATIONSHIP WITH GOD. CHRIST SAVES US TO WORKS OF RIGHTEOUSNESS, BUT OUR WORKS OF RIGHTEOUSNESS DO NOT SAVE US.

In a way what Titus does for us on this Christmas morning is to remind us that the coming of the child has consequences. We do not just kneel at the manger and then get back to life as usual. That was then, this is now. We live in a new relationship to God and a new relationship to society. We are made right (justified) and we act righteously, uprightly. The letter to Titus does not show forth the most exciting picture of Christian discipleship: No one finally is called to take up the cross or love to the full measure of devotion. In the light of Christ's appearing we do good works, do not slander, act gently, and show every courtesy. A gentleperson's faith. Maybe it's not the fullness of the life of Christian discipleship, but it's a start. And in most communities (and churches) I know, a little gentleness and courtesy could go a long way.

RESPONSIVE READING

PSALM 97

In many ways, the affirmations of the psalm fit with the affirmations of the epistle to Titus. God upholds the righteous. As God is exalted above the idols, so God exalts upright people above the wicked. "Light dawns for the righteous / and joy for the upright of heart." God is not defined by power alone but by righteousness and equity; so in righteousness God judges in favor of the righteous (Mays, 311–12).

This is moderately good news, as opposed to the unreservedly good news of the angels' announcement to the shepherds. I dare guess that on Christmas morning some of those who come to wait and worship will not consider themselves among the righteous or the upright of heart. The psalm holds forth a kind of imperative for them: May they repent! May they straighten up!

In the meantime, you might tell them that on this day, of all days, the light dawns for them as well.

PRAYER

Kind God, let us go and see; let us go and speak. This year let the seeing precede the speaking, so that we bear witness only to what we have witnessed. Let us know in our hearts the joy we would proclaim to your people. Let your word be our word, too. Yours the great word, ours the small, but healing words, graceful words, Christmas. Through Christ our Lord, Amen.

NATIVITY OF OUR LORD 3
CHRISTMAS DAY

DECEMBER 25, 1999

REVISED COMMON	EPISCOPAL (BCP)	ROMAN CATHOLIC
Isa. 52:7–10	Isa. 52:7–10	Isa. 52:7–10
Ps. 98	Ps. 98 or 98:1–6	Ps. 98:1–6
Heb. 1:1–4, (5–12)	Heb. 1:1–12	Heb. 1:1–6
John 1:1–14	John 1:1–14	John 1:1–18 or 1:1–5, 9–14

ALL THE TEXTS REMIND US THAT God did not simply wake up one day and say, "I'll try something brand new; I'll send a Messiah." Jesus is brand new, of course, but also he is the Word by which creation was made—the pattern that shapes cosmos and history alike. Jesus is brand new, of course; but the same God who speaks through him has spoken in many and diverse ways to our fathers and mothers through the years. We sing a new song on every Christmas day, but the psalmist's New Song helps shape our song. We are surprised by Christmas. God is not.

GOSPEL

JOHN 1:1-18

As Robert Morgan of Oxford University points out, in many ways the prologue to John's Gospel provides the context in which we read all the other Gospels. Certainly that is true of the Advent and Christmas narratives. Given Mark's Gospel, we would have the preacher and miracle worker anointed by the Spirit at his baptism. Given Luke's Gospel, we would have the child born to a maiden, offspring of David, perhaps even savior of the world. But because of John's Gospel, we celebrate Jesus as God Incarnate, word become flesh. That celebration shapes all the other celebrations and informs our liturgies, our hymns, and our sermons. We may think we know and love the synoptic gospels better than we do John, but it is John's Gospel that provides the interpretive lens through which we view the Christian story and the perspective from which we tell that story.

The beginning of the prologue echoes the beginning of the Bible, the beginning of the world. "In the beginning God"; "In the beginning the Word." In part, this is a reading of Genesis that takes seriously the fact that in Genesis 1 the creation of light and life, of all creation, takes place through a word. "And God said, 'Let there be light, and there was light.'" The saying is the making. In the beginning, the word.

In part, the Fourth Gospel certainly also draws on some of the Wisdom traditions that were available to the evangelist—the claim that divine wisdom provided the blueprint for the creation of the world. Sometimes, as in Proverbs 8, that wisdom was personified, as if wisdom were a person and not just a concept. Sometimes, as in Sirach 24, Wisdom comes to earth and seeks those who will follow her way. Of course, wisdom is never precisely incarnate. Writer and reader alike know that this is a kind of metaphor. John turns the metaphor into metaphysics. Wisdom not only visits humankind, Wisdom becomes humankind. The plan that was with God from the beginning, by which God created the universe, now joins the universe that God has created. Word become flesh.

Like Mark 1, John 1 plays John the Baptizer off against the one whom he baptizes. In John (as we have noted), the Baptist has become entirely witness; the importance of his baptism fades entirely into the background.

What he witnesses is this one who from the beginning was with God.

While Mark starts with John the Baptist and Luke starts with Jesus' birth and the announcements leading up to it, Matthew starts with Adam (as a kind of prologue to the birth) and John starts with the first word spoken on the first day of creation. The story of Jesus Christ is not a divine afterthought in the great drama of human history. It is the beginning of that story, its middle, and its end—both its finish and its goal.

The prologue foretells the great themes of the Gospel of John, which are also great themes of the gospel itself. The word becomes flesh, flesh that joins with humankind in celebration (John 2) and sorrow (John 11). We behold his glory—the glory that does miracles, the glory that reveals the Father, the glory that will return to the Father.

Symbols drawn from the creation story illumine the story of Jesus and in turn illumine our story as we are confronted with Jesus. The light shines in the darkness, and then there is a pun. The darkness does not comprehend it; that is one reading. The darkness does not overwhelm it; that is another. John's Gospel is full of darkness failing to get the light—notice the accusations of John 9 that Jesus is not a savior but a sinner. John's Gospel is also full of darkness unable to overcome the light. On the cross Jesus cries out: "It is finished." He means: "It is completed." He means: "I have won." The resur-

JOHN'S GOSPEL IS FULL OF DARKNESS UNABLE TO OVERCOME THE LIGHT. ON THE CROSS JESUS CRIES OUT: "IT IS FINISHED." HE MEANS: "IT IS COMPLETED." HE MEANS: "I HAVE WON." THE RESURRECTION IS THE SIGN OF GOD'S APPROVAL ON JESUS' VICTORY. THE DARKNESS DOES NOT OVERCOME THE LIGHT.

rection is the sign of God's approval on Jesus' victory. The darkness does not overcome the light.

The word "incarnate" is full of grace and truth. "Truth" appears often in John's Gospel. Jesus speaks truly; often says "Amen"—Amen, which can be translated "truly, truly"—and then makes his inescapably true claims. At the end, Pilate looks for truth, but Jesus has already told him that Jesus is truth, so Pilate turns away. "Grace" appears only here in this Gospel and seems almost to have wandered in uninvited from one of Paul's letters. And yet, if grace is the unexpected and undeserved way in which God enters human history to bring people to God's self, then in John's Gospel Jesus is full not only of truth but of grace.

The whole of John's Gospel, I suspect (tutored by J. Louis Martyn and Raymond Brown), is written to deepen faith and to deepen courage for first-century churches who are needing to make a break from their old and comfortable place in the synagogue. One way of reading verse 11 is this: "He came to his own home, and his own people did not receive him." The prologue encourages its readers and hearers to receive Him. The prologue reminds them that what is at stake here is not only local but cosmic. They can choose the light, or they can choose the darkness.

All this reminds us that Christmas is not only a time for the old, old story, it is time to make or renew the old, old choice: to choose for the incarnate Word is to choose light; to choose against the incarnate Word is to choose darkness. Blessed are those who choose the light.

First Reading

ISAIAH 52:7-10

Again we need the twofold vision. In the context of sixth-century Judah and Jerusalem, we have the promise that God will redeem the city, and the hope of a messenger sent to tell the city the triumph of a king. We do not know if a particular king or a particular victory are in mind, but that this is a celebration of military victory there can be no doubt.

In the context of Christmas Day and of our Gospel passage, the messenger is not the King's messenger but God's, the good news not simply the news of victory but the news of incarnation. In one sense, John the Baptizer is the messenger who declares good news. In another sense, Jesus himself announces the salvation that he embodies.

The reign of God which John and Jesus announce, however, is still hidden from most of the world. At the first Christmas it was by no means obvious to the powers that be that the history had shifted on the fulcrum of this incarnation.

Not all the ends of the earth saw the salvation, but those who had eyes to see, those who beheld the glory hidden in and behind the flesh, those whom God gave the power to become God's own children, who were born, not of human power nor of fleshly might, but were born of the quiet and surprising Spirit.

> How silently, how silently
> The wondrous gift is given
> So God imparts to human hearts
> The wonders of his heaven.
> No ear may hear his coming
> Yet in this world of sin
> Where meek souls will receive him still
> The dear Christ enters in.
> (Phillips Brooks, "O Little Town of Bethlehem")

Nor can we forget that the prophet sees God's vindication coming to Jerusalem. When this Incarnate One comes to Jerusalem, once in John 3 and again in John 11, the people do not shout for joy. Some accuse him; some arrest him; some crucify him. Even on Christmas day we cannot forget.

Second Reading
HEBREWS 1:1-12

Here is continuity and discontinuity; expectation and surprise. (We really need verses 13-14 to understand the epistle's claims.)

The God who speaks in Jesus Christ is the same God who spoke by the prophets. That, of course, is what we have seen through all the prophetic texts of Advent and Christmas. However one interprets the specific expectations of the prophets, the God of hope speaks through them, and then speaks again—clearly, sweetly—through Jesus Christ.

Verses 2-3 are almost a gloss on the Gospel of John. For Hebrews, as for the Fourth Gospel, the Son, the Word, is the one through whom the world was created. For Hebrews, as for the Fourth Gospel, the Son reflects the very glory of God. In some ways Hebrews goes farther: The Son is not only creator of the universe, he is its sustainer.

Yet the story also recapitulates John's story. The Son becomes incarnate; the Son atones for sin; the Son is raised to the right hand of the Majesty on high.

Verses 5-14 reflect a controversy undoubtedly lively in the first-century churches to which Hebrews was written, but (I would have thought until recently) rather foreign to the concerns of twentieth- and twenty-first-century

Christians. Using a series of proof texts that probably originally had to do with the king's anointing, the author shows the superiority of a "Son" to mere angels, who are only ministers of God and not God's own heir. The Son is the anointed one; the angels are hired hands.

Amidst the current popularity of angels, I still doubt that anyone would claim that angels are superior to Jesus, God's son. Yet it does sometimes functionally seem that they have taken over for him: prayers to angels; confidence in angels; homilies on angels. Bizarre that the one who was to mediate between God and humankind now sometimes seems to have been replaced by mini-mediators. Maybe it is because even in his grace Christ bears the unmistakable gravity of majesty: the one who intercedes for us also created the world. It is hard to cozy up to the Word Incarnate; cute angels seem easier, whether of the greeting card or the TV series variety.

Whatever real angels may be, they are probably not as cute as that. The one true mediator, Christ Jesus, is nowhere near as cute. But he is strong enough to be God's agent for the making of the world and therefore for its healing, too. So when our lives need remaking and our hurts need healing, we might do well to turn to Him. The writer of Hebrews, at least, would have thought so.

RESPONSIVE READING
PSALM 98

This is the perfect psalm for Christmas. A new song celebrates an old promise. God has done an astonishing thing, and just what we might have hoped, if only we'd been paying more attention. Indeed, James Mays points out that this song provides the background text for Isaac Watts's great hymn: "Joy to the World" (Mays, 312). Here, indeed, heaven and nature sing.

The psalm uses virtually the same language as the Old Testament passage Isaiah 52:7-10. Here is a song to celebrate the victory that Isaiah announces.

In a way that foreshadows the conviction of the New Testament, the psalm speaks of God's covenant faithfulness to Israel but also beyond that, of the promise that God's salvation extends to the ends of the earth—not only to include all of humankind but to include the natural world as well. A student of mine tells of restoring his soul lying on the beach near New Haven; the gulls rising from the shore and the waves lapping on the shore seemed to move with one rhythm, and soon enough his heartbeat found that rhythm, too. Perhaps it is a parable of Advent hope: Let heaven and nature sing.

We clap our hands, but the world also claps its hands and joins in celebration. Creator of the world visits the creation; the Word comes to its own home; the

Son visits what He has made. No wonder hills are singing and floods are clapping. We are singing and clapping, too.

Of course, the psalm also provides the steady Advent and Christmas reminder: the one who comes to establish righteousness. Of course we welcome him; but we wait, and wait to obey.

PRAYER

Your light shines in the darkness, O Christ, and we seek to comprehend it. Mystery beyond our naming, mercy beyond our escaping, we would live in your light and serve your light. Your light shines in the darkness, O Christ, and the darkness does not overcome it. Let your light shine in the dark places of our world for your name's sake and to your glory. Amen.

FIRST SUNDAY AFTER CHRISTMAS
THE HOLY FAMILY

DECEMBER 26, 1999

REVISED COMMON	EPISCOPAL (BCP)	ROMAN CATHOLIC
Isa. 61:10—62:3	Isa. 61:10—62:3	Sir. 3:2-6, 12-14
Ps. 148	Ps. 147 or 147:13-21	Ps. 128:1-5
Gal. 4:4-7	Gal. 3:23-25; 4:4-7	Col. 3:12-21
Luke 2:22-40	John 1:1-18	Luke 2:22-40
		or 2:22, 39-40

IT IS STILL CHRISTMASTIDE. It is still time to sing the carols and rejoice, though it gets harder as the days wear on. The press of every day is unavoidable and ineluctable. People who had church enough and more in the last weeks of Advent and the first days of Christmas think it's a good time to rest up a bit or clean up a bit. You yourself are on the way to the Xerox machine to copy these pages to hand over to your seminarian or your associate so that he or she can prepare for the liturgical event we all try to avoid: Let Down Sunday.

Yet our texts make clear it is not really Let Down Sunday; it is Move Ahead Sunday. The story moves forward from the manger in praise and proclamation. Simeon comes before God with praise; Anna proclaims good news to the people. Simeon continues the song of the angels; Anna prolongs the preaching of the shepherds. Galatians and Colossians show forth the shape of our response to the gift of Christmas—for Galatians, the freedom of the gospel, for Colossians, its responsibility. We are like the shepherds heading home from the manger, praising and glorifying God. Even our sheepherding will be different from now on.

GOSPEL
LUKE 2:22-40

The story begins with the Holy Spirit. The Spirit fills Simeon and drives him. Luke's Gospel and Acts are the books of the works of the Spirit. The Spirit overshadows Mary and a child is born (Luke 1:35). Filled with the Spirit,

Elizabeth blesses Mary (1:41). Zechariah prophesies under the influence of the Spirit (1:67). The Holy Spirit descends on Jesus (1:22), and filled with the Spirit he is able to thwart the devil (4:1). His first public sermon invokes the Spirit (4:18), and his last public prayer returns the Spirit to God (24:46). When the church is ready to continue its own ministry of praise and proclamation, God sends the essential gift—the Spirit (Acts 2:4). In the last scene of Luke's two-volume work, Paul interprets the Spirit to his listeners (Acts 28:25). For Luke, the Spirit is God's active presence among humankind, inspiring, motivating, enabling, endorsing human activity that is blessed and shaped according to the will of God. By no means is there a full-fledged doctrine of the Trinity in Luke; but there is the essential assurance that the Spirit links the Father to humankind and the Father to Jesus his Son.

The setting for this activity of the Holy Spirit is the fulfillment of the Torah; Law and Spirit come together in Luke as they do not in Paul. Jesus is circumcised according to the law, and according to the law is taken up to Jerusalem. Sacrifices are made for him according to the law (later, of course, he will be sacrificed to the law, but the story only foreshadows that by hints and warnings—see 2:35). Sharon Ringe points out that according to Levitical law it was really only Mary who needed to be purified after giving birth; but in Luke the whole family takes part in the purification and in the hope to which it points (45). In Luke, as we have already seen, Jesus is true Messiah, Israel's hope, and as Israel's hope he lives according to the commands and promises of the law.

What Simeon has awaited and what he sees in Jesus is really the anointed of the Lord (2:26). As a prophet, Simeon blessed God for a twofold mercy. Jesus *is* Messiah, God's gift to Israel. Jesus is also Isaiah's light to the nations. Precisely by being God's gift to Israel, he is God's gift to the whole world, since Israel serves a light that is not limited to Israel alone.

As a prophet, Simeon warns Mary and Joseph of the twofold danger. Precisely because he is God's representative among people, Jesus will separate people one from another, he will draw opposition as well as praise. Precisely because he is the light, he will draw the forces of darkness; darkness will hurt him; the sword will pierce Mary's heart. The story foretold by the prophets and lived out by them and by Jesus and by the apostles: the light shines in the darkness, and overcomes the darkness, but not without stirring up the forces of darkness to oppose it. Simeon knows this; he warns Mary.

He prepares to depart in God's peace, but he will leave not only peace but the warning of danger behind. How could it be otherwise?

Anna, like Simeon, represents the old waiting for and blessing of the new. She proclaims who he is to those who "look for the redemption of Jerusalem." Both Luke's Gospel and the book of Acts begin in Jerusalem. Luke's story ends in

Jerusalem as well, while Acts ends in Rome. Jesus is born in the time of Caesar Augustus and by the end of the two-volume story, he is being preached in Caesar's capital. But in Luke's Gospel, Jesus also knows that in the not-too-distant future Jerusalem will be destroyed—Jerusalem is redeemed only as part of the larger story of the redemption of the world (see Luke 20:41-44; 21:20-23). The temple is no longer the center of God's story; Jesus himself is that center.

There is no question in Luke's Gospel of the humanity of Jesus. Like every human, he grows, matures; with the blessed he grows in wisdom. God's favor, which was proclaimed to Mary by the angel Gabriel, now rests on Mary's Son.

JOHN 1:1-18 (BCP)

See the discussion for Christmas Day.

FIRST READING
ISAIAH 61:10—62:3

The Isaiah passage picks up the final promise of Anna in the Gospel passage—the hope for Jerusalem. It is hard to end the passage with 62:3, since the following verses pick up the imagery of the wedding which is so central to this oracle. It may be that there is here some sense that Israel has strayed adulterously after other gods, but now in this time of restoration she is like a bride, faithful to her delighted spouse. The celebratory note lifts the whole passage: Christmas delight is the delight of restoration, God's love for God's people, the faithful response of the beloved.

THERE IS NO QUESTION IN LUKE'S GOSPEL OF THE HUMANITY OF JESUS. LIKE EVERY HUMAN, HE GROWS, MATURES; WITH THE BLESSED HE GROWS IN WISDOM. GOD'S FAVOR, WHICH WAS PROCLAIMED TO MARY BY THE ANGEL GABRIEL, NOW RESTS ON MARY'S SON.

Again the restoration of Israel will be a sign and vision to all the people—perhaps they will envy Israel; perhaps they will learn from her of the beauty of the Lord's love.

SIRACH 3:2-6, 12-14 (RC)

Jesus Ben Sira, the Jewish sage of the second century before Christ, brings to bear the insights of Near Eastern Wisdom. The material goes well with the household obligations as spelled out in the section assigned from Colossians (see below). This is prudential wisdom about how best to serve God by living in an appropriately obedient relationship with one's parents. It is a kind of spelling out in wisdom terms of the commandment to honor thy father and mother

(*HarperCollins Study Bible,* 1158). In a way it seems self-evidently wise, but as with all such wisdom it runs the risk of glossing over the exceptions. There are fathers who use their rule to abuse and mothers who use their authority to intimidate. Again this is the kind of text which can lead to the most patent moralizing and generalizing. Seen in the larger context of God's intention for humankind it is helpful, but it needs extensive treatment in a larger context. I should think it is not the place to focus the homily for the first Sunday after Christmas. And if the idea is that Sirach somehow celebrates the kind of family we see in the Holy Family we need to remember that in the Holy Family the father is not really the Father, and the Son upbraids the mother on more than one occasion, in a most impolitic way (see Luke 2 and John 2).

SECOND READING
GALATIANS 4:4-7 (RCL) 3:23-25 (BCP)

You know the situation for which the letter to the Galatians was written. Paul founds the Galatian churches; but after he leaves, other Christian teachers arrive and insist that Paul has omitted an essential part of the Gospel. In order to be a believer in Jesus Christ, one must also take on the Jewish law (whether all of the law or only certain aspects of the law is not altogether clear). These teachers are especially insistent that Galatian (gentile) males receive circumcision as a sign of their incorporation into the community of faith. Paul writes the only one of his extant letters that is obviously and genuinely angry. The Galatians are falling away from the gospel he has taught them and following a false gospel. They are abandoning their Christian freedom for a slavery as oppressive as the old slavery they had to pagan gods and foolish superstitions.

We really need to look at the whole section, Galatians 3:23—4:7. A kind of parable is at least implied. The law functions for the childhood of humankind, but grace and adoption are the marks of maturity. Jesus Christ is the one who takes over for the law, which was both guardian and imprisoner.

Jesus is the Son through whom adoption is made possible. Through him believers become sons and daughters of God as well, mature heirs of the gifts of God's goodness. Paul has empirical proof of this adoption. In their worship services, the Galatian Christians cry "Abba," which means "Father." Perhaps this reflects a kind of ecstatic speaking in tongues among the Galatians. Perhaps it represents the first word of the Lord's Prayer, repeated in Aramaic with the rest of the prayer (presumably) recited in Greek. In either case, the very fact that these Christians can call God their Father shows that they have been adopted into God's family.

This assurance that we are part of God's family is what Paul calls "faith." It is itself a gift from God, but it is the gift that assures us that God does give us everything we need in Jesus Christ.

Note how closely the theme of Galatians picks up the themes of the affirmations in Luke. Jerusalem is no longer the center of God's dealing with humankind; Jesus Christ is that center. Therefore, the law that Jerusalem requires—especially the law of circumcision—is no longer the ground of the covenant relationship between God and God's people. The ground of that relationship is faith:"But now that faith has come we are no longer subject to a disciplinarian, for in Christ Jesus you are all children of God through faith."

The passage that the lectionary leaves out, 3:27-29, reminds the Galatians that their faith is sealed through baptism. Precisely in baptism the old distinctions between Jew and gentile, male and female, slave and free are washed away. Clothed with Christ, Christians need no longer be anxious about any external signs of their relationship to God—not circumcision, not diet, not gender or status. Faith alone brings all into the family.

Remember that it is still Christmastide. After all the "family" celebrations (or the deep loneliness that often comes when people feel excluded from such celebrations), this is the Sunday to recall that Christmas brings us into the family that counts above all—the family of God's own Son, who through faith becomes our brother. Joy to the world.

COLOSSIANS 3:12-21 (RC)

The passage combines portions of two major sub-movements within the letter to the Colossians. The first portion is a continuation of the apostle's description of the shape of life for the baptized in the community of faith (a section that begins with 3:1 and continues through 3:17). The second is the beginning of the so-called Household Table, a list of rules for Christian living within the household. The first part draws heavily on the imagery of baptism and new life; the second draws heavily on accepted standards of morality among sensible people of the first century, followers of Christ and "pagan" alike.

I SHOULD THINK THAT AT CHRISTMASTIDE WE WOULD BE MORE EAGER TO CELEBRATE THE WAY CHRIST INDWELLS THE CHURCH THAN TO FIGURE OUT WHO SHOULD BE SUBMISSIVE TO WHOM ON THE HOME FRONT.

I should think that at Christmastide we would be more eager to celebrate the way Christ indwells the church than to figure out who should be submissive to whom on the home front. Sermons on the household tables in the New Testament need to take serious account of the original setting of these texts (including the next injunction about slaves) and should not be simply nodded to as part of our exposition of other themes. If there is a central word to this rich text it comes at 3:15: "And be thankful." Colossians 3 is a spelling out of what such thankfulness might look like. It takes the gift of Christmas and shows how the gift lives and nurtures the ongoing life of the community of faith. It is evident especially in the love that we show to one another in the church. Lewis Donelson sums up the passage well: "Christian love is shaped by personal humility, by vulnerability to the community, by forgiveness" (Donelson, 46).

RESPONSIVE READING
PSALM 148

This great psalm of praise moves through the order of creation in Genesis 1, beginning (after the angels) with the heavenly bodies, moving through the beasts, and ending with "Kings of the earth and all peoples . . . young men and women alike." The great canticle of praise reaches out to include the whole cosmos. Everything created by the word of God returns to God the words of praise. James Luther Mays, with all his Calvinist reserve, nonetheless sounds like St. Francis here: "We [human beings] are in our obligation to praise no different from and no more than all the rest. Everything and everyone is identical in being addressed by the psalm. We human beings are one with all beings in our relation to One whose name alone is exalted and whose majesty is above earth and heaven" (Mays, 445). Of course, the psalm sounds like St. Francis, too.

Note that it begins with angels (we still hear the echo of angels from the services of last week); angels are not only messengers of God to us, they join us in the eternal praise of God, so says the psalm. Note that the psalm ends with Israel—the praise of all creation is also the praise of this people. The creation of all the cosmos moves toward the creation of this people (and Christians believe the creation of this people also moves toward the incarnation of the One by whose word the worlds came to be). Cosmos contained in him; cosmos unfolded from him. The still center of the turning world.

PSALM 147 (BCP)

There is comment on the final section of this psalm in the material for the second Sunday of Christmas. The psalm is a song of praise that praises God both for what God does in creating the world and for what God does in redeeming Israel. God's bounteous goodness in nature is replicated by God's mercy to those who are in distress. God also blesses the response of those who are blessed. People are to turn to God in reverence and hope. The psalm is almost a pastiche of themes and images, all of them providing praise for God's astonishing bounty. At this Christmas season the psalm helps move us away from too great a stress on the material bounty we may have received beneath the tree to the greater bounty that sustains the universe and uplifts the downhearted.

PSALM 128:1-5 (RC)

If at all possible, I would encourage attending to the whole psalm (which is only six verses). The psalm is almost proverbial, pronouncing a kind of providential blessing upon those who are faithful (compare Psalm 1). The first verses proclaim a blessing and the last verses pray the blessing. Finally the psalm relates this blessing to God's presence in Zion. The City is the sign of God's blessedness and the place from which God bestows blessing. This seems a cheerful psalm for a cheerful season.

PRAYER

In Jesus Christ you have set us free, O God. Free from bondage to ourselves but also free from bondage to the devices and desires by which we would commend ourselves to you. We acknowledge our unworthiness of your gift, but we acknowledge that it is sheer gift—granted us even in our unworthiness. Fill us with your Spirit and our hearts with gratitude. Through Jesus Christ our Lord, Amen.

FEAST OF ST. STEPHEN

DECEMBER 26, 1999

REVISED COMMON	EPISCOPAL (BCP)
2 Chron. 24:17-22	Jer. 26:1-9, 12-15
Ps. 17:1-9, 16	Ps. 31 or 31:1-5
Acts 6:8—7:2a, 51c-60	Acts 6:8—7:2a, 51-60
Matt. 23:34-39	Matt. 23:34-39

THE CROSS ALWAYS SHADOWS CHRISTMAS (as Easter always interprets the cross). Simeon has warned Mary of the coming danger. The child grows in wisdom and stature but also grows toward sacrifice and loss. It is perhaps appropriate that on the day after we celebrate the gift, we remember the cost—the cost to Jesus, but also the cost to those who follow him. Stephen, one of the seven, helps open the Gospel to those who speak Greek and therefore, perhaps, in anticipation, moves the Gospel toward the gentiles, the celebration of epiphany. Both the Matthew passage and the Zechariah passage remind us of the cost of faithfulness—in Israel and for Christian disciples, too.

SECOND READING
ACTS 6:8—7:2a, 51c-60

Stephen's story, in Acts, vividly and deliberately calls us back to the story of Christ's martyrdom; Jesus' story vividly and deliberately points ahead to Stephen and to the risk that all faithful followers take on.

I always look out when the lectionary gives us 2a's and 51c's. One suspects there is a danger that the movement of the text will get lost, truncated.

As the story starts (not just as the story ends), Stephen reminds us of his Lord. He is full of grace and power, as in the text for the Feast of the Holy Family; Jesus is filled with wisdom and the grace of God is upon him (Luke 2:40). In both texts, God's favor is indicated by the Greek word usually translated "grace," *charis*. Like Jesus (and like the apostles), Stephen indicates that he is authorized by God because he performs "signs and wonders" (see Acts 2:22 for Jesus, Acts 2:43; 4:30; and 5:12 for the apostles). Stephen stands in the line that extends from the prophets through Jesus through the apostles. For him (as for the prophets and

Jesus before him and for other believers after him), fidelity to his mission will be fidelity to death. As with Jesus (and with Mary and with Simeon and Anna), the Spirit rests on Stephen, strengthening him and inspiring him.

What the lectionary leaves out is the bulk of Stephen's speech, a kind of history of Israel's salvation, or perhaps more accurately a kind of history of Israel's resistance to salvation. The whole story of God's sending prophets and kings to Israel only to see them rejected ends with the punch line that the lectionary also omits: "You stiff-necked people, uncircumcised in heart and ears, you always resist the Holy Spirit." (Acts 7:51ab. Then with the lectionary text: "As your fathers did, so do you.")

Now explicitly, the resistance to Jesus stands in the line of the resistance to the prophets; implicitly, Stephen stands in the same line. His sermon both brings about his death and interprets that death.

Stephen's martyrdom recalls Jesus. He forgives his enemies; he commits his spirit, not into the hands of the Father but into Jesus' own hands. He stands in the great line of the prophets and of the Messiah, and partakes both of the same Spirit and of the same destiny. Notice, too, that the kind of apocalyptic prediction in the gospels that at the end of time the faithful will see Jesus coming from heaven, from the right hand of God, is here somewhat re-interpreted. Jesus stands at the right hand of God and welcomes the martyr into heaven. (As Jesus said to the thief, "Today you will be with me in paradise," not "at the last day I will raise you up to Paradise." [Luke 23:43])

Saul consenting to Stephen's death in 8:1a is not only a fine touch of drama, it is a stunning reminder that (as with the resurrection) reversal always stands at the other side of martyrdom. Who will carry forward this cause, this preaching, this good news? The one who stands at the side consenting to the martyrdom will become the chief witness in this book of Acts, and just beyond the book, as the readers surely knew, himself a martyr (whose Gospel will also far outlast himself).

What do we see here? That you cannot know the story of Jesus without knowing the Old Testament, even if the lessons you draw from it are largely negative (a hermeneutic that seems insufficient to the richness of the texts). That the story of Jesus (who for Luke is in heaven) is prolonged on earth by the continuing faithful preaching and suffering of servants like Stephen. That while there is no guarantee that fidelity will mean martyrdom, there is no guarantee that it will not. That no one knows when her or his moment for heroism will come, so that one prays to stay faithful and seeks to live by the Spirit.

> WHAT DO WE SEE HERE? THAT YOU CAN'T KNOW THE STORY OF JESUS WITHOUT KNOWING THE OLD TESTAMENT

Dietrich Bonhoeffer, one of the martyrs of the century now passing, sat in prison and wondered if his reckless willingness to challenge the Third Reich was really recklessness for the sake of Christ. He decided that it was. Here is what he wrote to a friend: "At first I wondered a good deal whether it was really for the cause of Christ that I was causing you all such grief; but I soon put that out of my head as a temptation, as I became certain that the duty had been laid on me to hold out in this boundary situation with all its problems." (Bonhoeffer, 69–70).

GOSPEL
MATTHEW 23:34-39

It is striking that Matthew (not Luke) provides the best commentary on the passage from Acts. In this passage Jesus clearly identifies himself with the long line of prophets, and looks ahead to Christian "prophets, wise men and scribes." Martyrdom is apt to be the lot of a number of these early Christians.

Judgment is pronounced upon Jerusalem precisely because she has failed to acknowledge those who are sent by God's Spirit. That she stones the faithful points, of course, to the means of Stephen's execution, but that she turns from the faithful (from Abel until now) points to Stephen's speech and the long history of rejection on Israel's part.

The commentaries will tell you that Matthew (or Jesus) got the wrong Zechariah.

The sense that Jesus will now absent himself from Jerusalem until he "comes again" of course points to the eschatological hope. In Luke and Acts (somewhat differently from Matthew), that absence is mitigated by the presence of the Spirit and by the promise that Jesus comes again and again to honor the death of the faithful (martyrs) and to receive their spirits into heaven.

In Matthew's Gospel this whole passage is part of the much longer woe against the scribes and Pharisees and represents Matthew's sense that the people of Judah and Jerusalem stand under judgment both for their hypocrisy and for their rejection of Jesus.

It need hardly be added that both Matthew and Acts are written out of a context where church and synagogue are fighting over the question of who are the true heirs of Moses and the prophets, and that no faithful Jew of that time, or of this, would recognize either the woes of Matthew 23 or the list of rejections in Acts 7 as either a fair or an accurate description of Israel's story with her God. Nor should we.

BOTH MATTHEW AND ACTS ARE WRITTEN OUT OF A CONTEXT WHERE CHURCH AND SYNAGOGUE ARE FIGHTING OVER THE QUESTION OF WHO ARE THE TRUE HEIRS OF MOSES AND THE PROPHETS.

FIRST READING

2 CHRONICLES 24:17-22

This is obviously included as a kind of historical corrective to Matthew (or Jesus), who like students of the Bible before and since sometimes gets the wrong name for the father of famous daughters or sons. But more fully, we get an illustration of the kind of martyrdom to which Jesus refers and which Stephen enacts. Like Stephen, Zechariah is calling the people of Judea to a worship of the true God. Boldly, Stephen insists that the true God is the one who comes to humankind in Jesus of Nazareth, and to worship God without acknowledging Jesus is inadequate faith (if not the outright idolatry Zechariah fights against). Again, this martyr, like those in Jesus' oracle and like Stephen himself, is stoned for his faithfulness.

Notice a striking contrast, however. While the dying Zechariah cries: "May the Lord see and avenge!" (2 Chron. 24:22). The dying Stephen cries: "Lord, do not hold this against them" (Acts 7:60).

JEREMIAH 26:1-9, 12-15 (BCP)

Read in its own context, this is a story of a prophet without honor in his own country. Jeremiah warns the people that unless they repent and follow the one law of the one God they will be like Shiloh—an important sanctuary that had been destroyed, probably in the eleventh century B.C.E. (*HarperCollins Study Bible,* 1128).

Read in conjunction with the passage from Acts, we have here the story of another messenger from God who speaks truth, calls for repentance, and raises the ire of the people. His opponents accuse Stephen of following one who will tear down the temple, and Jeremiah predicts the destruction of Jerusalem unless the people repent. Unlike Stephen, Jeremiah escapes with his life—but just barely (see Jer. 26:24).

Jeremiah's story embodies Stephen's reminder to those who are about to execute him: "You stiff-necked people, uncircumcised in heart and ears, you are forever opposing the Holy Spirit, just as your ancestors used to do. Which of the prophets did your ancestors not persecute?" (Acts 7:52).

PSALM 17:1–9, 16

Here is a prayer for vindication and redemption addressed to God: "Guard me as the apple of the eye; hide me in the shadow of your wings." How does one sing this psalm in the light of the Stephen story, where in an important sense we see a faithful one who is not protected from the enemy?

Does the promise that he is received into the heavenly places become a kind of Christian solution to the problem of unjust suffering? Or is there a tension here between the faithful prayer that counts on God and the realism of both 2 Chronicles and Acts (and Matthew 23) that reminds us that sometimes the faithful pay for their fidelity with their deaths? The adversary is not always foiled, at least not at first, not visibly. Stephen does not see his vindication (does not see, perhaps, that part of that vindication is Saul who stands in the wings).

The narratives undercut the optimism of the psalm; or perhaps the psalm provides the hope that could drive the narratives. Had we no hope for deliverance how could we be faithful? In this life, or for the life to come, or in the lives that are touched by our life we pray God to use our living and our dying. In that sense the prayer endures: "I call upon you, for you will answer me, O Lord" (v. 6).

PSALM 31 (BCP)

Psalm 31:5 provides the source for Jesus' word from the cross in Luke 23, a word which Luke (or Stephen) then shifts to become a word about Jesus himself: "Lord Jesus, into your hand I commit my spirit." The assurance of the psalm, "You have redeemed me, O Lord, faithful God," is enacted only eschatologically for Jesus and for Stephen. The redemption is redemption beyond death, not redemption from death. The psalm itself shows forth a robust confidence in the power of God to deliver the righteous from their enemies in this life, but taken along with the passage from Acts can provide a reminder to have confidence in God both in life and in death.

PRAYER

We do not know, O Lord, when we may be called to bear witness, or what cost our witnessing may have. We know that you are God and that competing gods vie in every marketplace for the world's attention. Grant us to proclaim you so winsomely and to serve you so diligently that your name may be glorified. In our living, in our dying, may we serve your cause. Through Jesus Christ our Lord, Amen.

HOLY NAME OF JESUS / MARY, MOTHER OF GOD

NEW YEAR'S DAY

JANUARY 1, 2000

REVISED COMMON★	EPISCOPAL (BCP)	ROMAN CATHOLIC (RC)
Num. 6:22–27	Exod. 34:1–8	Num. 6:22–27
or Eccles. 3:1-13		
Ps. 8	Ps. 8	Ps. 67:2-3, 5-6, 8
Gal. 4:4–7	Rom. 1:1–7	Gal. 4:4–7
or Phil. 2:5-13		
or *Rev. 21:1-6a*		
Luke 2:15–21	Luke 2:15–21	Luke 2:16–21
or *Matt. 25:31-46*		

NOW WE HAVE A CORNUCOPIA, A MÉLANGE, A KALEIDOSCOPE of festive possibilities. Probably most preachers will have the good sense (or the liturgical compunction) to concentrate on one of these options. We begin with those texts that are appropriate to the celebration of the name of Jesus and of Mary, and then will conclude with texts from Ecclesiastes, Revelation, and Matthew 25 that are set to address the possibilities of celebrating the New Year and, of course, the new millennium.

GOSPEL
LUKE 2:15-21

Verse 21 stresses the naming of Jesus at the time of his circumcision. The combination of the name and the rite remind us that in Luke, as in the other Gospels, Jesus' story can only be told in the context of Israel. Here he is named as his parents are obedient to the requirements of the law. He enters into the history of a people and through that people into the history of the world. Without the people and without the history there is no understanding him. That does not mean, of course, that he only replicates or sums up the history; he also transforms

★ Italicized texts are used when January 1 is celebrated as New Year's Day.

it, but it is the history of Israel that he transforms in order to transform the history of the world.

The verse recalls the announcement of the angel in Luke 1:31. Unlike the giving of the name in Matthew, Luke's account does not rely on the etymology of the name—one who saves. However, the description of the one named Jesus implies the salvific meaning of the name: "He will be great, and will be called the Son of the Most High, and the Lord God will give to him the throne of his ancestor Jacob. He will reign over the house of Jacob forever, and of his kingdom there will be no end." Again we note how the naming and the circumcision give Jesus his place among the people of Israel and in their history.

More than that, because the name was announced by an angel, not simply chosen by Joseph and Mary, we see that the name, like the birth and the ministry to follow, are part of God's plan, using human actors but transcending human activity. Jesus had this name even before he was conceived! Put it another way; he was conceived in the mind of God before he was conceived in the womb of Mary.

> BECAUSE JESUS' NAME WAS ANNOUNCED BY AN ANGEL, NOT SIMPLY CHOSEN BY JOSEPH AND MARY, WE SEE THAT THE NAME, LIKE THE BIRTH AND THE MINISTRY TO FOLLOW, ARE PART OF GOD'S PLAN, USING HUMAN ACTORS BUT TRANSCENDING HUMAN ACTIVITY.

Mary is of course the other figure to whom the Gospel reading calls special attention, on this day that recognizes her. Though Luke never calls her the mother of God, she is the mother of Jesus who is the one sent from God to be ruler of Israel and a light to the gentiles. That she is God's own mother is a later expansion on the Lukan affirmation of her unique and important role—not necessarily inconsistent with Luke's picture but beyond Luke in its implicit appeal to trinitarian theology and the godhead of Jesus himself.

What Luke has shown through chapters 1 and 2 is that Mary is a uniquely faithful person who listens to the word of God and obeys; she is an evangelist who preaches the good news concerning her own son; she is a person of great spiritual depth who treasures the word she receives through the shepherds, holding them (as pious people should) in the depth of her heart.

The child in her womb and then the words in her heart—she bears the gifts of God for the people of God.

FIRST READING
NUMBERS 6:22-27

When God delivers to Moses the Aaronic blessing, he declares the way in which Aaron and the priests who follow are to name the divine name over the chosen people. When the angel delivers to Mary the name of Jesus, who will reign over Israel, he delivers that other name by which priests and laypeople alike can pronounce God's blessing on God's people.

In Jesus, the blessing, the peace, and the light extend beyond Israel to include the gentiles. For Christians he fulfills the promise (always implicit in Israel's story, too) that the blessing and the light extend beyond Israel to the whole creation.

For Christians this one named Jesus is the one in whom God's blessing comes, God's face shines, God's countenance appears, God's peace is bestowed. "For it is the God who said, 'Let light shine out of darkness,' who has shone in our hearts to give the light of the knowledge of the glory of God in the face of Jesus Christ" (2 Cor. 4:6).

ECCLESIASTES 3:1-13

Ecclesiastes 3 is often read as a comforting affirmation about the regularity of God's world. It can as easily be read as a statement, if not of cynicism, at least of resignation. We need to read on to the end of the paragraph: "That which is, already has been; that which is to be, already is" (Eccles. 3:15). One doesn't ask history to have a plot for life to move forward to meaning, because all is repetition and every promising good is counterbalanced by the equal and opposite bad. We don't know much, so we should make the most of the little that we have. This may be a text with which to confront a new year and even a new millennium, but it is shaded by Ecclesiastes' "anti–New Year" reminder: "There is nothing new under the sun" (Eccles. 1:9).

> ECCLESIASTES 3 IS OFTEN READ AS A COMFORTING AFFIRMATION ABOUT THE REGULARITY OF GOD'S WORLD. IT CAN AS EASILY BE READ AS A STATEMENT, IF NOT OF CYNICISM, AT LEAST OF RESIGNATION.

EXODUS 34:1-8 (BCP)

Now God delivers to Moses the tablets to deliver to the people—a replacement for the tablets shattered after the incident with the golden calf. On the one hand, the story stresses the re-giving of the law. It is a good reminder to those of us who are steeped in the distinction between law and grace that law itself can be a gift, and that a gracious God provides that gift faithfully, repeatedly, stubbornly.

Here again we have the stress on the holy name "the Lord," which in Hebrew is the unnameable name transliterated "Yahweh." In Exodus 34:5, the Lord pronounces the divine name, "YHWH." Then verses 6-8 spell out what the name means in the story of Israel, just as the Gospels spell out what the name Jesus means in the lives of believers.

PHILIPPIANS 2:5-13

The text provides a lens through which to read both Luke 2 and Numbers 6 (perhaps these are bifocals). A couple of issues about this passage are much vexed, but neither has much to do with the relationship of the passage to Jesus' name. The first issue is whether the passage contrasts the pre-existent Son with Jesus the humble servant or whether this is rather an implicit contrast between disobedient Adam and obedient Jesus without any necessary implication of Christ's preexistence. The other question is whether the function of the passage is to enjoin an ethical imitation of Christ on the Philippians (be humble as he was humble) or rather to remind them of their identity in him (have that mind in yourselves which you already have in Christ, the humble one). The action that Paul foresees is very much the same, but the motivation is different in subtle ways.

There is also considerable consensus that Paul here uses a hymn that he did not write, perhaps a hymn already known and loved by the Philippians, to make his points both about Jesus' special status and about the Philippians' special obligation.

In the context of this day, however, we note especially that the hymn Paul quotes talks of the name that is above every name. Since for this passage the naming comes after the crucifixion and glorification of Jesus, it seems unlikely that it is the name "Jesus" that Paul (or the hymn) has specifically in mind. More likely, the claim is that in the crucifixion and exaltation, Jesus receives the divine name *kyrios,* for Greek-speaking Jews a way of not quite speaking the divine name Yahweh. In English, *kyrios* is most often translated "Lord" as it is here. Now (reading Philippians and Numbers) it is Jesus himself who receives not only the name Jesus, but the name Lord. The Aaronic blessing "the Lord bless you and keep you" can also be read christologically. Jesus is the fulfillment of the priestly blessing, and he receives the name with which the faithful are blessed.

GALATIANS 4:4-7

Here the role of Jesus (if not his name) and the role of Mary (if not her designation as mother of God) come together. Paul is contrasting the old world of the Law with the new world that has come in Jesus Christ. Through a series of complicated analogies, he argues that in Jesus Christ the faithful pass from our minority (when we are under the care of a stern guardian) to the freedom of adulthood where we accept our place as sons and daughters of God. We are adopted into God's family by the Spirit of God's son; that is, his sonship makes our new status as sons and daughters possible. This is another way of stating that he has the name that is above every name, or that he is the one who saves people. Jesus is now the older brother whose sonship brings us into God's family.

The reference to Jesus' mother is not exactly an aside, but it serves in the larger argument to remind us that Jesus entered fully into human life: with a real mother, a real people. Yet because he entered human history "in the fullness of time," he redeemed the history and the humanity. Born under the law and born to a human being, he overcomes the law and liberates humanity.

Galatians takes an image, a metaphor, to proclaim what our other passages proclaim by stressing Jesus' name(s). We remember that for Old and New Testament alike images are not mere rhetorical ornamentation and names are not accidents. The image shows forth, embodies, the reality to which it points. The name is the revelation of the one named. Jesus as Son, the Son named Jesus, Jesus who is also *kyrios,* the Lord to whom every knee shall bow. The images point to that reality; the name names it.

ROMANS 1:1-7 (BCP)

This is the only Pauline letter we have that was written to a community of faith he had not yet visited. Many think that verses 1-7 include a kind of poem drawn from a tradition that Paul and perhaps the Romans also knew. For instance, the suggestion that Jesus was declared Son of God at his resurrection is here unique in Paul's writing, which elsewhere understands both sonship and resurrection somewhat differently. Like the other traditional material we have noted, in Philippians 2, this passage affirms that Jesus receives a name that indicates his particular power: in this case the name is "Son of God." The rest of the passage shows us what he is able to do as Son of God. He provides grace for all, apostleship for Paul, peace from God to all the saints (the believers). The right response of believers to him is twofold: it includes obedience, it includes faith. One way of understanding the great letter that follows is to suggest that Romans 1–11 gives us a picture of the shape of faith, and Romans 12–16 a picture of the shape of obedience.

Homiletically it might be a good time to think together about what names mean. Though we have robbed naming of some of its mystery, every parent knows something of the awe and hesitation that goes into the naming of a child. This will say something about who the child is, or what we hope for her or him. When our firstborn was born, we had two boys' names in mind and two girls' names. It was evident immediately that we had to choose from the first list, and more surprising, it was evident immediately which name was his.

How much more when God has chosen the name for Jesus as a sign and embodiment of what God intends to do through him.

Or another angle. How important it is for us to get names right. As a teacher, I try very hard early in the semester to get the right names for my students; it is discourteous and sometimes even hurtful to get it wrong. How much more with the gift that God has given us: let's get his name right. Who is he? Naming him is an important start in knowing him—and honoring him, too.

Of course, we also deal with New Years, and on this day the beginning (or one year before the beginning) of a new millennium. I have to begin by confessing my uneasiness with overemphasis on the detail of dating. The best guess of many scholars is that Jesus was born about 4 B.C.E., and if they're right we entered the third millennium some years ago with no hoopla whatsoever. We are now (almost) 2,000 years past the almost certainly wrong date assigned to Jesus' birth in the Middle Ages, and it's hard to get excited about the anniversary of a mistake. My spouse is not exactly thrilled if I show up with the anniversary flowers a couple of days late.

Ecclesiastes is really a good warning against excessive calendrical enthusiasm. While we're used to singing these verses to guitar in modest hopeful settings (both musically and socially), the fact is that the passage is written out of fairly profound cynicism, as part of the general Ecclesiastical reminder (or warning) that there is nothing new under the sun. Put another way, while it may be true that the year 2000 now begins, neither sun, moon, nor stars is keeping track. The calendar is a human device for coping with change and constancy. Nothing wrong with it, but hardly the stuff of profound theological enthusiasms.

> WHILE IT MAY BE TRUE THAT THE YEAR 2000 NOW BEGINS, NEITHER SUN, MOON, NOR STARS IS KEEPING TRACK. THE CALENDAR IS A HUMAN DEVICE FOR COPING WITH CHANGE AND CONSTANCY. NOTHING WRONG WITH IT, BUT HARDLY THE STUFF OF PROFOUND THEOLOGICAL ENTHUSIASMS.

Christians more millennialist than I, of course, delight in noting the times, especially when the times end in zeroes. And two of our passages open up attention to chronology.

REVELATION 21:1-6a (RCL)

Here, powerful imagery proclaims the hope toward which we believe history moves: new heaven, new earth. It is the shape of the hope, not its date, that seems central in our interpretation. It is impossible to know exactly what (if any) time scheme John of Patmos had in mind for his prophecies. And some calculations of the importance of this new millennium will already be disconfirmed if you actually get to deliver this week's sermon. The shape of the hope is worth holding forth this year or any new year: God with us; we as God's people; tears wiped away; mourning no more. And two new names for Jesus (while we are thinking about his name): Alpha and Omega. I read Philippians 2 the same way; Jesus is at the beginning and at the end. Certainly John's Gospel names him that way. The name of Jesus and the concern about the turning of the years come together. We do not worry about the turning of the years because the story, the history, begins in him, and will end in him, too. Alpha and Omega. The name is far more important than the date.

GOSPEL
MATTHEW 25:31–36 (RCL)

Matthew 25:31–36 follows two parables but is not itself a parable. It is an apocalyptic description of the end of time, and therefore appropriate for millennial moments and for the turning of each year as well. The question is, how are nations judged in God's history? The answer is that they are judged by how they treat the least. Originally "the least" were probably believers, poor missionaries struggling on their way to proclaim the Gospel, at the mercy of powers greater than their own. Now, often we Christians are the powers or wield power. What meek and lowly visitors make appropriate demands on our attention? Here is another name for Jesus: "The least of these."

PRAYER

We pray in your name, Lord Jesus Christ, trusting in the power of that name to bring us into the presence of God. We preach in your name, Lord Jesus Christ, trusting that our words will convey your Word to your people. We act in your name, Lord Jesus Christ, trusting that you are at work to drive the world toward your justice and your mercy. We pray in your name, Lord Jesus Christ. Amen.

SECOND SUNDAY AFTER CHRISTMAS

JANUARY 2, 2000

REVISED COMMON	EPISCOPAL (BCP)	ROMAN CATHOLIC
Jer. 31:7-14	Jer. 31:7-14	Sir. 24:1-2, 8-12
or Sir. 24:1-12		
Ps. 147:12-20	Ps. 84 or 84:1-8	Ps. 147:12-15, 19-20
or Wisd. 10:15-21		
Eph. 1:3-14	Eph. 1:3-6, 15-19a	Eph. 1:3-6, 15-18
John 1:(1-9), 10-18	Matt. 2:13-15, 19-23	John 1:1-18 or 1:1-5, 9-14
	or Luke 2:41-52	
	or Matt. 2:1-12	

ON THIS SUNDAY WE RETURN TO THE great affirmation of the incarnation in the prologue to John. Now we read that hymn in the light of the celebration of Advent and Christmas we have been enjoying, and in the light of these other scripture passages that help us to understand the central mystery of John.

John 1, Ephesians, the story of the Magi all remind us that history is in God's hands, and that God providentially brings us to Christ in worship and in praise.

GOSPEL
JOHN 1:(1-9), 10-18

We have visited this text during this season. The question now is whether we read it differently in the light of other texts assigned for the day, and that is a question best answered at the end of our considerations.

MATTHEW 2:1-12, 13-15, 19-23 (BCP)

Not only in Christmas pageants are the wise men or astrologers—the magi—a balance to the shepherds (one set grouped stage left and the other stage right for the obligatory final tableau). The shepherds are astonished by surprising mercy; the magi go seeking. Like the shepherds, the magi have to end up in Bethlehem; perhaps there is something to the fact that Bethlehem is not the great city where the great king is, but (like the stable) "outside." Certainly there is something to the fact that this is David's city. For Matthew, Jesus is David's son. Certainly, as always for Matthew, there is something to the fact that the birth in Bethlehem fulfills prophecy. Matthew believes that God has known the plot of this story all along and has sprinkled Scripture (our Old Testament) chock-full of clues—the prophecies. Here the clue comes from Micah.

There is good reason for the tradition that the visit of the magi is the beginning of the Gospel for gentiles. Whoever else these wise men may be, they are not Jews.

There is the sharp reminder that mercy already brings opposition. This happens in the time of King Herod, and before the verses are over, we know that King Herod is a force to be reckoned with and finally, of course, a force to be overcome.

In verses 13-15 the opposition grows stronger, more virulent. The prophecy is underlined. Another prophet speaks other words that foretell the visit to Egypt. In Luke's narrative, Simeon tells Mary that a sword will pierce her heart; in Matthew's Gospel the sword already begins to do its deadly work. He is driven to exile who will soon enough be driven to the cross. Why do the readings leave out the actual slaughter of the innocents? Is it too hard on our nice Christianity to see the price of mercy, to know that grace always breeds opposition? We like Christmas gifts wrapped under the tree. Alas, the first Christmas gift brought blood and tears. The prophet would not have been surprised. Rachel wept, now Rachel's daughters weep.

Verses 19-23 remind us that in Matthew especially, Jesus makes no move that is not prophesied and therefore included in the plan of God. The holy family comes to Nazareth, Joseph, like his ancient namesake, driven by a dream (see also Matt. 1:20). They come, not because it is their old home town—as in Luke—but because Jesus needs to fulfill the prophecy (whose source is not clear): "He will be called a Nazorean" (Matt. 2:23). Beginning to end, the story is in God's hands. The Scripture gives us the script that shows us God's providential control.

LUKE 2:41-52 (BCP)

Here is the Bible story every schoolchild learns to hate. Jesus as teacher's pet. Yet beyond the inescapable annoyance of the fact that the young Jesus sounds so much like the young (you fill in the name from your childhood), the story points out Lukan themes, Gospel themes.

There is the contrast between the worried earthly father and the confidence in the heavenly Father whose business Jesus does. There is the firm anchoring of

the story in the Temple and therefore in the story of the Jewish people. There is
Mary, once again the faithful servant of the Lord, treasuring precisely what God
has given her to treasure. There is the child growing in wisdom, so that for Luke
(despite the evidence of this temple scene), like every young boy, he really had
some growing to do. Perhaps that is a good theme for the Sunday after Christmas: how does our faith grow with his, starting with the manger but moving to
mysteries both deeper and more sad?

SECOND READING
EPHESIANS 1:3-19a

Those who study this epistle disagree on whether it was written by Paul
or by one of his followers. What they agree on is that the epistle advocates and
celebrates the unity of all humankind in Jesus Christ—especially as that unity is
made manifest in the relationship between Jews and gentiles.

Lewis Donelson reminds us that these verses are not a precise theological
explication but are liturgical, part of a blessing. Indeed, he suggests, all of Ephesians can be read as "a blessing to God" (Donelson, 64).

Unity is the great theme of the first chapter of the epistle: the unity between
God the Father and Christ the Son, the unity between Christ and the whole
creation; the unity of the church in Christ. In the Greek the whole section from
1:3-23 can be read as one paragraph—all of it part of the opening benediction of
this epistle. And 1:3-13 is really one long sentence, full of subordinate clauses.

The passage blesses God for the way in which God blesses believers in Christ,
and holds up both sides of that blessing: what we have in Christ, what we have as
believers.

What God bestows on Christ, God bestows from before the beginning of
creation. What God bestows on us, God bestows from before the beginning of
creation, too. Christ is destined for glory and believers are destined for glory
with him.

What the assigned passage leaves out, however, is the ground for this confidence. It is the resurrection that affirms predestination. We go from the end of
the story back to the beginning of the story.

What the assigned passage also leaves out is the somewhat surprising punch
line, that this destiny, this destining, leads to one destination: the church. There
the promises of God are embodied in community.

The structure of the passage underlines the unity of community. The "we" of
verse 12 surely signifies Jewish believers, the "you" of verse 13 refers to the gentiles. Though the Jews were the "first to set their hope on Christ," gentiles are no

less marked with the "seal of the promise." All are adopted in Christ and all are therefore heirs of the mercies of God.

We note how central both to Ephesians and to Galatians (see Gal. 4:1-7) is the theme of adoption. The notion that we are children of God by birth has its own theological power, but in these epistles there is perhaps a deeper claim. We are children of God by God's deliberate choice in Jesus Christ. Through Christ we become members of the family where (as Ephesians insists) God alone is Father.

Friends of ours have a large family; four children are adopted, one is the biological child of the parents. After one of the adopted children had heard his father explain how special was the act of adoption, the act of choosing, he said of the brother who was the biological son: "But Daddy, can't we adopt Chris, too? Otherwise he'll feel left out." In this story, the gift of adoption is open to all—Jews and gentiles alike, lest anyone seem left out.

Ephesians does in its own way what John 1 does. It reminds us that the story of the coming of Christ is not only an event in the life of one community or one family at one time long ago. It is the world-shaping, cosmic and powerful means by which God brings the whole world to Godself and humankind to one another. For Ephesians, more explicitly than for John, Jesus also shows the fullness of his power in the fullness of the church. The unity of creation is embodied in the unity of the church, and the fullness of Christ fills up not only the universe, but also and especially the community of believers.

While I suggested in my comments for New Year's Day that the excitement about the millennium is more cultural than biblical, if you feel called or required to think about the significance of this new millennium, Ephesians provides a good starting point. The millennium begins in God's intention in Christ and ends in God's intention in Christ. The clue to its meaning is the resurrection of Jesus, and our assurance against its dangers is that, in Jesus Christ, God is for us.

First Reading
JEREMIAH 31:7-14

The passage presents two prophecies of deliverance (7-9 and 10-14) predicting and celebrating the return of Israel from exile. Verse 9 speaks of Israel in ways that recall the adoption promises of Ephesians 1 to Jews and gentiles alike: "For I have become a father to Israel, and Ephraim is my firstborn." The text speaks both to the promises of Christmas and to the hopes for a new year. The God whose hand holds history is a God who wills joy and return for the faithful. The final word is always comfort and possibility. For Christians, of course, Jesus is the source of joy and the road home.

Here personified wisdom speaks of her role in the creation of the world and the blessing of Zion. Almost certainly the Fourth Evangelist draws on images such as these in presenting his picture of the Word that is from the beginning and then comes to dwell—not just with Jacob, but with the whole world. While there is no doctrine of wisdom as incarnate in human flesh, there certainly is the promise of Wisdom as present in human history. The passage helps us understand the strong affirmations of John 1—John believes that Jesus is himself the wisdom and purpose of God, present from the beginning and incarnate in ministry. Sirach's metaphor becomes John's faith: the Word does dwell among us. Beholding him we behold God as well.

RESPONSIVE READING
PSALM 147:12-20

Here we have stress, not on the wisdom of God, but on God's word. While the word does not seem to be a preexistent member of the godhead, the word does have power. It runs fast; it blows like the spirit; it melts the hail; it gives order and structure to Israel. Again we see another element of the Fourth Gospel's strong stress on God's word: the word is what God does; it is active and powerful. In John's Gospel, Jesus is what God does; he is active and powerful, bringing light to the darkness and the world to God.

PSALM 84 (BCP)

The psalm goes beautifully with the Lukan reading. The child Jesus is not just the prodigy who confounds his elders, he is the faithful Jew whose soul longs for the temple. Indeed, it may have been this psalm or one much like it that the pilgrims would have sung on their way to the Holy City. Later in the story, as Luke reminds us that the temple will be destroyed, we discover that now, instead of longing for the temple, faithful people will long for Christ himself, God's sun, our shield.

WISDOM 10:15-21 (RCL)

Here Wisdom, rather like the Holy Spirit in other texts, becomes the active agent by which God has worked with Israel. She delivers Israel from

Egypt, speaks through Moses, is present in the pillar of cloud and fire (Exod. 13:21-22), and inspires the songs of the children of Israel. For John's Gospel the gifts that came to Moses are outdone (and perhaps even undone) by the greater gift that comes in Jesus Christ where Wisdom, the Word, not only inspires but is incarnate.

GOSPEL

JOHN 1:(1-9), 10-18 (RCL/RC)

When we re-read the Prologue to John in the light of these passages from Jeremiah, Sirach, Psalm 147 and Wisdom, we certainly get a richer sense of the context for the great claim of the Fourth Gospel that the Word was in the beginning and that it became flesh.

John draws upon the image of wisdom as an extension of God's planning and doing that sometimes takes its place among human beings—as the law and ordinances of God. John draws upon the image of the word of God that is active and powerful; able not only to speak but to do.

The affirmation of this passage is that from the beginning God has shaped the world and intended history according to the pattern of the Word; we know what the Word looks like because we know what Jesus Christ looks like; and we know what the Word can do because we have seen what he can do.

Moses may have known the word, but Jesus *is* the word. In him we see the very glory of the Father. It is full of grace, because the word always actively does God's merciful will among humankind. It is full of truth, because this word is the full revelation of who God really is.

Ephesians, too, provides a context for declaring what John's Gospel declares. From the beginning, the intention of God is made known in Jesus. To know him fully is to know what creation means and where history turns. That is a strong word for the second Sunday of Christmastide and for the first Sunday of a new year (and by some calculations, a new millennium).

The second Sunday after Christmas therefore becomes the time when we declare not just the meaning of the manger but the meaning of history and the promise of creation. Mark begins his gospel with Jesus' baptism and ministry. Matthew takes him back to Abraham (1:2) and Luke takes him back to Adam (3:38). John takes him back to the beginning of creation. Jesus is not an afterthought, a Messiah sent when other plans had failed. Jesus is the forethought, the purpose and intention of God (so, too, Ephesians claims). He is the blueprint by which the cosmos was made, and he is the script for the drama of human history.

Christmas does not just celebrate the babe, it celebrates the eternal Word, as close as breathing and as powerful as the very breath of God. "Oh Come, let us adore him!"

PRAYER

Word of God, by whom the world is made and to whom the world returns, dwell richly in our hearts that we may serve you faithfully and proclaim you boldly. Son of God, by whom we are reconciled to God and to one another, draw us into your family that we may dwell in peace. Let the gifts of this season bear fruit in the lives of your people—always to the end that your name may be glorified. Amen.

Works Cited

As a General Reference

The HarperCollins Study Bible. New Revised Standard Version with the Apocryphal/Deuterocanonical Books. Wayne A. Meeks, general ed. New York: HarperCollins Publishers, 1993.

On Particular Passages or Themes

Bartlett, David L. Romans. Westminster Bible Companion. Louisville: Westminster/John Knox, 1995.

Brueggemann, Walter. First and Second Samuel. Interpretation. Louisville: John Knox Press, 1990.

Idem. Isaiah. 2 vols. Westminster Bible Companion. Louisville: Westminster John Knox, 1998.

Bonhoeffer, Dietrich. Letters and Papers from Prison. Eberhard Bethge, ed. New York: Macmillan, 1967.

Donelson, Lewis R. Colossians, Ephesians, 1 and 2 Timothy, and Titus. Westminster Bible Companion. Louisville: Westminster/John Knox, 1996.

Martyn, J. Louis. Galatians. Anchor Bible. New York: Doubleday, 1997.

Mays, James L. Psalms. Interpretation. Louisville: John Knox Press, 1994.

O'Day, Gail R. "The Gospel of John: Introduction, Commentary and Reflections." The New Interpreter's Bible. Leander E. Keck, ed. Vol. 9. Nashville: Abingdon Press, 1995, 491–865.

Ringe, Sharon. Luke. Westminster Bible Companion. Louisville: Westminster/John Knox, 1995.

Weiser, Artur. The Old Testament Library. Philadelphia: Westminster, 1962.

THE SEASON
OF EPIPHANY

NANCY KOESTER

Jesus is the light of the world. Epiphany, the season of light, reveals Jesus as the source of light. For those already in Christ, Epiphany is a season for increasing the light of faith. For seekers it may be a time of revelation, as they meet Christ for the first time through the church's proclamation.

It all begins with the mysterious star guiding the Magi to Bethlehem. Then the Gospel texts of the season take us from Jesus' baptism to his transfiguration on the mountain. In between these two events, the Gospel texts reveal Jesus' power as he makes disciples, heals the sick, forgives sinners, casts out demons, and dares to call himself "Lord of the Sabbath." These words and deeds both demonstrate Jesus' authority and bring him into conflict with the religious establishment, which does not appreciate Jesus' upstaging and outshining them. Because Jesus' enemies see him as a threat to their way of life, they seek to destroy him. Jesus' light of mercy and glory awakens faith and evokes hostility, setting the stage for Jesus' journey to the cross. Yet that difficult way to Calvary is lighted by God's own affirmation, "You are my Son, the Beloved; with you I am well pleased" (Mark 1:11).

The lectionary for Epiphany offers great adventures in preaching. Mark's Gospel (plus one reading from Matthew and one from John), is accompanied by vigorous and varied Old Testament lessons. Most of the "second" or epistle lessons are a running series from 1 and 2 Corinthians, exploring Christian freedom, leadership, and community in the light of Christ.

Preachers and pastors honor the Gospel as basic to the church's proclamation, appreciating the support and insight which the other lectionary texts provide for the Gospel. At the same time, however, preachers are free and should feel free to work with any of the assigned readings as preaching texts in their own right. This includes the psalms, which are customarily limited to use as responsive readings. But the psalms, with their raw honesty, militant faith, and jubilant praise, shed much light on our lives as the people of God and have inspired great preaching in several Christian traditions. The writer believes it is time for an Epiphany concerning the use of psalms and of other neglected texts for preaching. If we go to a restaurant and always order "the house special" it is not for want of other nourishing and exciting things on the menu. If the other foods were not also good to eat, they would not have been placed on the menu.

The writer acknowledges debt to the scholars whose works are cited and to all pastors whose preaching brings the light of Christ to congregations. May God's light brighten the church's worship and shine through its witness to Jesus Christ, the light of the world.

THE PSALMS, WITH THEIR RAW HON-
ESTY, MILITANT FAITH, AND JUBILANT
PRAISE, SHED MUCH LIGHT ON OUR
LIVES AS THE PEOPLE OF GOD.

THE EPIPHANY OF OUR LORD

REVISED COMMON	EPISCOPAL (BCP)	ROMAN CATHOLIC
Isa. 60:1-6	Isa. 60:1-6, 9	Isa. 60:1-6
Ps. 72:1-7, 10-14	Ps, 72 or 72:1-2, 10-17	Ps. 72:1-2, 7-8, 10-13
Eph. 3:1-12	Eph. 3:1-12	Eph. 3:2-3, 5-6
Matt. 2:1-12	Matt. 2:1-12	Matt. 2:1-12

WHEN THE STAR STOPPED OVER THE PLACE WHERE Jesus was, the Magi were "overwhelmed with joy." This great joy animates each text for the Epiphany of Our Lord. Isaiah 60 trumpets, "arise, shine, for your light has come!" Psalm 72 blesses the king who saves the poor and needy. Writing from a jail cell, the apostle Paul glorifies God for unveiling a mystery. Holy joy overwhelms old boundaries between Jew and gentile, captive and free, lighting up the night for all people.

FIRST READING
ISAIAH 60:1-6, 60:1-6, 9 (BCP)

Interpreting the Text

Isaiah 60 belongs to a third "Isaiah," who addressed the Jewish exiles shortly before the fall of Babylon in 539 B.C.E. Chapters 60–62 look forward to God's promised salvation, when Jerusalem regains its former glory. Israel is still captive but freedom is near. Isaiah 60 offers realism (v. 2a), hope (vv. 2b, 3, 5, 6, 9) and encouragement: "Arise! Lift up your eyes and look around" (v. 1, 4).

Knowing the place of this text within the multiple authorship of Isaiah is probably less important for the preacher during Epiphany than seeing the relation of Isaiah 60 to Matthew's Magi story. Isaiah 60 most likely informed Matthew's understanding of Jesus and his telling of the Magi story. The rising of the light (Isa. 60:1), the coming of gentile kings (v. 3), and the bringing of wealth (vv. 6, 9), particularly gold and frankincense, are all present in the Gospel.

From its setting in the lectionary, Isaiah 60 sheds light on the Christian proclamation that Jesus is the hope of the world. In Epiphany the Isaiah text itself works very much like the star of Bethlehem, guiding exiles and seekers through the darkness to reveal Jesus as the coming, shining light (v. 1).

Whether or not it is linked to Matthew 2, Isaiah 60 has its own integrity for preaching. The movement from realism to hope to exhortation is a good sermonic strategy because it re-enacts the journey of faith. With this text, pastors can boldly exhort their hearers, as well as themselves: "arise and look around!" Expect great things from God! Hymns that blend themes of light and exhortation include "Rise, Shine You People"[1] and "I Want to Walk as a Child of the Light."[2] Within Isaiah 60:1-6, 9 are all the elements needed for a sermon: realism, hope, and the call for a response.

IN EPIPHANY THE ISAIAH TEXT ITSELF WORKS VERY MUCH LIKE THE STAR OF BETHLEHEM, GUIDING EXILES AND SEEKERS THROUGH THE DARKNESS TO REVEAL JESUS AS THE COMING, SHINING LIGHT.

RESPONSIVE READING

PSALM 72

This psalm is a corporate prayer for blessing on Israel's king, that his reign may bring prosperity and that he may use power to show mercy. More than just a figure of interest for Israel, this king receives tribute and gifts from other kings (vv. 10-11). Psalm 72 probably informed Matthew 2:11. Early Christians probably identified "the king" (v. 1) with Jesus, and the Magi with the other kings (v. 11) who came to worship him with gifts. This may explain how the Magi of Matthew 2 came to be called kings.

In Epiphany, the season when God is made known to us in Jesus' life and ministry, Psalm 72 spotlights compassion at the heart of godly power. Verses 4 and 12-14 show the great king's mercy for his poorest and weakest people. Matthew shows us Jesus in this light too (Matt. 5:1-12). The king saves his people from oppression and violence. The king in Psalm 72 is the exact opposite of Herod (Matt. 2:3-18). The stark contrast between these two kings helps develop the theme of power and Jesus' unusual kingship (see John 18:36). Even without its association with Matthew 2, Psalm 72 could inspire a sermon on how God wants leaders to use power.

EPHESIANS 3:1-12

Interpreting the Text

Ephesians begins with doxology for God's great work of salvation in Christ (1:3-23). Ephesians 2 contrasts what life was like for the gentiles without Christ, and what life is like now with Christ—both for gentile believers and for the Christian community as a whole. It is worth going to jail for this! Paul is a prisoner for the sake of the gentiles, to whom and for whom he has proclaimed the gospel of Jesus Christ. Paul is in prison for setting the gentiles free. The second lesson describes Paul's mission, which is not the least bit hindered by his captivity. Two themes link this text with the Epiphany Gospel: the Gospel is for gentiles as well as Jews; the Gospel, hidden for ages, is now unveiled.

Responding to the Text

Ephesians 3:1-12 can hold its own as the primary preaching text for the day. It contains at least three dramatic reversals, all of which highlight God's saving work. First, a mystery hidden for ages is now revealed. Second, a treasure once tightly held by a few is now offered to everyone. Third, a man locked in prison is ecstatically, spiritually free, and his sufferings inspire him to praise God. When God seems hidden or absent, when we think we are shut out from God's promise and favor, when we or other Christians suffer for the sake of the gospel, Ephesians 3 can turn us inside out and move us from lament to praise.

Robert Duvall's recent film, *The Apostle,* portrays "Sonny," a passionate pentecostal preacher.[3] Enraged by his wife's unfaithfulness, Sonny kills his wife's lover. Sonny knows that, if caught, he'll go to jail. He flees to an obscure rural town in the South where he would be safe if only he could keep quiet. Yet he must preach! He cannot help it. Supporting himself with odd jobs, he refurbishes a shabby country church and builds up a small congregation of poor blacks and whites. He even preaches on the local radio station, assuming that the broadcast will not reach far enough for anyone back home to recognize his voice. He is wrong. During a revival meeting one night, police cars wait outside the country church, lights flashing. Inside the church, a young seeker is converted through the preaching of Sonny, the very man the young seeker has betrayed. With the congregation praying, singing, and clapping, Sonny walks down the aisle and submits to his own arrest. A new church has begun and Sonny is finally free.

MATTHEW 2:1-12

Interpreting the Text

The Magi are the last ones on the scene in Sunday school Christmas pageantry, and the church year places them in Epiphany. But when Matthew's Gospel has its own voice, the Magi are the first ones—perhaps the only ones—who come to Bethlehem seeking Jesus. Matthew says nothing of shepherds or angel choirs. Instead, foreign astrologers are the first to worship Jesus.

According to Raymond Brown in *The Birth of the Messiah,* Matthew's Gospel was probably written to a mixed community of Jews and gentiles.[4] The Magi's journey shows that Jesus was born for the gentiles as well as the Jews (Matt. 8:11). But the Magi's message is not "It's a small world, after all." No sooner do the Magi leave Bethlehem than the ruthless king Herod orders the execution of innocent children (2:16-18). Unaware of the terrible pangs soon to attend the new kingdom's birth, the Magi are "overwhelmed with joy" (v. 10). They avoid Herod and return home safely.

The mysterious Magi have inspired hymns, folk tales, and art. Traditions about the Magi (they were kings, there were three, one of them was African, they rode on camels) come from later elaboration; the text leaves much unsaid. The Magi were "from the East" which could mean Persia, Babylon, or Arabia. The gifts they brought, their astrological interpretation of the star's meaning, and the term "Magi" itself provide mixed clues about their homeland(s). "Magi" comes from the Greek word meaning "magic" and can include many occult practices. Here it most likely refers to astrology—the practice of reading the influence of the stars on human events. Astrology was a problematic practice in Israel (Isa. 47:12-15), so it seems strange that these star-readers find a place at Bethlehem's manger. People are also curious about the star. Exactly what was the "star" that guided the Magi? It has been called a poetic device or a miracle, a comet, a planetary conjunction or a nova (new star). No one knows.

Above all these unknowns, two things stand out. First, the coming of the gentiles to worship Jesus is very important for Matthew (8:10-12; 21:42, 43; 28:19). Second, an event in the natural world points the Magi to Jesus (see also Matt. 14:32).

The Magi seek Jesus because the star draws them. But nature alone cannot reveal Jesus. Apart from Scripture, there is no telling who Jesus is. So nature and Scripture shine together in this Gospel. The Magi's question, "Where is the child who has been born king of the Jews?" echoes Jeremiah 23:5 and Numbers 24:17. If this new king is to be so powerful, no wonder Herod trembles (2:3). The scribes and chief priests consult Micah 5:2 and 2 Samuel 5:2 to determine where the new king is to be born and what his role will be.

Responding to the Text

"Do not expect more light until you follow what you have," says a Quaker proverb. Epiphany begins in starlight. No wonder, then, that the Magi are such shadowy, mysterious figures. The Magi follow the star through open country to hidden dangers in Herod's court. But their journey leads to the manger, God's grace at sunrise.

One way to preach on this text is through storytelling about our own quest for light amid life's shadows. The text itself provides the best story, but don't overlook some of the seasonal stories inspired by the text. For example, Carlo Menotti's passionate and winsome operetta, "Amahl and the Night Visitors," tells of a poor family's hospitality to three traveling kings, a midnight confrontation, and a miraculous healing.

Like the Magi, we must travel without knowing many things. Yet God reveals what we need to know, one step at a time. Following God's light finally leads into God's presence. The Magi do not know exactly where to find Jesus (v. 2). The star guides them to Jerusalem where from Scripture they receive further direction to Bethlehem. Not knowing Herod's true character, the Magi unwisely say too much (v. 2).

> LIKE THE MAGI WE MUST TRAVEL WITHOUT KNOWING MANY THINGS. YET GOD REVEALS WHAT WE NEED TO KNOW, ONE STEP AT A TIME.

The Magi probably do not know that their journey heralds the gentiles' coming to God through faith in Christ, nor do they know that this baby they honor will grow up to be crucified. They do not know that God, rather than astrology, leads them—for the star does not shape events, rather events call forth the star. They only know that the mysterious star somehow compels them to leave home and seek the newborn king.

Following the light they have, they travel further along. On their way to Bethlehem the star shines again for them. Overwhelmed with joy on finding Mary, they kneel down to worship and to offer gifts. The light of the star and of the Scriptures has led them to Jesus. Being wise, then, does not mean knowing and understanding everything. It means following the light into ever greater light, seeking Jesus' brightness as God-with-us. A story sermon on this text will be truthful about what we do not know. We venture through ambiguity and darkness, following the light. A story-telling sermon on this text will help people follow the light to the place of overwhelming joy.

Another approach is a teaching sermon. Ask the universal question: How do we know God? This question animates Epiphany, when God is revealed through

Jesus' incarnation and ministry. Matthew 2:1-12 gives a twofold response to the question: Both nature and Scripture point to Christ. Guided at first only by the star, after reaching Jerusalem the Magi hear Scriptures that point specifically to Jesus. Leaving Jerusalem, they follow both Scriptures and star. Their eyes and ears lead them to Christ who infuses all life with light. Nature and Scripture point to the Lord who is greater than both. The Epiphany hymn "Bright and Glorious is the Sky"[5] compares God's Word to a guiding star in our lives.

Christian spiritual traditions place varying emphases on the importance of seeing and hearing in the life of faith. For example, in Eastern Orthodoxy seeing is most important; icons are windows to eternity, visual invitations to faith. Meanwhile for Lutherans and many others, faith comes by hearing God's Word. These approaches are not mutually exclusive; they can complement each other.

The quest for God in nature draws countless people who, like Ralph Waldo Emerson, reject all Christian truth claims and seek God only in the dew, the stars, and the blowing clover. Those who seek God only in nature disdain Scripture, tradition, or proclamation. People do experience a sense of God's majesty in nature, but nature alone does not reveal Christ. On the other hand, it is possible for Christians to become so fixed on hearing and reading that they don't see God's creation and our part in it.

This Epiphany Gospel could well inspire a seeker sermon. Ask people what they are looking for and where they are searching. Then invite them, following what light they have, to come to the manger at Bethlehem to worship Jesus.

A third approach to preaching this text is to focus on the gentiles coming to Christ, a theme of great importance in Matthew's Gospel. As noted above, this Gospel was probably intended for a mixed community of Jews and gentile Christians. The Magi were gentiles who most likely practiced one or more other religions, yet they were the first to worship Jesus. How easy it would be to jump from this to a sermon on inclusivity. The point, however, is not merely that the Magi are included in God's grace, but that these wanderers leave home, seek Jesus, and worship him. If inclusion were an end in itself, there would be no need for the Magi's journey. Matthew does not want to remove all boundaries, but rather to re-draw these boundaries along the lines of faith. The main point is that the Gospel is for all who believe.

THE BAPTISM
OF OUR LORD

JANUARY 9, 2000

FIRST SUNDAY AFTER THE EPIPHANY

REVISED COMMON	EPISCOPAL (BCP)	ROMAN CATHOLIC
Gen. 1:1-5	Isa. 42:1-9	Isa. 42:1-4, 6-7
Ps. 29	Ps. 89:1-29 or 89:20-29	Ps. 29:1-4, 9-11
Acts 19:1-7	Acts 10:34-38	Acts 10:34-38
Mark 1:4-11	Mark 1:7-11	Mark 1:7-11

JESUS' BAPTISM REVEALS HIS OBEDIENCE TO God and his solidarity with us as sinners reconciled to God. Bold creation themes in the first readings and psalms help us to see the baptism of Jesus as the beginning of a new creation. Isaiah's Servant Song shows Jesus' ministry in light of justice and mercy. Readings from Acts show the astonishing growth of God's new creation, the community of believers in Christ. Mark's account of Jesus' baptism may inspire preaching on John the Baptist, Jesus' baptism, or God's astonishing love that approved of Jesus' perilous mission. Taken together or singly, these Scriptures show God's Word creating the world anew.

FIRST READING
GENESIS 1:1-5

Interpreting the Text

Before God spoke, the world was formless, empty, and dark. First God created light. Then God separated light from darkness. Throughout the Bible, God is at work giving light and separating light from darkness (Isa. 9:2, John 1:4-5, 1 Peter 2:9). God's voice began creation. Each time God spoke, good things happened as the world came, in the words of a beloved hymn, "fresh from the word."

Responding to the Text

As the first lesson for The Baptism of our Lord, this text asks for a response of faith, faith that in Jesus a new creation has begun, in Jesus the light of the world has come. Just as God's joyful "Good!" greeted each new creative event, so God's word of approval graces Jesus' baptism. God separated light from darkness at creation, and God used John the Baptist's message of repentance and forgiveness to separate light and darkness in human life. While surely Genesis 1:1-5 is a great preaching text in its own right, its context in the lectionary brings us a full, rich reading of the Gospel.

ISAIAH 42:1-9 (BCP), 42:1-4, 6-7 (RC)

Interpreting the Text

This is the first Servant Song in Isaiah (see also 49:1-6; 50:4-11; 52:13— 53:12). The Servant in these songs could be the people of Israel, the prophet, or someone else sent into a world that needs justice and compassion. In the beginning God created the world (Isa. 42:5); and now the world needs to be re-created through this chosen Servant, bringer of light to the nations (42:6). Through this Servant, as through God's voice at creation, new things happen (42:9).

Responding to the Text

God sees people and countries infected with a deadly disease whose symptoms are cruelty, oppression, and injustice. A sermon could work with Isaiah as the primary preaching text to show God's dealings with the world. A framework of malady and remedy (or our need and God's response) may work best, especially when compared with what God chooses *not* to do. God does not prescribe a flood to purge away sin, nor is God's glory and holiness (Isa. 42:8) compromised by making sin OK. Instead of destroying evil or blandly affirming it, God sends a beloved servant to establish justice, show mercy, bring light, and set prisoners free. The preacher can look at his or her own community for a story of local "Servants" who bring light to the neighborhood.

There are Christian servants working on a larger scale, too, whose stories vividly illustrate God's saving work among us. Congregations involved in or attracted to Habitat for Humanity need to know about the prophetic Christian roots of that organization, which so far has built 26,000 homes in the United States and over 45,000 homes internationally. The June 14, 1999, issue of *Christianity Today,* entitled "The Coming of the Pragmatic Prophets," includes an article about Habitat activist Millard Fuller, "God's Contractor." The article tells how Fuller took "a radical Christian vision (building homes for poor people), inspired in the midst of a radical Christian community (Clarence Jordan's Koinonia Farm), and sold it to corporate and mainstream America. And they bought it." While people of all faiths are involved in Habitat, Fuller says that Habitat builds homes "because of Jesus."

Inner-city congregations inspired by Isaiah, and their partner churches, will want to know of an active servant who pleads their cause. Another article in the same issue of *Christianity Today* describes the work of Catholic political scientist John Dilulio, "The Criminologist Who Discovered Churches." Believing that inner-city churches can help at-risk youth and work for urban renewal, Dilulio is working to get foundations and corporations, and yes, even governments, to support urban, faith-based ministries. Dilulio is an urban Catholic who, like John the Baptist, knows that conversion is central to change, and that change happens in very specific, practical ways. Churches can reach and change at-risk urban youth, and these churches need financial support from outside.

Christians naturally identify the Servant with Christ (Luke 4:17-21), and tend to see the Servant Songs as prophecies about, or hymns to, Jesus' work. The musical setting of Isaiah 53 in Handel's *Messiah* is one of the finest examples. Most people are more familiar with the Gospels than with Isaiah, so the way in which texts are heard and understood in congregations may be the reverse of the chronological order in which those texts were written. For preaching on the Baptism of Our Lord, the Isaiah 42 text both supports and enriches the Gospel and can readily be used to describe Jesus' ministry. A welcome supplement to Mark's terse narrative, Isaiah's vigorous, intimate poetry has the power to evoke responses of gratitude, love, and praise.

RESPONSIVE READING
PSALM 29

A raging storm is the backdrop for this psalm. Beginning with a call to worship (vv. 1-2), the psalm takes us over ocean, forest, wilderness (desert), and mountain. The psalm ends with God enthroned in heaven, and the people appealing to God for strength and peace. A preacher may link this stormy psalm with "the heavens torn apart" in Mark 1:10.

It is common in our time for people to think of God primarily as gentle and above all "nice." But this psalm ascribes destructive power to God. What we may think of as impersonal forces of nature are here attributed directly to God. A sermon on this psalm could break through our climate-controlled comfort level to help us to see, once again, our total dependence upon the mighty Creator God. One response to the all-powerful, storm-wielding God is protest: such a wild

God seems cruel and irrational. But this psalm is not interested in the question of theodicy (explaining God's actions in a way that will satisfy us). Its whole intention is to contrast human smallness with God's majesty, and thereby evoke prayer and praise.

PSALM 89:1-19 (BCP)

Psalm 89 celebrates God's covenant with David (89:3, 20-37). The selected portion of the psalm, however, celebrates God's power in nature and proclaims God's righteousness and justice. Verses 15-18 suggest a worship setting in which a community gathers to praise God. In the context of the Baptism of our Lord, verses 3 and 19 may call to mind Jesus as God's chosen one.

As a hymn of praise, this psalm will accomplish its work as it is sung or read responsively. As a preaching text, its big-screen view seems quite the opposite of Mark's focus on one baptism for one person, Jesus, who may have been the only one to hear the heavenly voice and see the Spirit-dove. But that strange contrast of macro and micro is a good sermonic strategy. Jesus Christ, through whom the world was made (macro) submits to John's baptism for repentance and forgiveness (micro). With the psalm as a backdrop, the Baptism of Jesus moves (like Phil. 2:5-11) from heights to humility to worship, with the "faithful one" (Ps. 89:19) at the center.

SECOND READING
ACTS 19:1-7

Interpreting the Text

This text comes near the beginning of Paul's third missionary journey when he arrives in Ephesus for his long sojourn there. There Paul encounters some disciples (19:1) who identify themselves with John's baptism. These disciples know nothing about the Holy Spirit, nor do they look for "one who was to come after John" (19:4). Paul helps these disciples advance from the preparatory work of John the Baptist into the fullness of Christ's work on their behalf. Through their baptism "in the name of the Lord Jesus" the Holy Spirit comes upon them. The interpretive issues are: differentiating the baptism of John from that of Jesus and advancing the gospel mission through proclamation, baptism, and the gifts of the Holy Spirit.

What we believe matters! Until Paul found these "disciples," they had but a partial understanding of God's grace and only a prelude to discipleship. Few if any of us wonder about the difference between John's baptism and that of Jesus. But many people nurture hopes and promises that are quite compelling, especially if these things do not appear to be religious! Some religious schemes borrow from or overlap with Christianity in some way. Aside from making obvious didactic connections between Acts 19 and Mark 1, the preacher could respond to this text by doing what the Apostle Paul did: start with where people are—for example, the religion of self-fulfillment, good deeds, or comfort—and then show that the fullness of God's promises is found only in Christ. For a clear, brief resource on practical apologetics in our time, see Richard Mouw, *Consulting the Faithful.*[6]

> START WITH WHERE PEOPLE ARE—FOR EXAMPLE, THE RELIGION OF SELF-FULFILLMENT, GOOD DEEDS, OR COMFORT—AND THEN SHOW THAT THE FULLNESS OF GOD'S PROMISES IS FOUND ONLY IN CHRIST.

ACTS 10:34-38 (BCP/RC)

Interpreting the Text

God wants the gospel of Jesus Christ to be proclaimed to gentiles as well as Jews (Acts 10:9-16), and Peter's sermon to Cornelius and his household is part of this larger theme. Peter, who has prided himself on living the life of an insider (1:14), now finds himself preaching the gospel to outsiders—gentiles. Peter names this mission's starting point: it all begins with Jesus' baptism by John, when God anoints Jesus with the Holy Spirit. Acts 10:39-43 completes this text by proclaiming Jesus' death and resurrection and promising forgiveness of sins to all who believe in Jesus.

Responding to the Text

This text has at least two wonders. The first: a whole new world grows from a tiny seed. When Jesus submits to John's baptism of repentance and forgiveness, God gives the Holy Spirit and power. This sets in motion Jesus' ministry, death, and resurrection, so that all who believe in him are reconciled to God.

The second wonder is that Peter is the one to preach this message. Peter is Apostle to the Jews as Paul is to the gentiles. But Peter finds himself moved by a message that he does not control, a message that does not stay at home within Peter's world. God has to do considerable work with Peter before Peter can preach this message to Cornelius' household. The Gospel is too lively and expansive for us to control, but if God uses us to spread the Word we are blessed.

GOSPEL

MARK 1:4-11

Interpreting the Text

Mark's Gospel opens onto the peak of John's career. The rugged Baptizer draws "all the people of Jerusalem" and "the whole Judean countryside" out to the hard wilderness to hear a hard message. John preaches repentance and forgiveness. Confessing their sins, crowds of people are baptized. John has such a strong following that many people take him as a prophet in his own right, not a forerunner of Jesus. John's clothing (v. 6) links him with Elijah (2 Kings 1:8) and the Old Testament's closing promise of Elijah's return (Mal. 4:5-6). Yet John preaches to prepare the way for someone greater. John contrasts his baptizing (in water) with Jesus' baptizing (in the Holy Spirit). This contrast between these two baptisms has been understood in different ways: between water baptism (preliminary and preparatory) and Spirit baptism (complete and eternal); between the cleansing of repentance (which humans do) and the cleansing of grace (a gift of God); or simply a way of setting apart John's ministry from that of Jesus, and noting which was greater.

The Spirit's descent and the voice from heaven mark Jesus as God's beloved son, blessed with divine approval. But the scene is not meant to be blandly affirming. Donald Juel notes the "dynamic, violent and final" imagery of the heavens being "torn apart" (v. 10).[7] There is no going back, no containing God. The voice and the Spirit-dove are just the beginning of grace and danger as Jesus' baptism rips heaven open. Full of God's Spirit, Jesus will finish the story with his own crucifixion when the temple curtain, like heaven at his baptism, is torn apart (15:38).

Responding to the Text

Those who preach on the Baptism of Jesus may well begin their work with a reality check. For most people in congregations, even in liturgical traditions, the importance of Jesus' baptism is not self-evident. Most likely it is just one more thing that pastors seem to be interested in but people patiently endure. This problem can be overcome, first of all, by allowing the Gospel text to be as rough, angular, and surprising as it really is.

There are at least three foci in the Gospel, which could stand alone or work together in a sermon. First is the strange figure of John the Baptist. Working outside the lines of temple-worship, drawing people away from what seems to be their religious center, John the Baptist is abrasive and unconventional. Let us ask: Why have so many powerful religious movements flourished outside of established, respectable churches? People flock to hear John preach a message of repentance and forgiveness of sins. Could such a message appeal today? The conventional middle-class wisdom—that sin and repentance lower our self-esteem and deepen the oppressive alliance between religion and guilt—has produced very few new Christians. In our day, experimental churches which preach repentance and forgiveness are often packed to overflowing with young adults who seek a stronger, more bracing message than they expect to hear in mainline churches. A sermon on this text could put John's message in stark, plain language and then ask: Why are people still drawn to John's message? Can it be that people need and want something more from God than bromides and entertainment?

> CAN IT BE THAT PEOPLE NEED AND WANT SOMETHING MORE FROM GOD THAN BROMIDES AND ENTERTAINMENT?

Second, the preacher may choose to focus on Jesus' baptism. Jesus was without sin, yet he is baptized by John. This seems like a person who is perfectly healthy taking prescription medicine intended to treat a deadly illness. Why is Jesus baptized? Jesus' baptism is not so much for him as it is for us. It shows his obedience to God and his solidarity with us in our human condition. His baptism begins his living, dying, and rising for us. As a sinless one receiving John's baptism of repentance, Jesus who knew no sin dared to become sin (2 Cor. 5:21). The Epiphany hymn expresses this well:

> When Jesus came to Jordan to be baptized by John,
> He did not come for pardon but as the Sinless One.
> He came to share repentance with all who mourn their sins,
> To speak the vital sentence with which good news begins.
> He came to share temptation, our utmost woe and loss,
> For us and our salvation to die upon the cross.
> So when the dove descended on him, the Son of Man,
> The hidden years had ended, the age of grace began.[8]

Third, there is God's response to Jesus' baptism (Mark 1:10-11). The heavenly voice, the Spirit-dove, and the tearing of the heavens may have been unknown to anyone but Jesus. But their presence in the Gospel lets us glimpse something of God's love for Jesus the Son. Explore this through analogy: What is it like for parents when children grow up and leave home? Taking a cue from Don Juel's emphasis on the tearing of the heavens, we know that parents' hearts are torn when they let go of children and release them into the world. The parents accept danger and live in hope when the beloved child ventures out into the world. For Jesus, this baptism begins a risky mission to bring estranged people back into relationship with God (1:8). Jesus' baptism meant that he left home and came to live with us sinners. That God was willing to be torn this way and still be "well pleased" with Jesus is a sign of grace for us all.

SECOND SUNDAY AFTER THE EPIPHANY

JANUARY 16, 2000

SECOND SUNDAY IN ORDINARY TIME

REVISED COMMON	EPISCOPAL (BCP)	ROMAN CATHOLIC
1 Sam. 3:1-10, (11-20)	1 Sam. 3:1-10, (11-20)	1 Sam. 3:3-10, 19
Ps. 139:1-6, 13-18	Ps. 63:1-8	Ps. 40:2, 4, 7-10
1 Cor. 6:12-20	1 Cor. 6:11b-20	1 Cor. 6:13-15, 17-20
John 1:43-51	John 1:43-51	John 1:35-42

GOD KNOWS US AND CALLS US TO FOLLOW AND SERVE CHRIST. The texts for this Sunday are entwined by themes of God's knowing and calling. Intimate knowledge of us does not prevent God from calling us, but sometimes it is hard for us to recognize God's voice. The Apostle Paul insisted that the Corinthians follow Christ's call rather than the call to self-indulgence. Samuel needed help discerning God's call. Nathaniel expected the caller to come from anywhere but Nazareth. We too are called, both to discern and to follow God's voice. As we follow, we come to know God better.

FIRST READING

1 SAMUEL 3:1-10 (11-20)

Interpreting the Text

A prophet in Israel at the end of the time of Judges, Samuel anointed both Saul and David as kings. Samuel was born to Hannah, a woman long barren who prayed to God for a child. God granted her request and when the child was weaned, Hannah brought Samuel to "the house of the Lord at Shiloh" (1 Sam. 1:24). There he assisted Eli, a judge of Israel and priest at Shiloh. During the twelfth century before Jesus' birth, Shiloh was a religious and administrative center for Israelite tribes then settling in Palestine. As Samuel grew up, visions were rare and people seldom heard from God.

Into the long silence, God calls. But Samuel, not yet knowing the Lord (v. 7), does not recognize God's voice. God calls three times. Samuel wakes Eli, whose eyesight has grown dim but whose discernment is sharp. Sensing God's call, Eli tells Samuel what to do. Next time Samuel is ready: "Speak, for your servant is listening."

It would be easy to sentimentalize this story if it ended here. But God's message to Samuel is hard and uncompromising: God will destroy Eli's family ("house") and no sacrifice or offering will change God's mind. Eli's sons Hophni and Phinehas have treated the people's offerings to God with contempt (1 Sam. 2:12-17). The sons seem also to have engaged in some form of cult prostitution (2:22-24). Even before Samuel's call, an unnamed "man of God" has warned Eli that God will severely punish Eli's sons and the whole family (2:31-36). Now Samuel has the painful honor of hearing God speak judgement on the family of Eli his mentor. When Eli asks to hear God's message, Samuel holds nothing back.

Responding to the Text

God's voice launches Samuel on a turbulent career that contributes to the falling and rising of prophets and kings. At first Eli helped Samuel discern God's call. But no one inventoried Samuel's gifts or tried to match him up with an apt vocation. No one advised him to do work that energized him. No one tested his personality type, charted his likes and dislikes, interpreted his grades, or took him on a retreat to seek his vision for the future. Samuel did not fill out a form listing places he would like to serve or the compensation he should receive. Not even loyalty to a mentor was allowed to shape his ministry, for Samuel's first message was bound to hurt Eli. It is a lonely business being a prophet. We should all think twice before saying "speak Lord, for your servant hears." Samuel's call story stands in vigorous tension with current practices of vocational discernment.

To be sure, suffering does not necessarily guarantee that one's call is from God. And it does make sense that God wants us to use our gifts, serve with our strengths, and thereby find some happiness. Despite this reasonable approach, however, the fact remains that God sometimes calls us to very uncomfortable work. God may ask us to say things that no one wants to hear; we might have to say things that will anger people who have helped us. God might ask us to do things we are not good at, things that we were not trained to do or did not sign up for.

GOD SOMETIMES CALLS US TO VERY UNCOMFORTABLE WORK.

God finds us and calls us in particular moments in history, to situations we did not create and did not choose. Though our historical context is different from Samuel's, the world is constantly under construction as God wields judgement, works redemption, and wins reconciliation. We do not know what will happen when God calls. At first Samuel was not at all sure of God's voice. That voice can stretch us far beyond our choices, so everything depends on who does the calling.

RESPONSIVE READING

PSALM 139:1-6, 13-18

This psalm addresses the urgent questions: Does God know me? Does God care? Every Sunday people bring these questions with them to church. This psalm, therefore, is a slow pitch over the plate. This psalm—in its entirety—deserves to be treated as a sermon text in its own right. Use plain speech and pictures from everyday life. Invite hearers to ponder just how well God knows each one of us. Humor has a place in such preaching, and so does daring. Look over the edge of what it means to be human and to be known by God. Name situations in which God's knowing us is comforting, and name situations in which God's knowing is disturbing or even frightening.

The cry for deliverance and revenge (139:19-22) both mars the psalm and keeps it honest. God sees our rage too, especially if we have been abused, wronged, or exploited. Then focus on the gracious promises in the psalm (vv. 8, 10, 12, 18). End with a gospel proclamation—it makes all the difference just *who* knows us so completely. Even at a distance, Jesus knew Nathaniel and could read his character. So too God knows and calls each one of us.

PSALM 63:1-8 (BCP)

The first eight verses of this psalm voice our longing to be in God's presence. Using this psalm in corporate worship, we promise our prayers and praises to God, both at appointed times of worship (v. 2) and in the private nighttime hours (v. 6). The psalm has a past, present, and future dimension: "for you have been my help"; "my soul is satisfied"; "I will bless you as long as I live." This is an excellent text for personal prayer within the context of corporate worship; it also sets the right tone for Nathaniel's joy (John 1:49) at coming into God's presence.

PSALM 40:2, 4, 7-10 (RC)

This psalm combines thanksgiving and petition in a corporate liturgy. The verses selected for this responsive reading celebrate God's deliverance (v. 2), teach wisdom (v. 4), and present a public testimony to the worshipping congregation (vv. 7-10). The psalmist has not "restrained" or "hidden" or "concealed" God's saving help. Eagerly the psalmist gives credit where credit is due. This calls to mind Jesus' description of Nathaniel as "an Israelite in whom there is no deceit" (John 1:47).

1 CORINTHIANS 6:12-20

Interpreting the Text

This reading is part of Paul's response to issues and questions posed by the Christian community at Corinth. Paul's basic principle here is that freedom means freedom for relationship, freedom to love and serve the neighbor. Some Corinthians took Paul's preaching (that we are free from the law) to mean license to do anything they please—quotation marks in vv. 12 and 13 identify their slogans and arguments. But Paul warns that such self-serving liberty is a new kind of bondage to sin.

Some of the Corinthians compared sexual relations to eating, a morally neutral activity that satisfies a natural appetite (vv. 13-15). But Paul says there is no morally neutral sexual activity. The body is made for the Lord. God claims the whole person, body and all. What we do in and with our bodies is important to God. Moreover, God has a future for our bodies, because God will raise up the whole person (15:35-49).

Verses 15-17 deal with the specific issues of prostitution. Paul might have chosen to blame women for prostitution, but instead he calls men to account. Paul challenges men to use their bodies in a way consistent with their relationship with Christ. Quoting Genesis 2:24, Paul insists that sexual relations have their proper place within marriage. This is further developed in 1 Corinthians 7.

Responding to the Text

Does Christian faith deny bodily expression? Does God care only for unseen, spiritual, or intangible things? No, says Paul; God values our bodies so much that God makes us the Holy Spirit's dwelling place. A temple is a holy place, set apart for God. So our bodies are intended to glorify God. God's people wrestle with very physical issues—from excess weight to anorexia, chemical dependency, and sexual immorality. Our quest for freedom with food, sex, or chemical substance can lead to deep and deadly bondage. Rather than be enslaved by these things, we are to glorify God in our bodies.

> BENEATH OUR QUEST FOR FREEDOM LIES THE DEEPER PROBLEM OF IDENTITY. WE CANNOT BE WHO WE ARE UNTIL WE KNOW *WHOSE* WE ARE.

Beneath our quest for freedom lies the deeper problem of identity. We cannot be who we are until we know *whose* we are. Paul says that we are bought with a price (v. 20) because Christ died to save us. He offered his whole self in order to bring us as whole people into relationship with God. Such love calls us to glorify God with our whole selves, body and soul. True freedom comes when God calls us to our identity as persons for whom Christ died, free to live in Christ for our neighbors. In "The Freedom of a Christian" Martin Luther wrote that a Christian is "perfectly free, lord of all, subject to none," and "a perfectly dutiful servant of all, subject to all."[9] Christians live this paradox: true freedom comes through serving others in Christ. This message daily constrains us and liberates us.

GOSPEL
JOHN 1:43-51 (RCL/BCP), 1:35-42 (RC)

Interpreting the Text

One person's testimony brings another person to Jesus. John the Baptist begins the pattern, which continues as Andrew brings Peter to meet Jesus. Philip—the one disciple Jesus calls directly—tells Nathaniel about Jesus. Philip establishes a context for the encounter with Jesus by referring to the Scriptures: "We have found him about whom Moses in the Law and also the prophets wrote, Jesus Son of Joseph from Nazareth" (v. 45). Nathaniel is skeptical: "Can anything good come out of Nazareth?" His question is well founded. Nazareth is never mentioned in the Old Testament; there was no hint of a Messiah coming from that obscure village. Knowing that Nathaniel's question can only be answered by meeting Jesus himself, Philip simply invites Nathaniel to come and see.

Jesus' conversation with Nathaniel unfolds through a series of allusions to the Scriptures already mentioned by Philip. Craig Koester explores the meaning of this complex passage.[10] Calling Nathaniel "an Israelite in whom there is no deceit," Jesus subtly contrasts Nathaniel with Jacob. Recall that in Genesis 27 Jacob, later named Israel, stole Esau's birthright through deceit. Nathaniel's forthright question shows him to be an honest man. When Nathaniel believes in Jesus, Jesus promises him even greater things than Jacob saw long ago. (In Gen. 28:12 Jacob saw angels ascending and descending on a ladder.) Now Nathaniel and others who follow Jesus will see "angels of God ascending and descending upon the Son of Man" (John 1:51). God's glory is revealed in the crucified and risen Son of Man.

Through playful allusions to the Scriptures Jesus makes his own identity known to Nathaniel. The law and the prophets (John 1:45) have promised God's Messiah, the Branch of David (Zech. 3:8). When the Messiah comes, "you shall invite each other to come under your vine and fig tree" (Zech. 3:10). Nathaniel wonders: Is Jesus really the one whom the Scriptures promise? Jesus points to the promise coming true in Nathaniel's own experience: Wasn't Nathaniel under his fig tree when Philip called him? Nathaniel's ecstatic response (v. 49) makes sense in the light of prophetic hope.

The season of Epiphany proclaims Jesus Christ revealing God in word and deed. But in John's Gospel, people start to follow Jesus even before they see any miracles or hear Jesus teach: "Blessed are those who have not seen and yet have come to believe" (John 20:29). On the basis of others' testimony, especially the witness of Scripture, people still come to meet Jesus.

Early in his Gospel, John establishes this pattern for evangelism. The first two disciples hear John the Baptist say "Here is the Lamb of God!" (1:35). That message provokes their curiosity and willingness to follow. At this early stage they do not fully understand Jesus as the Lamb of God. Nevertheless the message prompts them to seek Jesus and to learn more of him. For those who are outside the faith looking in, this is a very encouraging message (note that even active church members may see themselves as outsiders if they have major questions about the faith). The preacher proclaims God's invitation to "Come and see."

In John's Gospel, Jesus' first words ask a question: "What are you looking for?" (v. 38). Contrast this with Mark 1:14 where Jesus begins with a command: "Repent and believe in the good news." In John, Jesus asks a question. The disciples respond with another question: "Where are you staying?" (v. 38). Jesus does not answer the question directly; instead he invites them: "Come and see." In John's Gospel, people follow Jesus before they understand him. Their questions are not answered ahead of time but only as their life with Jesus unfolds. Preachers can promise that Jesus does not ask people to park their questions at the church door before entering.

Today's Gospel provokes two preaching themes, both related to evangelism. First: How do people get started following Jesus? No one can inherit faith from another person; but the testimony of Christians does point people to Christ, opening the way for a personal encounter with him. In John 1, Philip is the only person called directly by Jesus. All the others come through the witness of someone else—John the Baptist, or a friend or family member. This is the simplest and best form of evangelism: one person tells another about Jesus and follows this with the invitation to "Come and see."

The second theme: How do we deal with questions—our own or those of people we hope will follow Jesus? Many Christians are afraid to say anything about Jesus, lest someone ask a question they cannot answer. Others are confused about the place of questions in faith. It is common to think that if you have faith you can have no questions; and if you have questions you have no faith. John's Gospel offers a better approach. In John, faith and questions often work together. Faith is the basis from which understanding grows.

IT IS COMMON TO THINK THAT IF YOU HAVE FAITH YOU CAN HAVE NO QUESTIONS; AND IF YOU HAVE QUESTIONS YOU HAVE NO FAITH.

Faith welcomes honest questions. Jesus' own invitation is the key: "Come and see." This is the classic approach to Christian thinking: faith seeks understanding.

Very few people come to faith because of an academic argument. Rather, they are invited or brought into a community of people centered on Jesus Christ. In the community they can ask their questions and search the Scriptures. In the community people meet the Christ to whom Scriptures bear witness. John 1:35–51 is full of questions. In the community we may question Jesus and Jesus may question us. The Gospel invites honest questions, pointing us to the one who is God's living answer.

THIRD SUNDAY AFTER THE EPIPHANY

JANUARY 23, 2000

THIRD SUNDAY IN ORDINARY TIME

REVISED COMMON	EPISCOPAL (BCP)	ROMAN CATHOLIC
Jonah 3:1-5, 10	Jer. 3:21—4:2	Jonah 3:1-5, 10
Ps. 62:5-12	Ps. 130	Ps. 25:4-9
1 Cor. 7:29-31	1 Cor. 7:17-23	1 Cor. 7:29-31
Mark 1:14-20	Mark 1:14-20	Mark 1:14-20

IN THIS SET OF READINGS THE THEME OF "CALL" continues with some dramatic contrasts and intriguing counterpoints. Called by God, people may follow like Simon and Andrew, or run the other way, like Jonah. And those who do follow Christ may sometimes follow him by leaving home and at other times by staying put, but for new reasons. Yet even those who stay put find that God's call changes them.

FIRST READING
JONAH 3:1-5, 10

Interpreting the Text

God has told Jonah to go to Nineveh, one of the oldest and greatest cities of Mesopotamia, and proclaim its wickedness against it (v. 2). Jonah runs from God's call and serves out his time in the fish's belly. When the fish spews him out of its mouth, Jonah makes an inglorious entrance to his new assignment. And before Jonah even has time to take a shower, God is after him again, with the triple command: "Get up . . . go . . . proclaim!"

Nineveh is so large it takes three days to walk through it (v. 3), yet Jonah does not even begin preaching until he is one day's journey inside the city. Jonah's stark message neither promises mercy nor calls for repentance: "Forty days more, and Nineveh shall be overthrown" (v. 4). Despite Jonah's forced obedience and his grim sermon, the whole city turns to God (3:5-9). Nineveh's all-out repentance—so complete that even the animals wear sackcloth—is comic contrast with Jonah's stingy ways. God wants Nineveh to be saved and Jonah wants it to be destroyed (4:1-3). God wins. Yet God is not satisfied that Jonah remains angry and unrepentant. As God's dealings with hard-boiled Jonah continue in chapter 4, God calls not only Nineveh but Jonah to repent.

Responding to the Text

If it is isolated from the Jonah story the first lesson sounds flat and moralistic. But in its natural context this lesson is the high point of a tall tale. The tale includes exaggeration: the storm, the fish, Nineveh's all-out repentance. It has zany humor, such as the role reversal in 1:14 where the sailors pray and the prophet sleeps ("Will the real religious leader please stand up?"). But in spite of himself, Jonah succeeds (1:16; 3:5). The first response is to enjoy retelling the story.

The tall tale has an edge. It calls us as God's people (represented by Jonah) to repent. The sin to be repented of is stinginess with God's word. Do we assume in advance that people can not hear God's word, or that they are so wicked as to be beyond repentance? Do we think that nothing we can say or do will move people anyway, so why bother? Jonah didn't want people to be reconciled to God because he would rather see them punished.

And perhaps we, like Jonah, do not see that people all around us in post-modern Nineveh are hungering and thirsting for God, trying to find God in the most unlikely places. When people do respond to the Gospel, we are amazed that it still happens. If we see ourselves in this picture, then the book of Jonah is indeed a joke on us; but it is a joke with divine intent: God dares us: "Try speaking my word and see what happens. Get up . . . go . . . proclaim!"

JEREMIAH 3:21—4:2 (BCP)

Interpreting the Text

During his reign (639-609 before Jesus' birth), King Josiah attempted to remove all traces of foreign worship from Judah, moving Judah toward purity in its relationship with God. Jeremiah approved of Josiah's reforms (Jer. 22:15). Jeremiah 3:21–4:2 includes pronouncements against foreign religious practice in Judah and Jerusalem, sometime before Babylon besieged and conquered that city in 587/6.

For Jeremiah, repentance is more than a remorseful feeling. True repentance honors God's claims through specific actions, such as removing pagan shrines and ceasing from pagan religious practice (3:4). Jeremiah 3:21—4:2 includes God's call to repentance (vv. 21, 22); the people's response (vv. 22b-25); God's conditions (4:1-2a), and God's promised blessing (v. 2b).

God's call *to* something usually involves a call away from something else. For example, in Mark's Gospel the fishermen leave their nets behind. In Jeremiah, the prophet calls people away from pagan worship practices. Whether or not God's call includes a condemnation of our actions, it brings about a change. It is not possible to hang on to the old life and still follow God.

Jeremiah asks the prickly question: What and whom do we worship? The prophet tells us, 'accept no substitutes for God.' Martin Luther said that our God is whatever we fear, love and trust the most.[11] God calls us to turn away from false idols and worship the one true God. A change of heart transforms actions as well as attitudes so that our lives lean toward justice, truth, and uprightness. Repentance is not just a private matter; indeed God promises that others will benefit from our repentance. Repentance is part of a larger work of grace through which others will be blessed (4:2b).

RESPONSIVE READING
PSALM 62:5-10

If our hope and trust lie in something other than God, we naturally resist God's call. But since Psalm 62 expresses the psalmist's complete trust in God, it prepares the worshipping community to hear God's call. Verses 5-7 express the psalmist's own testimony, followed by an exhortation to "trust in the Lord at all times" (v. 8). The next two verses (vv. 9-10) offer wise advice: neither poverty nor wealth lasts, so we should not rely on schemes or robbery. The warning in v.10 calls to mind Jesus' saying that it is harder for a camel to pass through a needle's eye than for a rich person to enter the kingdom of heaven (Mark 10:25).

PSALM 130 (BCP)

All the prayers of the church may be included in this plea, which moves from confession to confidence in God's mercy. Silent watching and waiting (vv. 5, 6) comprehend all individual and corporate needs. The psalmist exhorts Israel to "hope in the Lord" (v. 7) because of God's love and power. God saves us and brings us "out of the depths" to a place of steady, confident faith.

This psalm is painted on the canvas of human experience, but the true subject of its art is God's character of "steadfast love" and "great power to redeem" (v. 7). In our time, sermons quite naturally dwell on human experience, and the cry from the depths (v. 1) offers abundant entry points for preaching. A once common but now underused approach is to explore God's own character, especially God's *steadfast* love and great *power to redeem*. These are not remote or static qualities, but dynamic, relational ones. Charles Wesley's hymn "Oh, for a Thousand Tongues to Sing" celebrates God's redeeming power and steadfast love at work in our lives.[12]

PSALM 25:4-9 (RC)

This psalm asks God to deliver, forgive and guide us. The selected portion can stand alone as a prayer from the heart of the congregation. Verse 7 voices an intriguing request: that God remember us selectively. We ask God to forget the wrongs we have done, forget the good things we have left undone, and remember us only "according to your steadfast love . . . for your goodness' sake." When we pray or sing "Jesus, remember me when you come into your kingdom" (Luke 23:42), we are asking God to forget our sins and remember us in Christ's steadfast love.

SECOND READING
1 CORINTHIANS 7:29-31

Interpreting the Text

Leaving their nets to follow Jesus, the fishermen in Mark 1:14-20 exemplify Paul's urgent hope (vv. 29-31). It is easy enough to connect the dots between second reading and Gospel; but those who preach on the second lesson will need to do more. For the alert listener, this second lesson sounds strange enough to evoke a "you've got to be kidding" response. For example, Paul says "time is short" (v. 29a); but how short is two thousand years? Does Paul call husbands to be indifferent to their wives (v. 29b)? Does Paul expect us to ignore grief and joy (v. 30a)? Does Paul really expect us to live as though we do not own anything (v. 30b)? Does Paul ask us to withdraw from the world (v. 31) and have no role in society?

If these verses were all Paul ever said, his message would be completely otherworldly. But elsewhere Paul's writings are deeply integrated with life. The apostle calls men and women alike to faithfulness in marriage (1 Cor. 7:1-16); he consoles those who grieve (1 Thess. 4:13); he understands physical suffering (1 Cor. 4:11, 12). If it is not a call to otherworldliness, what then is Paul's point in 1 Cor. 7:29-31?

Sometimes we cannot see the forest for the trees. Paul wants us to see the forest. Apart from Christ, we are like people wandering in the woods without a map or compass. Paul wants us to look at the compass and see all things oriented to Christ. Paul recognizes that this life is real but not final. If we orient our lives solely by our day-to-day experiences of grief and joy, or buying and selling, we lose the larger picture of what God is doing. We get lost in the forest and see only trees.

Himself a tentmaker (Acts 18:3), Paul knows that Christians engage in commerce; but to make business the governing factor in our lives elevates something incidental to a position of ultimate worth. Paul insists that the present form of this world is passing away. Even as we live in this world, the gospel orients us to God's goal: Christ's final triumph of life over death, love over hatred, God over evil.

> TO MAKE BUSINESS THE GOVERNING FACTOR IN OUR LIVES ELEVATES SOMETHING INCIDENTAL TO A POSITION OF ULTIMATE WORTH.

1 CORINTHIANS 7:17-23 (BCP)

Interpreting the Text

Paul's advice, "let each of you remain in the condition in which you were called" (1 Cor. 7:20) is cut from the same cloth as the second reading (RCL) discussed above. Before, the Civil War pro-slavery arguments used verse 20 to keep people "in their place." But Paul is not indifferent to slavery. When dealing with a real runaway slave named Onesimus, Paul urges his owner to receive Onesimus back—no longer as slave but as a brother (Philemon 16). 1 Corinthians 7:23-24 is a dialectic in which Christians are set free to serve Christ. Any interpretation that tries to collapse this dialectic (by justifying oppression or by requiring social advancement) misunderstands and misuses Paul. Paul's point is that each of us, regardless of social station, can serve God where we are.

Responding to the Text

Paul says that faith is to be lived in any and every situation. Jesus continued his ministry from a point of absolute dereliction on the cross. Either the ambition to rise in society or the determination to keep others down can distract us from serving God here and now. All people in Christ are *already* free to serve. All are *already* slaves to Christ. This message both constrains and liberates us, depending on which side of the dialectic we most need to hear. In the free-to-serve dialectic, the part we most need to hear is usually the part that is hardest for us to hear. For example, for many people "vocation" gets swallowed up by career and servanthood gets confused with advancement. How easily we become slaves to upward mobility! Even pastors can wear these chains!

But faith is to be lived in every situation, and those who climb status ladders are not necessarily better servants than those who labor at the bottom.

GOSPEL

MARK 1:14-20

Interpreting the Text

After John's preaching and baptizing in the wilderness, Mark shifts the scene to Galilee where Jesus walks alone beside the sea. In *Mark as Story,* David Rhoads, Joanna Dewey, and Donald Michie describe Galilee as the place of Jesus' greatest popularity.[13] He begins there alone, calls four men, and is followed by bigger crowds each time he returns. The promise "I will make you fish for people" comes true at the beginning of the Gospel and continues to be fulfilled throughout the church's story.

The call story beside the Sea of Galilee follows a two-step progression common in Mark. First, Jesus calls Simon and Andrew (v. 17) and then James and John (v. 19). No mere repetition, Jesus' call gathers force toward a larger goal. The fishermen's immediate response is one of the most striking things about this Gospel. Some interpreters argue that in order to respond "immediately" the fisherman must have had some prior contact with Jesus, even though Mark says nothing about it. Whether or not the fishermen knew Jesus before he called them, they respond to the power of God's Spirit (v. 10). Mark's focus is not on what the fishermen knew or did not know, but on Jesus' compelling call.

Responding to the Text

Jesus calls us to follow him. This means that we are always in the process of leaving something behind and moving into new life in Christ. Few things in life can be more important than hearing and following God's call. People often wonder "what does God want me to do with my life?" This question can be addressed at many levels, including both the individual's vocation and God's call to the church to "fish for people." For addressing the question "what does God want me to do with my life?" this passage from Mark affords both opportunity and peril.

> WE ARE ALWAYS IN THE PROCESS OF LEAVING SOMETHING BEHIND AND MOVING INTO NEW LIFE IN CHRIST.

The opportunity is to proclaim Jesus' call: "follow me and I will make you fish for people." This call competes with other calls to achieve success, gain a particular status, enjoy comfort, be entertained, or simply to escape. God calls all Christians to tell others the good news of Jesus. Sometimes this means staying put and seeing opportunities to "fish" where we are (1 Cor. 7: 21-31). Sometimes this means leaving an old life behind and starting something new, as did Simon and Andrew, James and John. Their leaving the nets "immediately" implies radical discontinuity between their old life and the new life. Yet there is continuity: Jesus tells them that they will still be fishing, but using different bait for a different catch. A sermon on this text could take one or two local stories of Christians called to serve God—one story of leaving an old life behind and another story of staying put but with new goals and new bait.

Preachers can take this opportunity to encourage those who might sense a call to ordained ministry. But the peril of conveying the message that only clergy are "called" is great. If it comes across as ministerial preening, people may excuse themselves from fishing because they are not experts and don't have the right fishing gear, or are just plan not interested. Fortunately the text contains its own antidote to this problem: Jesus did not call the professional religious to follow him, but fishermen.

Another peril is that we merely affirm God's call to various vocations and stop short of Jesus' call to "fish for people." In *American Evangelicalism,* sociologist Christian Smith documents that self-identified "evangelicals" are much more likely to tell others about Jesus than are self-identified "main-liners" or even "fundamentalists."[14] For too long Christian witness has been polarized in a false dichotomy of evangelism and social action. But one without the other is not good bait. The church of the future must "fish for people" in both word and deed. Jesus calls whole persons and churches to follow him, bearing witness to him in all we say and do.

FOURTH SUNDAY AFTER THE EPIPHANY

JANUARY 30, 2000

FOURTH SUNDAY IN ORDINARY TIME

REVISED COMMON	EPISCOPAL (BCP)	ROMAN CATHOLIC
Deut. 18:15-20	Deut. 18:15-20	Deut. 18:15-20
Ps. 111	Ps. 111	Ps. 95:1-2, 6-9
1 Cor. 8:1-13	1 Cor. 8:1b-13	1 Cor. 7:32-35
Mark 1:21-28	Mark 1:21-28	Mark 1:21-28

WHO HAS SPIRITUAL AUTHORITY TO SPEAK FOR GOD, and how should this authority be used? Every faith community grapples with these questions. The questions press hard when congregations are in transition and in search of leadership. The first reading assures the people about to enter the promised land that, after Moses is gone, God will raise up a leader. It is one thing to have authority and another thing to use it well; the psalms call us to worship God who uses authority to provide for us and guide us. Religious authority is to be used for the sake of the neighbor, and in 1 Corinthians 8 Paul argues that there are times when the best use of freedom is self-restraint. In the Gospel, Jesus' authority shines through in his teaching and his power over spiritual forces, expressing God's truth and mercy.

FIRST READING
DEUTERONOMY 18:15-20

Interpreting the Text

Attributed to Moses, the first reading is addressed to the people of God as they prepare to attack and enter the land of Canaan from the east. Moses warned that false religion abounded in the promised land. The Canaanites practiced magic, fortunetelling, and sorcery, and made their sons and daughters "pass through fire" (Deut. 18:9-12). Moses declared that amidst all these false religions, "you must remain completely loyal to the LORD your God" (18:13). Moses himself would not be there to lead them, but God promised to raise up a prophet like Moses from among the people, a prophet to speak God's word and to hold the people accountable for the message. Moses knew that people would wonder how to tell a true prophet from a false one. So Deuteronomy 18:21-22 offers a test of religious authority: if the prophet's word does not come true in due time, that prophet is not from God. In contrast, God's word, spoken with authority, brings results.

Responding to the Text

We live in a world of many religions, but even within Christian communities, competing voices can pull in opposite directions. Leaders make conflicting claims. Christians wonder: how do we know who speaks for God? Sometimes, time alone can tell. Still, it is hard not knowing whom to believe and whom to follow, even though false leaders are eventually exposed for what they are. But leadership is only one side of the coin. As Moses well knew, good leaders are not always followed! God wants the people to be faithful, too, and holds us all, leaders and people alike, accountable for the word of God entrusted to us.

When it comes to leadership, Deuteronomy 18 stresses both continuity with the past and readiness for the future. Some leaders stress one or the other, but faithfulness to God's word gives us both. We can expect that God's word is active and able to accomplish God's purpose among us. This text from Deuteronomy would make an excellent preaching text for a congregation in transition, seeking to define its mission and to call and empower its leaders.

RESPONSIVE READING
PSALM 111

This psalm praises God for showing "his people the power of his works" (v. 6). Thus Psalm 111 is thematically linked with the Gospel in which Jesus "shows the power of his works" by casting out unclean spirits. The Gospel has a clear focus on authority over spiritual powers, but the psalm celebrates God's mercy in providing food, keeping promises, establishing just laws, and redeeming the people. Power and mercy do not always go together in this world, but they do in God's love for us. God's authority over the whole world works through acts of righteousness, providence, and mercy.

PSALM 95:1-2, 6-9 (RC)

Through song, praise, thanksgiving, and prayer, Psalm 95 calls the community to worship God. The selected verses also include a warning against unbelief (vv. 8, 9); this refers back to Israel's many rebellions in the years of wilderness wandering (e.g., Exod. 17:1-7). The psalmist wants everyone who sees God's work in creation (95:4, 5) and in human history (95:9-11) to live faithfully and worship God. If we live as though we are not under God's authority, we do so at our own peril.

SECOND READING

1 CORINTHIANS 8:1-13

Interpreting the Text

In 1 Corinthians 8, Paul addresses a question raised by the Corinthian congregation: should we eat meat offered to idols? In towns like Corinth, there was no "secular" slaughter of animals for meat. Virtually all meat came from animals that had been offered to Greek and Roman deities. Sometimes the meat was given away during a celebration, sometimes it was sold in the marketplace, and sometimes it was eaten by worshippers in the temple of a particular god. The Christians at Corinth knew that the idols did not really exist because there is only one God (v. 4). But did this knowledge allow them to eat meat offered to these so-called gods—or did eating this meat actually support the worship of false gods?

The problem also reflected economic differences. Well-off people were more likely to eat meat on a regular basis, often conducting business over a meal in which the meat being served had been offered as a sacrifice. Christians who refused to eat this meat could lose business. Meanwhile poor people rarely ate meat unless it was part of a pagan religious festival where meat was freely distributed. For poor people, meat almost inevitably had religious implications. For many Christians, eating meat or seeing a fellow Christian eat meat meant support of idol worship. What to do?

Paul agreed with the Corinthians that "all of us possess knowledge" (8:1). What matters is how we use that knowledge: knowledge puffs up (the self), but loves builds up (other people). For the Corinthians to use their knowledge in self-serving ways (rather than helping others) was to abuse that knowledge. In verses 4-6 Paul affirmed the basic principle that there really is only one true God. Paul next explored what this meant for those who assume that eating meat offered to idols implied support of idol worship (vv. 7-13). In principle Christians were free to eat or not eat meat. But Christians should consider how their actions affect other people. If eating meat signaled acceptance of idolatry, then Christians should refrain.

This text can and does evoke protest: must we always defer to the sensibilities of others, even to the point of compromising our convictions? There was a time when some Christians were deeply troubled by people of different races associating with each other, and for some this remains an issue. In such a case, would Paul tell us to defer to the wishes of others? It is difficult to answer exactly what Paul would say or do in every situation. In his own ministry, Paul sometimes chose to offend and sometimes chose to defer. But Paul's goal was to build up faith in Christ and strengthen Christian community. The best response to the text is to let it question us: what is the best way, in our own context, to build up faith in Christ and strengthen Christian community? One pastor said, "When preaching, I try not to offend through carelessness. But if my words offend, it must be on purpose and for a good reason." Paul's point is not just that we should be nice, but the Gospel is such an important message that it ought not to be confused with other, accidental messages.

> IN HIS OWN MINISTRY, PAUL SOMETIMES CHOSE TO OFFEND AND SOMETIMES CHOSE TO DEFER.

We may make different choices in different situations. A classic example concerns the use of alcohol: adults may decide to have wine with supper in their homes, but decide not to make alcohol available on a youth retreat. Others will insist that the best way to keep the message clear is to refrain from all use of alcohol. Another example has to do with cross-cultural contacts. Western standards of dress—both for men and women—are often offensive to people in non-western cultures. To help ensure that our witness has integrity, we need to consider what messages we send by our clothing and conduct. Not that all Christians will make the same choices about dress and conduct, but we should at least consider that our words and actions may send messages we do not intend. Paul arranged his life and ministry around what would best communicate the Gospel, and he challenges us to live so as to send the Gospel message—not unintentional messages—wherever we go.

1 CORINTHIANS 7:32-35 (RC)

Interpreting the Text

This passage is part of a lengthy discussion of marriage and singleness. Paul affirms the value of marriage at the beginning of 1 Corinthians 7, and later (vv. 32-35) he affirms the value of singleness for the sake of Christian service. Christians were counter-cultural in that they recognized the value of single people within their communities. Paul does not make singleness the norm for all people, but he insists that singleness is an estate valued by God. It has its own dignity and opportunities for service within the wider community. Singleness allows people a certain freedom that is more difficult for those with family obligations.

Responding to the Text

Many churches today rightly stress the importance of community life for the well-being of married couples and families. Some single people may therefore find it difficult to see themselves as fully valued members of congregations. So churches also need to rightly stress the importance of Christian community for single people. And single people bring great gifts to the community as a whole. People may remain single for various reasons, just as people may remain married for various reasons. But Paul calls us all to be full partners in the Gospel. The key to our identity and calling is not singleness or marriage, but being born anew in Jesus Christ.

GOSPEL
MARK 1:21-28

Interpreting the Text

This Gospel text begins and ends with exclamations about Jesus' authority (1:22, 27). The readers and hearers of Mark's Gospel are told right away that Jesus is the Christ, the Son of God (1:1); but those who hear him in Capernaum have no inside knowledge. All they have to go on are Jesus' words and deeds. The people have already noticed that Jesus' authority is unlike that of the scribes (v. 22) whose authority rested on consensus and tradition. It is one thing to wonder where Jesus fits into the *human* ranks of authority; but now the people see him cast out unclean spirits, demonstrating that his authority extends into the *spiritual* realm.

Bruce Malina and Richard Rohrbaugh note that in the first-century Mediterranean world, people believed that everything was caused by personal forces. Greater forces could control lesser ones. The Most High God was at the top, followed by "other" gods, sons of god or archangels. Next came angels, spirits, and demons. Then came humankind with its own layers of social status. It seemed reasonable that Jesus, who had no high rank in society, would not speak with authority in public unless he were possessed by some greater power. In the last rank were the creatures over which people have power. In such a hierarchy, the unclean spirits—who were higher up and had greater knowledge of spiritual powers—recognized Jesus' true identity and the source of his authority (v. 24; see 1:13 for Jesus' conflict with evil).[15]

In Jesus' time it was commonly believed that demons (to use the Greek term) or unclean spirits (the Semitic term) could control human behavior. According to Malina and Rohrbaugh, a person with "deviant" behavior or someone "embedded in a matrix of deviant social relationships" was thought to be controlled by unclean spirits. Such a person was a threat to the community and could be expelled. To set someone free from demons not only got rid of the demons but restored that person to a place in the community.

Demons, of course, resisted any attempt to dislodge them from their host. In Mark 1:23-24 the unclean spirits try to protect themselves by using Jesus' name and recognizing his authority. This may be some attempt at magic, or it may be the logic of deference, so common in hierarchies: if the demons admit Jesus' greater power, maybe he will leave them alone with their own little fiefdom. After all, why should the "Holy One of God" care about a bunch of unclean spirits inhabiting some worthless human being—especially if those unclean spirits know and confess who is boss! But Jesus will have none of it. For Jesus, authority is not merely the right to wield power over those of lesser rank, but it keeps in view the ends for which that power is used. Jesus does not make little compromises with evil. He has the authority to deliver, heal, convict, forgive, cleanse, and raise from the dead. He aims to defeat evil so that we can be set free.

Responding to the Text

Because it declares Jesus' authority, this Gospel may awaken or strengthen faith, arouse curiosity, or expose unbelief. Jesus' claim to authority continues to do all these things today. The very nature of the text calls for a strong proclamation, not a tentative or half-hearted one. The first challenge is to find a vantage point from which to proclaim this vigorous word of Jesus' authority.

The text offers at least two points of entry; the first one is authority. Even in a postmodern society where traditional forms of authority are absent or greatly compromised, people still recognize authority based on professional status, talent, personal charisma, success, beauty, and perhaps even moral and religious integrity.

Most people try to use their own authority as they are able. And everyone has to acknowledge higher authorities—for example, in seeking medical or legal help, honoring a family obligation, paying taxes, or slowing down for a police car lurking in a speed trap just up the road. Some church and community leaders always seem to get a response when they ask for volunteers or contributions. Perhaps their authority comes from the fact that they themselves are giving so much. Where does authority come from? How is it exercised and to what ends is it used? A few well-chosen vignettes can prepare people to hear the Gospel proclaim Jesus' authority.

112

THE SEASON
OF EPIPHANY
―――――――
NANCY
KOESTER

Jesus' authority amazed people because they did not know where it came from. Unlike the scribes, Jesus did not need professional status. Unlike the Romans, he did not have military or administrative clout. He had no authority from wealth or social standing. Jesus does not fit into authority patterns in our time either. Yet Jesus makes a claim on us, above all through his death and resurrection for us. The preacher can ask: Who or what has authority over us? Who or what has authority in our congregations and communities? The truth is twofold: Jesus makes a claim on us and so do other powers.

We sometimes find ourselves possessed by powers much larger than ourselves, and this leads to the second entry point for preaching: demon possession and unclean spirits. This is not a suitable topic for "Sunday Morning Lite"; for some people church is a place to avoid anything unpleasant—being nice is the ultimate goal. Even those who are more pugnacious usually prefer a rational explanation and enjoy the sense of being in charge. All this can leave us quite naïve about the presence of evil, even in church. Christians in developing countries are generally more alert to spiritual forces than their North American brothers and sisters. Indeed, Christian churches in many parts of the world use exorcism routinely. They know that sometimes evil needs to be named, rebuked, and cast out so that people can be restored to God and to each other.

SOMETIMES EVIL NEEDS TO BE NAMED, REBUKED, AND CAST OUT SO THAT PEOPLE CAN BE RESTORED TO GOD AND TO EACH OTHER.

It is not that North Americans (and North American Christians) have no demons, but rather that we tend not to "see" them or name them. Indeed, there are powers that can possess us and ruin our lives, both individually and collectively. As one unclean spirit said, "my name is Legion, for we are many" (Mark 5:9). The legion we commonly encounter includes greed, immorality, self-serving ambition, revenge, racism, gambling, materialism, hatred, substance abuse, pride, violence as entertainment. Sometimes all hell breaks loose, as in the 1999 high school massacre in Littleton, Colorado, or the "ethnic cleansing" in Kosovo, or—more subtly—the senior citizens ruined by their late-blooming addiction to gambling. The preacher asks: Who is in charge here? What authorities do we obey? Jesus claims ultimate and final authority over us. He can name and cast out the unclean spirits that separate us from him. He uses his authority to cleanse, heal, and set people free. Being free in Christ is better than being "nice" in bondage.

The recent film *Simon Birch* works with themes of religious authority, freedom, and leadership. A zany prank turns a Sunday school Christmas pageant into chaos. At the center of it all is Simon Birch. Born a dwarf, Simon is popular among his classmates, but not for reasons of stature, money, or family connections. If anything, Simon's "authority" seems to come from his wild, comic honesty and his conflicts with certain adults. Meanwhile the unhappy pastor, possessed by a long unconfessed sin, is unable to show grace, especially to Simon.[16]

On the way home from a winter youth retreat, the bus driver swerves to avoid a deer. The bus skids off the road into an icy river. As freezing water begins to fill the bus, Simon cuts through the panic and gives orders on how to evacuate. The kids obey him and reach safety, but Simon forfeits his own life. Simon's story explores what religious authority really is, how it is used, and how we know it is the real thing.

FIFTH SUNDAY AFTER THE EPIPHANY

FEBRUARY 6, 2000

FIFTH SUNDAY IN ORDINARY TIME

REVISED COMMON	EPISCOPAL (BCP)	ROMAN CATHOLIC
Isa. 40:21-31	2 Kings 4:(8-17), 18-21, (22-31), 32-37	Job 7:1-4, 6-7
Ps. 147:1-11, 20c	Ps. 142	Ps. 147:1-6
1 Cor. 9:16-23	1 Cor. 9:16-23	1 Cor. 9:1-19, 22-23
Mark 1:29-39	Mark 1:29-39	Mark 1:29-39

"WHO'S IN CHARGE HERE, ANYWAY?" We would like life to make sense, and it feels good to know that we (or someone we trust) is in charge. Yet sometimes things spin out of control in world politics, in our bodies, and in congregations too. Wars, cancer cells, and conflicts make so much havoc in our lives that it is hard to believe God reigns. The texts for the fifth Sunday after the Epiphany are bluntly honest about the hard things people go through and about our pleas for help. The texts are just as strong in proclaiming that Jesus Christ has come to make things right. Jesus Christ has come to do battle with sin, death, and evil. Whether we are weak or strong, free or constrained, Christ is our hope.

FIRST READING

ISAIAH 40:21-31

Interpreting the Text

A prophet whose work was collected under the name of Isaiah wrote this text in the wake of the fall of Babylon, when exiled Israel longed to go home.

THE VERY SAME GOD WHO MADE THE WORLD WATCHES OVER AND DIRECTS HUMAN HISTORY.

"Isaiah" saw God's plan stretching from creation through Israel's history and beyond. The forceful cry "Have you not known? Have you not heard?" (40:21, 28) resounds twice, as though the prophet wants to shake his hearers from sleep. The prophet alerts God's people to their approaching deliverance. The very same God who made the world watches over and directs human history. To us, human rulers may seem invincible; to God they are like stubble which a tempest carries away from the field (vv. 23-24). And this same powerful God keeps track of and cares about Israel. Freedom is coming. Meanwhile God renews the people's strength so that they can live to see a better future. Isaiah's promise—"he gives power to the faint, and strength to the powerless"—has often made Christians think of Jesus' mighty acts of healing and exorcism (Mark 1).

Responding to the Text

This text reads much like the Psalms (for example Psalm 25, 33, 34, 36 and many more). Isaiah 40:21-31 is meant for those who are weary or feel abandoned, thinking that God had forgotten them (v. 27). The message of comfort, hope, and confidence inspires prayer and song. For example, "You Who Dwell in the Shelter of the Lord," the beloved hymn by Michael Joncas, says:

> You who dwell in the shelter of the Lord,
> who abide in this shadow for life,
> say to the Lord: "My refuge, my rock in whom I trust!"
> And I will raise you up on eagle's wings, bear you on the breath of dawn,
> make you to shine like the sun, and hold you in the palm of my hand.[17]

2 KINGS 4:(8-17), 18-21, (22–31), 32–37 (BCP)

Interpreting the Text

The story of Elisha resurrecting a child from the dead (2 Kings 4:8-37) echoes Elijah's ministry (1 Kings 17:17-24). Christians have traditionally understood this text to anticipate Jesus' powerful acts. The woman's quest for Elisha on Mt. Carmel is like the disciples' seeking of Jesus in a deserted place, because people needed his help (Mark 1:35-37). In 2 Kings 4, 1 Kings 17, and Mark 1, God's chosen one uses power and authority to restore people to life.

Responding to the Text

If 2 Kings 4 is chosen as a preaching text, it is best to work with the entire narrative (4:8-37). Vividly retold, the story can stand on its own and offers many connecting points with contemporary experience, especially the anguish and hope and fear we face when death threatens a loved one, even a child. 2 Kings 4 tells how a devout woman gives hospitality to Elisha, who in turn rewards her with an unasked-for blessing: the promise of a child in her old age (4:16a). This wise woman knows that the hope of having a child will hurt if it does not come true and may still hurt if it does come true. She would rather not risk it (4:16b) but in due time the promise is fulfilled.

The family does not live happily ever after because several years later the child falls gravely ill. Parents who have faced the death of a child will know this woman's agony when her son dies in her arms (4:20). The woman's desperate search for help (4:4:21-25) strikes a chord with all parents who have taken their child to an emergency room or waited through surgery. Elisha's surprise and dismay is something most pastors can relate to, as is the woman's aggrieved reproach: 'Whose idea was this, anyway, Elisha?' (4:28). Elisha's struggle to save the child (4:29-35) and the final victory over death express God's authority and power. Our own desperate encounters with death and near-death lead us to places we do not want to go. The story can evoke faith, courage, and hope in God's saving power.

JOB 7:1-4,6-7 (RC)

Interpreting the Text

Job has lost health, family and wealth (1–2). As if that isn't enough, he must contend with inept comforters who instead of simply hearing his lament, try to explain it away. Job's lament goes to the bottom of human suffering. It is the cry of one who has abandoned hope, yet for no discernable reason must continue living.

Responding to the Text

If we were to respond to this text by trying to make it all better, we would fall into the same trap as Job's would-be comforters. Unless a preacher wishes to tell the whole story of Job, the best response is to listen as the text is read and accept the lament for what it is. Meanwhile there are two faint rays of hope in this text. First, people who experience great suffering can read or hear this text and know that others have walked this path too. Second, in 7:7-11 Job addresses God directly. Even the most abject prayer implies some faith that God is there, and the hope that God hears our cry. When paired with the Gospel text, Job's lament shows our human condition and our profound need for Jesus to fight for us against death, despair and evil.

RESPONSIVE READING
PSALM 147:1-11, 20c

"The Lord . . . heals the brokenhearted and binds up their wounds" (Psalm 147:3). This psalm praises God for intervening on our behalf, for works of creation and providence, mercy and healing. The emphasis on healing works especially well with the Gospel text for February 6. In our time, there are some people who believe only in a God of creation, others who believe only in a God of political justice, and still others who believe only in a God who helps individuals gently and privately. This psalm combines all three in a rich hymn of praise for the many ways in which God shows mercy. Here is no distant God, but a God on whom we depend and in whom we place all our hopes (v. 11).

PSALM 142 (BCP)

This psalm could very well express the desperate hope of the Shunammite woman in 2 Kings 4, or the people who clamored for healing and deliverance from unclean spirits in Mark 1. Because this psalm combines honest complaint (142:4) and sturdy trust (vv. 1-3; 5-6), it is a fine example of prayer. It works very well as a congregational prayer, setting a tone of expectant hope in the Gospel. On its own, it provides a fine model for a sermon on prayer.

> HERE IS NO DISTANT GOD, BUT A GOD ON WHOM WE DEPEND AND IN WHOM WE PLACE ALL OUR HOPES.

SECOND READING
1 CORINTHIANS 9:16-23 (RCL/BCP), 9:1-19, 22-23 (RC)

Interpreting the Text

In 1 Corinthians 8, Paul urged the Corinthians to use their knowledge and their freedom to show love for other people. Chapter 9 continues these themes. Here Paul teaches by example. When Paul asks the Corinthians to use their freedom in ways that build up others, he encourages them to live as he himself already lives.

In Christ, Paul's way of life includes both restraint and flexibility. Concerning restraint, Paul lists several ways in which he refrains from making full use of his rights in the Gospel. For example, Paul understands that he has a right to be supported by those he serves (vv. 6-7) and that he has a right to marry (v. 5). But Paul lays aside these rights because to claim them would interfere with serving other people. Christians are free. Out of love, however, we do well to abstain from self-serving freedom, aiming instead to build up others.

Concerning flexibility, Paul says "to the Jews I became as a Jew" or "to those outside the law I became as one outside the law" (vv. 20-21). Here he uses freedom for the sake of the Gospel. Specifically, this could mean eating kosher food with Jews and eating non-kosher food with gentiles. It might sound like Paul is just a chameleon, adapting his colors to blend into his surroundings, doing what is most convenient. That charge would be true if Paul were adapting only to serve himself or spare himself some trouble. But his goal is to bring others to faith. Paul chooses flexibility "for the sake of the gospel" (v. 23). In exercising both restraint and flexibility, Paul proclaims the Gospel and brings people into faith.

Responding to the Text

One of the principle challenges of Christian evangelism is to make the Gospel accessible in a given cultural context. Missionaries have long recognized this. The integrity of the Gospel remains, but cultural forms change—and must change—if the Gospel is to be made known to all peoples. The challenge is to communicate the Gospel so that people really hear it. A translator must be faithful to the message and yet find ways to express it in a new language. We are always "translating" the Gospel and hearing the Gospel translated, whether across cultures or across generations.

Many Christians in North America seek to convey the Gospel message to those with little or no acquaintance with Christianity. Even small matters, like styles of music and dress, can help or hinder the message about Jesus. But by using varied styles of music and preaching, together with new forms of congregational life, Christians adapt themselves in order to convey the Gospel message.

Without a passion for the Gospel and without a clear commitment to the centrality of Jesus Christ, such adaptation is pointless. But Paul calls us to be all things to all people so that by all means some might be won to faith in Christ. The future of evangelism in our time cries out for faithful innovation: people who communicate the Gospel in ever new ways. The best sermon illustrations on this theme will come from local context. If possible, get to know at least one innovative church or outreach ministry in your area, and use its story for 1 Corinthians 9. Look for themes of flexibility, restraint, and faithfulness. If you yourself are already involved in such a ministry, you already know that you "do it all for the sake of the Gospel" (v. 23).

GOSPEL

MARK 1:29-39

Interpreting the Text

Movement, momentum, and miracle all animate this text. In *Mark as Story,* David Rhoads and Donald Michie discuss how Jesus goes from place to place "in order to proclaim, exorcise and heal."[18] This movement conveys a sense of urgency, turmoil, and activity. In Mark 1:29-39, Jesus' movement also highlights his growing popularity with the crowds. In other parts of Mark, Jesus' movement highlights conflicts with his adversaries and sometimes with his followers. Jesus goes from the synagogue to the house of Simon and Andrew, then to a deserted place to pray. His disciples search him out, saying, "Everyone is looking for you." But rather than return to Capernaum, Jesus keeps circulating throughout the region. Jesus' drive to reach more and more people inspires his followers in each generation to help make Christianity a world religion instead of the property of one people or culture.

The momentum of Jesus' ministry quickly builds, so that more and more people who need help seek him out. Indeed "the whole city was gathered around the door" of Simon and Andrew's house. These people clamor for healing. They also want Jesus to cast out unclean spirits. Whether they will hear and believe Jesus' message the text does not say. Sharp contrasts abound: Jesus attracts crowds (v. 32), yet Jesus seeks solitude (v. 35). People seek Jesus out (vv. 36-37) and Jesus moves on (v. 38). Jesus succeeds (vv. 33-34) and yet Jesus is restless (v. 38). Clearly Jesus is not content to belong to one group of people; his message and power must reach everyone.

Miracle is basic for this Gospel. At the start of his ministry Jesus' miracles attract crowds. Paul Achtemeier notes that Mark brims with stories of the miracles Jesus performed; proportionate to its length, Mark contains more miracle stories than the other Gospels. Commonly translated as 'miracles,' the Greek word *dynameis* has the same root as our word "dynamite." Achtemeier writes that *dynameis* is best translated as "acts of power."[19] Beginning with the Spirit's descent at Jesus' baptism and continuing through and beyond his wilderness temptation (1:10-13), Mark understood Jesus' dynamic acts of power as part of a running conflict with the forces of evil. Jesus' miracles helped the people who were healed or set free from unclean spirits; but their larger import is Jesus' victorious conflict with Satan and with death itself.

> MARK UNDERSTOOD JESUS' DYNAMIC ACTS OF POWER AS PART OF A RUNNING CONFLICT WITH THE FORCES OF EVIL.

We are not told why Jesus forbids the demons to speak (v. 34). Elsewhere in Mark, Jesus tells people to keep silent about him (for example, 1:44). Perhaps Jesus wants to be in charge of what will be revealed about him, as well as how, when, and by whom it will be revealed (Mark 14:61-62).

Responding to the Text

It may be tempting to reach for the sermonic tidbits in this text: we are healed to serve others (v. 31); Jesus took time out to pray and so should we (v. 35). These are important themes for the Christian life but they are not at the center of this text. Two cries of human longing lie at the core of this Gospel. One is plainly spoken: "Everyone is searching for you!" (v. 37). The other cry is implied by all those who need to be healed or set free from demons: "Deliver us from evil!" Both of these express our profound need to be in relationship with God. Jesus is the only person who can completely fill that need, because he alone reveals God to us and he alone has power over sin and death.

The two cries, "Everyone is searching for you," and "Deliver us from evil" are intertwined. The people in this text search for Jesus not just because they want to have a nice day but because they need help and they need it now. The people of Capernaum reveal much about the human condition: we are vulnerable, we are mortal, we want to be set free from suffering and evil. We want more life. We thirst for God.

A sermon on the first cry, "Everyone is searching for you," could pursue a set of leading questions: How do we search for God? What do we expect to find? Is Jesus the one we seek? Is he less—and more—than we bargained for? Is Jesus the one we wanted to find when we began our search for God? The local context can provide stories and illustrations, as can a vivid retelling of the text. The conclusion of the sermon, rather than summarizing what has already been said, can show that Jesus is searching for us—actively, passionately, restlessly searching for us (v. 38). *His* search for us is the Gospel.

The second "cry" of the Gospel text, "Deliver us from evil," is a plea for deliverance from many sufferings. This includes demon possession and "unclean spirits" (discussed in context with the Gospel for January 30). The cry also is a plea for healing from sickness and injury. In the huge topic of healing, this Gospel may raise more questions than it answers. Not everyone who sought Jesus was healed by him, for contrary to the disciples' pleas, Jesus did not return to Capernaum (v. 38). He moved on to new places. There is a sense of unfinished business in Capernaum: many people there likely wanted to be healed but were not. So the Gospel does not promise that everyone who seeks healing will receive it. It does, however, proclaim Jesus' power to heal. And it does place this power in the larger context of Jesus' battle with evil and death. No one can answer every question about healing, but preachers can encourage and model prayer for healing. (See the books by William Barclay, Alvin Rogness, and M. T. Kelsey).[20]

Our need for healing is one important part of the larger cry which Jesus himself taught us to pray, "Deliver us from evil" (Matt. 6:13; Luke 11:4). Martin Luther, in his *Large Catechism* (Lord's Prayer, last petition), works with militant conflict between good and evil similar to that of Mark's Gospel. Luther writes:

This petition seems to be speaking of the devil as the sum of all evil in order that the entire substance of our prayer may be directed against our arch-enemy. It is he who obstructs everything that we pray for: God's name or glory, God's kingdom and will, our daily bread, a good and cheerful conscience, etc.

Therefore we sum it all up by saying, "Dear Father, help us to get rid of all this misfortune." Nevertheless, this petition includes all the evil that may befall us under the devil's kingdom: poverty, shame, death, and in short all the tragic misery and heartache of which there is so incalculably much on earth . . . for if God did not support us, we would not be safe from [Satan] for a single hour.

Thus you see how God wants us to pray . . . for everything that affects our bodily welfare.[21]

SIXTH SUNDAY AFTER THE EPIPHANY

FEBRUARY 13, 2000

SIXTH SUNDAY IN ORDINARY TIME / PROPER 1

REVISED COMMON	EPISCOPAL (BCP)	ROMAN CATHOLIC
2 Kings 5:1-14	2 Kings 5:1-15ab	Lev. 13:1-2, 44-46
Ps. 30	Ps. 42 or 42:1-7	Ps. 32:1-2, 5, 7, 11
1 Cor. 9:24-27	1 Cor. 9:24-27	1 Cor. 10:31—11:1
Mark 1:40-45	Mark 1:40-45	Mark 1:40-45

IN HIS MOST CONTROVERSIAL ACT SO FAR IN Mark's Gospel, Jesus touches and heals an outcast. God's word has the power break down boundaries of sin and death and restore us once again to health, peace, and fellowship. The first reading recounts Elisha's healing ministry with his vociferous patient, Naaman. The psalms lead the way in praising God for such great mercy. And the Apostle Paul shows how God's grace redefines freedom and discipline for Christian living. God re-draws the boundaries of our lives in order to make us whole.

FIRST READING
2 KINGS 5:1-14 (RCL), 5:1-15ab (BCP)

Interpreting the Text

In this story, Naaman, an army commander from Aram (Syria), wants to be healed from leprosy, and the prophet Elisha heals him. That is the obvious link with the Gospel text for the Sixth Sunday after the Epiphany. Another more direct New Testament connection with 2 Kings 5 is Luke 4:27: Jesus' reference to Naaman's story shows God's freedom to heal and save beyond the boundaries of Israel. Jesus' hearers resent being told, in effect, that God can color outside the lines.

Responding to the Text

God's mercy comes in surprising ways. One response to this text is to retell it, savoring its humor and pathos and setting up a contrast between human expectation and God's mercy. The preacher might use playful anachronisms to engage the congregation.

Naaman is a great man and a mighty warrior (v. 1) who is afflicted with leprosy. He hears that healing can be found in Israel. So with his king's permission, Naaman goes to Israel, bringing along a great fortune of silver, gold, and fine garments (v. 5) and a letter from his own king to the king of Israel ("Let's have my people talk to your people"). But all this wealth can buy no healing from the King of Israel ("The difficult we do immediately; miracles take a little longer"). Israel's king thinks this is a setup, but his protest, "Say what? Am I God?" points the right way. Elisha saves face for the king by sending Naaman a message, "Go, wash in the Jordan seven times and your flesh shall be restored and you shall be clean" (v. 10). But Naaman goes into a blue funk. Elisha has prescribed no state-of-the-art healing technique and has used no expensive equipment! What did he waste his time for if he could have just washed in a river at home? Besides, Naaman is an important man (his big daily planner has more entries for one day than Elisha probably has for a year) yet Elisha barely gives him the time of day. Naaman fumes but his servants persuade him to "chill" and just try following Elisha's directions. You never know—maybe for Israel's God, less is more.

Naaman washes seven times in the Jordan and is healed. Still wanting to do things up right, he tries to pay for the healing (5:16), but Elisha says there is no bill. The prophet does not even demand that Naaman abstain from worshipping in a pagan temple, but just tells Naaman to "go in peace."

If the story is told in a lively, engaging way, we may look over Naaman's shoulder and see that God's way of saving us is different from our expectations. We may overhear that God simply loves us, and that, beyond what God has already paid, there is no bill.

LEVITICUS 13:1-2, 44-46 (RC)

Leviticus 11–15 describes what is clean and unclean. The people are to avoid anything that would contaminate their health and well-being. All of chapter 13 is devoted to diagnosing and dealing with leprosy, and much of 14 deals with ritual cleansing for people who are verifiably cured of leprous symptoms. (The term "leprosy" includes a range of skin diseases.) In dealing with people who have a disease, the priest's role is to apply diagnostic standards and perform the proper religious rites.

In its lectionary setting, this text highlights the plight of people who had "leprosy." As outcasts from society, their distress was both physical and spiritual. The text prepares worshippers to appreciate the Gospel story when in mercy Jesus touches and heals an outcast.

RESPONSIVE READING

PSALM 30

A song of praise and deliverance, this psalm may call to mind the man healed from leprosy by Jesus. Psalm 30:5 is an often-quoted verse in the Bible, because it brings hope and rings true to our experience. Later (v. 9), the psalmist recounts having bargained with God, something we are taught not to do—yet sometimes life brings us to places where trying to make deals comes naturally. Even then, God can turn our mourning into dancing and our sorrow into joy. Because it connects so vividly with human experience and so confidently praises God's mercy, this psalm can well be treated as a preaching text in its own right.

PSALM 42 or 42:1-7 (BCP)

Psalm 42 is a prayer for healing in preparation for pilgrimage. The prayer continues in Psalm 43, which shares a common refrain with 42 (42:5, 11; 43:5). An illness (v. 10) prevents the psalmist from undertaking the sacred pilgrimage, making memories of past pilgrimages bittersweet (v. 4). This psalm of petition and hope has inspired many choral works, including William Billings's tender and austere "As the Hart Panteth."[22]

> GOD CAN TURN OUR MOURNING INTO DANCING AND OUR SORROW INTO JOY.

PSALM 32:1-2, 5, 7, 11 (RC)

Psalm 32 is a song of thanksgiving for healing. The selected verses promise joy in God's forgiveness. Verse 5 has long been used by the people of God both as a statement of God's forgiveness already received, and an invitation to people to confess their sins and receive forgiveness. The exhortation in verse 11 sets a joyful tone, preparing the way for the Gospel message.

SECOND READING

1 CORINTHIANS 9:24-27 (RCL/BCP)
10:31—11:1 (RC)

Interpreting the Text

The ancient world placed high value on athletics. The Greeks were famous for their athletic competitions, and Paul was writing to a congregation in Greece. Corinth and many other cities had stadiums where athletic events drew spectators from all over the region. Major events for any town, athletic competitions were celebrated with religious festivals and public displays. Often the events would extend over a period of days. Among the Greeks the most prestigious event was the foot race. Successful runners spent long hours in training and achieved considerable fame for themselves because of their abilities. Boxing was another event that required considerable self-discipline, but it was a more painful sport. Athletes wrapped their fists in leather to protect their hands and to deliver the most powerful blows to their opponents.

Paul harnesses the widespread esteem given to athletes and applies it to the life of faith. He urges the Corinthians to devote the same amount of energy to living out their faith as athletes devote to winning the race. Despite the rhetoric of competition in verse 24, Paul is not suggesting that only one person will be saved or that Christians compete with one another for a single prize. Rather he speaks to the whole congregation, urging everyone to strive to their utmost in their living the life of faith. In verses 26-27, Paul also adapts the athletic imagery to better fit the Christian life (boxers normally seek to subdue their opponents, but Paul urges Christians to subdue themselves). Unlike boxers, Christians do not strive to defeat others, but to serve.

This becomes clear at the end of chapter 10. Here Paul resumes his general theme of exercising self-discipline for the sake of Christian witness. As in chapter 8, Paul comments on the issue of eating meat offered to idols (see also the comments for 1 Cor. 8:1-13, January 30). He repeats that the great concern is how actions affect others. If what we do makes it hard for another person to hear the Gospel, then out of love we should restrain ourselves. On the other hand, we may receive with thanks whatever God has given us. In either case our actions have the same goal: that many may be saved (10:30).

Responding to the Text

In modern America, as in first-century Greece, athletes are among the most widely honored members of society. The kinds of service to which Paul has called people can lack the drama and glory of athletic competition because serving one's neighbor often takes place in quiet and unnoticed ways, without public acclaim. But by comparing the Christian life to a race, Paul heightens our commitment to servanthood. Salvation is ultimately God's gift, but that does not mean we can become complacent. Instead, the hope of receiving God's glory and honor infuses everyday life with energy and ennobles it with self-respect.

Many people have a negative view of self-discipline because it seems to be a resounding "no" to most things that we find enjoyable. Paul puts the notion of self-discipline in a different light. For an athlete, discipline is not simply a "no" to enjoyment, but a "yes" to a greater purpose. Because we have not yet arrived fully in the kingdom of God, living the Christian life requires discipline. Sin remains a reality in our world and in ourselves, yet God calls us to the way of Christ, serving others in love.

GOSPEL

MARK 1:40-45

Interpreting the Text

Jesus' miracles continue in 1:40-45 as Jesus heals a leprous man. This particular act of healing, however, reveals a new dimension of Jesus' work: he violates boundaries held to be important by the community. Don Juel writes, "Jesus' healing of the leper is the first of several stories that deal with Jesus' violation of ritual boundaries."[23] Established by the Torah, these boundaries were meant to protect the community from danger and to keep people who were "clean" from being infected by those who were "unclean." A "clean" person could be defiled by touching a leper and would have to go through purification rituals—even if he or she did not contract the disease. Thus the disease(s) called leprosy affected not only one's body, but one's relationship with other people and with God. Yet none of this stopped Jesus from touching the diseased man.

> BECAUSE WE HAVE NOT YET ARRIVED FULLY IN THE KINGDOM OF GOD, LIVING THE CHRISTIAN LIFE REQUIRES DISCIPLINE.

In Jesus' time, many different skin diseases were called "leprosy"; these may or may not have included "Hansen's disease," typically called leprosy today. People who suffered from these skin diseases were cast out from their communities, lest the affliction spread to other people. Leviticus 13–14 instructs priests on how to diagnose leprosy, when to pronounce a person "clean" or "unclean," and what kinds of rites could restore a healed person to ritual purity.

At least two aspects of this Gospel text are unclear. First, some ancient texts describe Jesus' emotion as "anger" rather than pity (v. 41). We are not told why Jesus might have been angry. The stern warning and sending away at once (v. 43) make one wonder if an exorcism as well as a healing has taken place. Nevertheless, Jesus' actions (touching and healing the leper) and his words ("I do choose. Be made clean!") are plain and bold.

A second issue concerns the action in verses 43-45. Here Jesus orders the cleansed man "say nothing to anyone" (v. 44), yet the man flagrantly disobeys Jesus' command. This raises questions: Why wouldn't Jesus want others to know about the healing? And if Jesus could heal the man, why could he not also silence him? Interpreters have posited a "messianic secret" in Mark, in which Jesus tries to keep his true identity hidden. Paul Achtemeier says that the overriding point here is not "secrecy disobeyed" (1:45; 7:36) but Jesus' popularity.[24] The (disobeyed) order to remain silent highlights how impossible it was to keep people from talking about Jesus and seeking him out. The larger message is Jesus' power at work in his words.

Responding to the Text

"Out of bounds!" The official blows the whistle and takes the ball. As compensation, the other team gets the ball. It would be impossible to play basketball, or most other team sport games, without boundaries of time and space. Societies and families need boundaries too, to keep people safe and to make things run smoothly. Even on a very crowded bus or subway train most people usually try to respect each other's boundaries. Boundaries make the difference between a crowd and a mob. Co-workers who violate professional or sexual boundaries can make even the best position a "job from hell." In the beginning God created boundaries by separating light from darkness and sea from land (Genesis 1). The Ten Commandments include boundaries that make it possible for people to live together.

Yet some boundaries have defaced God's good creation. Sin and evil have made chasms between us and God, between us and other people. Jesus came to remove these boundaries. He removed or bridged them through his word which forgives, heals, and exorcises, and finally through his own death and resurrection.

The Gospel in Mark 1:40-45 is full of boundary violations. An unclean man begs for help from a holy man. The holy man touches the unclean one. And instead of Jesus being made unclean (the expected result), the man with leprosy is healed. Then, against Jesus' command, the healed man freely proclaims Jesus' work. And people come to Jesus from everywhere, most of them probably crossing some kind of boundary. The professional religious types of Jesus' day see him as in interloper, a claim-jumper, a base-stealer.

Jesus' mighty words and deeds remove boundaries that separate us from God and from each other (Mark 2:5; 3:28; 5:41-42). The preacher should avoid, however, the glib notion that all boundaries are bad and that therefore removing boundaries is always good. Many boundaries are God-given. We could not live without some of them. And to avoid overstatement, allow the text itself to set some boundaries. It is Jesus who reaches out, touches and heals the leprous man. Jesus bridges the gap between us and God. Whenever we pray, we are crossing the boundary between ourselves and God, because Jesus has already opened the way. Jesus also gave us some new boundaries (3:29; 32-35; 6:11; 7:15) which reflect God's will for our new life in Christ.

The Gospel story encourages us to pray for healing and to look forward to the time when God will remove, once and for all, everything that tries to separate us from God. Jesus' mighty words and deeds cross boundaries that once seemed impassable. The Gospel word says that nothing can separate us from the love of God which is ours in Christ Jesus.

SEVENTH SUNDAY AFTER THE EPIPHANY

FEBRUARY 20, 2000

SEVENTH SUNDAY IN ORDINARY TIME / PROPER 2

REVISED COMMON	EPISCOPAL (BCP)	ROMAN CATHOLIC
Isa. 43:18-25	Isa. 43:18-25	Isa. 43:18-19, 21-22, 24-25
Ps. 41	Ps. 32 or 32:1-8	Ps. 41:2-5, 13-14
2 Cor. 1:18-22	2 Cor. 1:18-22	2 Cor. 1:18-22
Mark 2:1-12	Mark 2:1-12	Mark 2:1-12

"I AM ABOUT TO DO A NEW THING," says the Lord. God's new thing is a walking miracle. God's new thing is a forgiven sinner. God's new thing is an awe-struck crowd: "never before have we seen anything like this!" Jesus Christ is the new "yes" to all God's promises. Yes to the Word made flesh!

FIRST READING
ISAIAH 43:18-25

Interpreting the Text

In Isaiah 43:14—44:5, the prophet looks forward to Israel's redemption and restoration. (Comments for the first reading, Fifth Sunday after the Epiphany, describe the historical setting of this text.) In the first reading God is the "I" who speaks directly to the people. Recalling the Exodus from Egypt (43:16-17), God promises even greater deliverance to come. 'If you think parting the Red Sea was something, wait until you see what I'm going to do now for you, my chosen people.' Isaiah 43:18-21 alerts the people to God's new plans.

In verses 22-24, however, the tone changes from vibrant hope to lament—God's lament because the people's love has grown cold. God is an unrequited lover. The people have not returned God's love; worse yet, they have run away by sinning against God (v. 24b). But instead of pronouncing doom, Isaiah's next words proclaim mercy: "I will not remember your sins" (v. 25).

Responding to the Text

God's promise to forgive and forget (43:25) works well with Mark 2:1-12 in which Jesus announces forgiveness; thus Isaiah 43 prepares the way for the Gospel. It also presents several fresh themes for preaching: the bracing newness of God's work (v. 19) and creation's renewal (vv. 19-20); the purpose of human life (v. 21) and God's lament when we turn away from that purpose; God's promise to blot out and forget our sins (v. 25). God leads us into an open future and makes all things new.

RESPONSIVE READING
PSALM 41

As a prayer for healing, Psalm 41 anticipates the Gospel in which Jesus forgives and heals the paralyzed man. Unlike the man in Mark 2, however, the psalmist receives no help from others; instead, antagonists take pleasure in the psalmist's sufferings, expecting him to die soon (v. 5). The psalmist alone awaits help from God (v. 10). This sufferer cries out in complaint (vv. 4-10) but also praises God's mercy and justice (vv. 1-3; 11-13). In our prayers we too can lament, praise God, and expect God's help.

PSALM 32 (BCP)

When this psalm was written, illness was commonly understood to be punishment for sin. This text describes how the psalmist experienced healing as evidence of forgiveness. Our understanding of the relationship between sin and illness has changed a great deal, though many questions remain. While some illness is directly linked to behavior (e.g., smoking can make us more vulnerable to lung cancer) many other illnesses cannot be similarly traced. At the same time we know that profound stress—including the burden of a troubled conscience—can erupt into physical suffering. The link between spirit and body is complex, but the psalm assures us that God wants life and health for the whole person. God's mercy gives us confidence to pray and to hope.

2 CORINTHIANS 1:18-22

Interpreting the Text

For the past several weeks, the second reading has come from 1 Corinthians. Now attention shifts to 2 Corinthians, a letter written some time later. Between the writing of the two letters Paul made a brief visit to Corinth (2:1). During that visit someone had deeply offended him. Paul went away. Although he hoped to return to Corinth, questions about his relationship to that congregation held him back. Paul wrote a letter expressing his pain over the way he had been treated (2:4). The congregation responded by disciplining the member who had hurt Paul (2:6, 7) and by letting Paul know of their continued concern for him. In the wake of these painful incidents, Paul wrote 2 Corinthians. Chapter 1 speaks of the consolation that we have in Christ Jesus. Chapter 2 shows compassion for the person who had caused the pain in the first place.

In the reading for the seventh Sunday after the Epiphany, Paul responds to questions about his travel plans. Apparently the Corinthians were expecting Paul to visit, and he had not come. Was Paul toying with them? Paul denied this, insisting that he deliberately stayed away out of concern for the unity of the church.

The theological heart of the passage is God's faithfulness. Through the gift of the Spirit, Christians are assured that God is faithful. The Spirit is God's "first installment," which guarantees greater joy and life to come. The Greek word *arrabon* (2:22)

> THE SPIRIT IS GOD'S "FIRST INSTALLMENT," WHICH
> GUARANTEES GREATER JOY AND LIFE TO COME.

means downpayment—the part of a purchase price which is paid in advance. It makes a contract valid and assures that further payments will be made. The gift of the Spirit guarantees that God keeps promises. Having received a taste of his grace through the Spirit, the Corinthians can be sure that God will bring them to everlasting life.

Responding to the Text

The Corinthians lived in a conflicted congregation. There were tensions among members of the congregation and between the congregation and Paul. Those who spend even a modest amount of time in Christian community soon discover how far short of the kingdom we can fall. Many pastors, after leaving a congregation, understand how it feels to have to express their love for that congregation by staying away. The church is a work in progress and the down payment of the Spirit counts for more than the presence or absence of one individual. We know that everything necessary for salvation was accomplished on

Good Friday and Easter. But as long as sin disrupts our relationships, God's redeeming work continues.

Just as Jesus' miracles were a down payment on his complete defeat of death and evil, so too the gift of the Holy Spirit is a down payment on God's will and purpose. The Spirit gives faith here and now. The Spirit is God's down payment rather than God's full payment. When we must deal with pain and broken relationships in the church, the "down payment" brings hope and healing.

Sometimes even faithful Christians, if they have had painful experiences, are tempted to say "no" to God. So Paul declares Jesus as the "yes" to all God's promises (v. 20). Note that Paul does not say that God affirms every situation. God's word comes as threat and promise, law and Gospel, "yes" to life and "no" to sin. Paul does not say that God only affirms us; for insofar as we remain sinners, God's word challenges us. We can be thankful that God does not say "yes" to our sin.

Paul does say that in Christ God's promises find their "yes." God promised new life and has kept that promise through Jesus' resurrection. God's "yes" stands overagainst our sin and saves us from it. A sermon on this text could use a three-part strategy: First, sketch a rosy ideal of the church. Second, admit some harsh realities. Third, proclaim the "down payment" and rejoice in it. Charles Wesley's exuberant hymn "Love Divine, All Loves Excelling" prays for the Spirit's coming and reaches eagerly for God's completed work, the new creation.

GOSPEL
MARK 2:1-12

Interpreting the Text

Of the healing stories in Mark's gospel so far, this one is the most detailed and theologically developed. A few comments will shed light on the text. The house where Jesus was staying had a flat roof which could be "dug through" (v. 4). It may have been made of mud and sticks, though Luke 5:19 mentions a tile roof. Either way, determined people could make an opening big enough to lower a man down into the house. It must have been a dramatic entrance!

The scribes have already been mentioned in a negative comparison with Jesus (1:22). Now they appear in person (v. 6). Scribes were learned people who worked with written records. Scribes could work in courts, for the military or religious establishment, or anyplace that needed administration and record keeping. In Mark's Gospel, scribes are especially concerned with the interpretation of the law. They appear in connection with high priests and elders. They usually oppose Jesus, and are associated with Jesus' death (14:53).[25]

Paul Achtemeier describes the structure of this text; an awareness of structure can help the preacher make some basic decisions about what to emphasize in the sermon. The *problem* (vv. 2-4a) is how to get the paralytic man within reach of Jesus. The *solution* is given in verses 4-5, 11, and the *proof* occurs in verse 12 where the amazed crowd confirms that a miracle has occurred. This simple structure houses what may be a later insertion, a *dialog* between the scribes and Jesus over who has the authority to forgive sins (vv. 6-10).[26] Whether or not this dialog is original to Mark, Jesus' authority to forgive has great importance for the Gospel and for all Christians. As Achtemeier notes, "we can no longer benefit directly from the physical presence of the healing Jesus but . . . can still experience his power in the forgiveness of sin he offers."[27]

Forgiveness of sins is the key theological issue in the text. Sin separates people from God. In Jesus' day, because disease and disability were thought to manifest the power of evil, these were commonly linked with sin (for a contrast, see John 9:3). Our desire to be God or to take God's place is the root of all sin. Sin violates the boundary between God and people as well as the boundaries between people. Forgiveness can restore the person to relationship with others.

God alone has the power to forgive sins. This power was expressed through the proper observance of sacrificial rites overseen by the religious establishment (to which the scribes belonged). For Jesus to pronounce forgiveness of sins was to claim special access to God's power, thus violating the boundary between human and divine. Adding insult to injury, Jesus' action also undercut the formal means already in place for dealing with sins, thus violating the boundary between Jesus and the religious establishment. So on hearing Jesus say "Son, your sins are forgiven" (v. 5) the scribes, professionals in religious boundary-keeping, think that Jesus commits blasphemy (see Mark 14:64). But instead of arguing with the scribes, Jesus does something entirely new. The key to the whole passage is verse 10, where Jesus asserts his authority and demonstrates his power.

Responding to the Text

The structure of the text suggests two major options for preaching. The first is to work with faith and healing, with a special focus on intercessory prayer. If forgiveness is the key theological issue of the text, intercession is the key practical issue. Most congregations and many individuals pray regularly for people who need healing. The Gospel dramatizes active intercession which can also be called advocacy. Friends of the paralyzed man are willing to do whatever it takes to bring him into Jesus' presence. If you can't go in through the door, go in through the roof! These people did not give up. Their actions were prayers, expressing faith, hope, and love. The text gives Christians strong encouragement to intercede for those who are ill or in special need, and to allow those prayers to evoke deeds of love. A story from the local context could illustrate such active intercession. For stories of advocacy for Christians persecuted for the faith, contact "The Voice of the Martyrs" at (918) 337-8015 or www.persecution.com.

Mark says that Jesus "saw their faith" (v. 5). The plural "their" is important. It may include the faith of the paralyzed man and it definitely includes the faith of his advocates. We need to pray for others and we need others to pray for us. The paralytic was not healed as a reward for his own private faith, but because Jesus was moved by the faith of his community. Yet Jesus' first action, pronouncing the paralyzed man's forgiveness, may not have been exactly what the advocates were hoping for. Would they have dug their way through the roof for a pronouncement of forgiveness? Only if they were good theologians as well as good friends! God's response to community intercession may not always be what we ask for or expect, but by faith we trust God's mercy. Clearly, restoring the man to right relationship with God was "Job No. 1" for Jesus. This was his highest priority. The physical healing dramatized restoration to God, which was the most important thing.

> GOD'S RESPONSE TO COMMUNITY INTERCESSION MAY NOT ALWAYS BE WHAT WE ASK FOR OR EXPECT, BUT BY FAITH WE TRUST GOD'S MERCY.

It took faith to bring the man to Jesus for healing. It also took faith to see God's power at work in Jesus. We are not told if the scribes joined in glorifying God (v. 12) but it seems unlikely. Faith was necessary both to intercede and to praise God for mercy.

The second approach is to work with Jesus' power to forgive sins. Preachers can no longer assume that their hearers are familiar with "sin and forgiveness" or that they accept it. This text provides a good opportunity to teach: what sin is (rebellion against God); what sin does (separates us from God and other people); and what forgiveness does (restores us to right relationship with God and others). Most people respond better to story than to lecture. Tell a story of a human relationship that moves from love, to misunderstanding, to alienation, to restoration.

Many people today are offended by talk of sin and forgiveness. Some say that sin-talk is bad for our self-esteem. Others think that forgiveness comes from within ourselves, not from God. Cleanly used, objection and response can make for a lively sermon. The goal of the sermon is to proclaim that Jesus forgives sin and opens the way to God. But the strategy recognizes obstacles (or objections), names them, deals with them, and lays them aside. Now the way is clear, for the Gospel is God's reconciling work. That's good Gospel news.

People often object to the Gospel because we want to stay in control. The scribes maintained control by monitoring religious rules and regulations. We maintain control by making choices. The scribes looked to the religious establishment for authority; we tend to look within the self for authority. But the forgiveness of sins is God's powerful word. It is true that sometimes we do need to forgive ourselves; but such self-forgiveness takes place as a result of God's forgiveness coming from outside ourselves. It is God doing something new. Jesus has authority to forgive sins. And he wants to use it for us.

EIGHTH SUNDAY AFTER THE EPIPHANY

FEBRUARY 27, 2000

EIGHTH SUNDAY IN ORDINARY TIME / PROPER 3

REVISED COMMON	EPISCOPAL (BCP)	ROMAN CATHOLIC
Hosea 2:14-20	Hosea 2:14-23	Hosea 2:16-18, 21-22
Ps. 103:1-13, 22	Ps. 103 or 103:1-6	Ps. 103:1-4, 8, 10, 12-13
2 Cor. 3:1-6	2 Cor. 3:(4-11), 17—4:2	2 Cor. 3:1-6
Mark 2:13-22	Mark 2:18-22	Mark 2:18-22

NO ONE PUTS NEW WINE INTO OLD WINESKINS because new wine will burst old skins, destroying both the wine and the skins. Old religious forms cannot contain or inhibit the new Gospel of Jesus Christ, for he will either burst through those old forms or rip them open. People like to think that God wants to keep respectable folks separate from sinners. But Jesus came to call sinners back to God. So he ate with despised tax collectors and sinners and called them to follow him. Long before Jesus, the prophet Hosea demonstrated God's love by marrying a prostitute. And inspired by Jesus, the Apostle Paul insisted that the best recommendation we can have is the Holy Spirit's work within us. As the new Gospel bursts through old forms, forgiven and healed people shout, "Bless the Lord, O my soul!"

FIRST READING
HOSEA 2:14-23

Interpreting the Text

God had plenty of reasons to abandon Israel. After all, Israel had been unfaithful to God so many times! Like a wounded lover or a betrayed spouse, God was torn between anger and hope that some day Israel would love in return. Israel's religious affairs were not just "options" or neutral choices; they were betrayals. God told the prophet Hosea to reenact all this by taking "a wife of whoredom" (1:2; 3:1). "See how it feels, Hosea! Then when you speak for God, you will know what you are talking about."

Using the language of romance, marriage, and infidelity, Hosea vents God's fierce anger in 2:1-13. But in verses 14-23, he declares God's new courtship of Israel (vv. 14-15), Israel's response (v. 16), and God's intention to renew the covenant with Israel (vv. 17-20). Israel's relationship with God will express complete devotion. False gods will be removed forever (v. 17). God's anger will turn to tenderness. Instead of estrangement there will be faithful love (v. 23). Not only Israel but the whole earth will benefit from this restored covenant (vv. 21-23). Throughout the book of Hosea, these fervent hopes are dashed many times. Gomer embraces other lovers, just as Israel worships other gods. But Hosea never loses sight of the way things are supposed to be. God will not give up.

Responding to the Text

Can this marriage be saved? What could be more painful than being married to someone who is repeatedly unfaithful? At what point do you call it quits? God knows the pain of betrayal all too well. Every time we let something or someone else be our god, we betray the true God.

Hosea's marrying the prostitute Gomer is even more shocking than Jesus eating with tax collectors. Hosea's message declares God's passionate, persistent love. Hosea gives us a rare glimpse into God's own heart, showing us what it is like to love, to be betrayed, to smolder in anger, and then to risk again. Loving people—loving us—is a risky venture for God.

> HOSEA GIVES US A RARE GLIMPSE INTO GOD'S OWN HEART, SHOWING US WHAT IT IS LIKE TO LOVE, TO BE BETRAYED, TO SMOLDER IN ANGER, AND THEN TO RISK AGAIN.

Hosea is not one of the better-known books; this text presents an excellent opportunity to tell its story. Like a flower overrun by weeds, Hosea's love blooms stubbornly and beautifully. Recently this writer heard a fine sermon on Hosea. The preacher did two simple things. First he helped us to picture Hosea's marriage with Gomer. People can identify with Hosea's pathos and stubborn love. They can well imagine friends saying, "That guy must be crazy to take her back again." Second, the pastor told us that God loves us like this. The sermon helped us experience "amazing grace." Jesus came to call sinners to repentance.

RESPONSIVE READING
PSALM 103

Too few sermons have as their object the simple act of praising God. Within the lectionary, this psalm prepares us to hear the Gospel with gratitude. As a preaching text in its own right, this psalm gives us a walking tour of God's great acts of mercy: healing, forgiveness, justice, and compassion. It also tells the truth about our mortality (vv. 14-16) and our complete dependence on God's mercy (vv. 8-12). In a culture where we never seem to have enough, this psalm lets us bask in God's mercy. How refreshing to receive God's blessing, singing joyfully "It is enough! We are satisfied."

SECOND READING

2 CORINTHIANS 3:1-6, 3:(4-11), 17—4:2 (BCP)

Interpreting the Text

Early congregations were often founded by traveling evangelists. Those bringing the gospel message would travel from place to place, sometimes visiting established congregations. When evangelists came to a community they had not visited before, they often brought letters of recommendation from Christians elsewhere. These letters helped establish trust so that the church could receive the travelers, most likely providing them with lodging and food. Perhaps with tongue in cheek, Paul asks if, in light of his previously strained relations with the Corinthian Christians, they now expect him to furnish a fresh letter of recommendation. Paul agrees that such letters are important, but the kind of letter he offers is not one written with pen and ink. The Corinthian congregation is itself his letter of recommendation. When he proclaimed the gospel, their faith was awakened, demonstrating the integrity of his ministry and showing him to be an ambassador of God and Christ. They already know his character by his preaching and its fruits.

Paul recalls promises that God made through the Old Testament prophets. One promise is particularly important. Jeremiah looked for God to establish a new covenant, in which God's law would be written on the "tablets" of people's hearts (Jer. 31:31-34). Paul declares that this new covenant has come to pass in Christ. God promised that the new covenant (written on human hearts) would be unlike the old one (written on tablets of stone). The law of Moses told what God expected from the people. The new covenant declares what God does for us. This gift of grace is the basis of new life with God through Christ Jesus and the power of the Holy Spirit.

In 3:17—4:2, Paul continues the contrast between the new and the old covenants. After Moses received the covenant written on stone, he was not permitted to see God's face but was allowed to glimpse God's back (Exod. 33:17-22). And when Moses came down from Mt. Sinai his face so radiated God's glory that he had to wear a veil (Exod. 34:29-35). Paul declares that through Christ, Christians are privileged to experience God's presence through the Spirit.

Because of the Spirit at work within them, their faces too show God's glory and presence.

Responding to the Text

Credentials matter. They can make the difference between getting a job or not getting a job, being admitted to school or being turned away. Credentials are supposed to let people know that a person can do the job. One of the most important credentials is the letter of recommendation. A good letter from the right person can even help someone with few other credentials to be given a chance. Through a letter of recommendation, a person with higher status can help someone else move a little higher, too. All of this can be told in a story— perhaps of a young person applying for college entrance or for a job. Once people are thinking about credentials, the preacher can apply this idea to Christian life and community.

In Christian communities, the best letter of recommendation is not written with paper and ink but upon human hearts. The call of Christ brings the community together, and the gift of the Spirit works among us. By living and dying for us, Jesus has "recommended" us to God, once and for all. And we continually recommend one another to God in prayer. Within the Christian community, we may recommend someone for leadership and service. Professional credentials can tell us some things, but they do not tell everything; neither do interviews. The Holy Spirit must guide decisions about calling and hiring. For Paul, the best recommendation was the one written on the hearts of the people by the Spirit of God.

The matter of credentials, hiring, and advancement applies not only to what happens within the walls of a church but to the whole of Christian life. Our baptism into Christ's death, grasped by faith, is the basic credential. The Spirit works in and through us, transforming us gradually into the image of Christ (2 Cor. 3:18). In life there can be no greater credential, no more powerful recommendation, than that which Jesus himself has written with his own blood, shed for us. Worldly credentials are mere junk mail when compared with Christ's own personal letter of recommendation written in blood for us.

GOSPEL
MARK 2:13-22

Interpreting the Text

This text asks two questions: Why does Jesus eat with tax collectors and sinners (v. 16)? Why don't Jesus' disciples fast (v. 18)? In Jesus' day, eating meals together implied shared values and a common position in society. Usually one ate with one's "in-group" of family, friends and household. Bruce Malina and Richard Rohrbaugh note that, since there was almost no privacy in first-century Palestine, people generally knew who kept company with whom and who shared meals together. These associations demonstrated each person's place in society. Since honor was a key value, most folks naturally avoided people whose association would bring shame. Hardly anyone would want to be seen with despised people like tax collectors.[28]

The Roman tax system had several layers. Levi is not identified as a chief tax collector or as being rich (see Luke 19:2). Levi and his comrades may have been "toll collectors" working for a "chief tax collector" who in turn answered to the Roman government. Toll collectors were stationed at gates, bridges, or other crossover points where they could inspect, search, and tax merchants' goods, and exact fees—frequently over-charging in order to insure a profit for themselves. Because they supported the Roman occupation by preying on their own people, toll and other tax collectors were despised.

If Jesus wanted a good reputation, he would not have associated with people like Levi. Yet Mark says that many tax collectors and sinners followed Jesus (v. 15). Jesus called Levi, a tax collector, to follow him, and went to eat in Levi's home where there were many tax collectors. Verse 17 shows Jesus' complete lack of interest in proving or improving his social standing. His interest is in healing the sick and calling sinners to follow him.

Not only did Jesus eat with the wrong people; his followers seemed to enjoy feasting too much. People wondered why Jesus' disciples, unlike those of John the Baptist and the Pharisees, did not fast. Fasting or going without food was a ritualized form of mourning. It was deliberate self-humiliation, typically accompanied by lack of concern for one's appearance (torn clothing or sackcloth, disheveled hair, ashes on the head). Fasting could be done for many reasons: to obtain God's help or protection, to express repentance, or to mourn the death of leaders. Like other acts of devotion, fasting could be misused to shape public opinion and create desired impressions. In the Gospel text, however, the issue seems to be fasting as an expression of mourning.

> NOT ONLY DID JESUS EAT WITH THE WRONG PEOPLE; HIS FOLLOWERS SEEMED TO ENJOY FEASTING TOO MUCH.

In verses 19-20, Jesus says that it is not time for his disciples to be mourning. Instead, they should celebrate, like wedding guests making merry with the bridegroom. There will be time enough to mourn after the bridegroom (Jesus) has been taken away. Unless people want to show disapproval and insult their hosts, there is no reason to fast at a wedding. The question "Why don't your disciples fast?" shows that people do not know what time it is; they do not know that Jesus' time with them is a day of divine grace. Jesus could have quoted Eccles. 3:4 ("a time to dance and a time to mourn"); instead he told a parable (vv. 19-20). The Gospel text includes several small parables (vv. 17, 19-20, 21-22), each revealing something of Jesus' ministry. By telling parables, Jesus could both teach his followers and deflect his opponents.

Responding to the Text

The quickest response is to exhort each other to show hospitality: "Jesus ate with the outcasts of society and so should we, so get busy." To be sure, practicing hospitality—especially to those whom the world rejects—is a vital expression of faith. But it is all too easy to romanticize the tax collectors as victims of cruel, snobbish Pharisees. Nearer to the truth, these tax collectors were money addicts to the Roman tax system, preying upon their own people like vultures. For a picture of how others recoiled when they saw Jesus eating with tax collectors and sinners, imagine a dove sitting with buzzards around a feast of carrion.

A first step in proclamation is to show how shocking Jesus' association with the tax collectors really was. This can be done by vividly retelling the text, or by telling about a holy person spending time with someone who is undeniably evil. Perhaps the best film along these lines is *Dead Man Walking,* in which a nun visits a death row prisoner convicted of two horrific murders. Sister Helen's family, colleagues, and neighborhood community are appalled by her ministry to this man. This very riveting story, while offering no easy answers, holds up the possibility of redemption in the face of radical evil.[29]

Jesus' call (v. 17) includes a "no" and a "yes." If we consider ourselves to be righteous on our own merits, Jesus did not come for us (v. 17)! If we know ourselves as sinners, then we are called to leave our old way of life behind and follow Jesus, feasting in his presence as we would at a wedding.

The parables in vv. 21-22 show old forms of religion to be incompatible with Jesus' mission. That critique seems safe enough until we ask ourselves what religion in our churches is based on. Just as Gomer in the first lesson continually went after other lovers, human beings continually pursue other gods. Our god may be material success, or the polite culture of churchly niceness. It may be a hierarchy or it may be nostalgia in which Jesus makes a mild appearance and leaves us basically unchanged. These parables of new and old cloth and of wine and wineskins could provide a leading image for a sermon that would move as follows. Goal: we would like to have a little bit of Jesus. Problem: It won't work. Jesus will not be domesticated by our small views of religion or our personal spirituality. Proclamation: Jesus wants our whole selves, all of us. Jesus makes us completely new.

The preacher may choose to work with one of the text's four small parables, or with one of the questions asked of Jesus (vv. 16, 18). To preach on the whole text, the theme that holds it all together is Jesus' own statement of mission in verse 17. This text is bound to be unsettling both for the self-righteous (who exclude themselves from needing Jesus' help) and sinners (who are called to follow). Don Juel says that Jesus' religious audience responded with "considerable disquiet" because Jesus was saying that compromises will not work. Jesus' ministry will eventually destroy the old ways, which is "precisely what his questioners fear."[30]

LAST SUNDAY AFTER THE EPIPHANY

MARCH 5, 2000

NINTH SUNDAY IN ORDINARY TIME / PROPER 4

REVISED COMMON	ROMAN CATHOLIC
Deut. 5:12-15	Deut. 5:12-15
Ps. 81:1-10	Ps. 81:2-8, 10-11
2 Cor. 4:5-12	2 Cor. 4:6-11
Mark 2:23—3:6	Mark 2:23—3:6 or 2:23-28

O day of rest and gladness, O day of joy and light,
O balm for care and sadness, most beautiful most bright,
On you the high and lowly, through ages joined in tune,
Sing, "holy, holy, holy," to the great God triune.
New graces ever gaining from this our day of rest,
We reach the rest remaining to spirits of the blest.
To Holy Ghost be praises, to Father and to Son;
The Church its voice upraises, to you blest Three in One.[31]

FIRST READING

DEUTERONOMY 5:12-15

Interpreting the Text

The commandment to keep the Sabbath is the last in the "first table" of the law, which defines the people's relationship to God. An integral part of that relationship was the Sabbath or seventh day. By not working, God's people set the Sabbath apart from other days. Embracing rich and poor, slave and free, male and female, people and animals, the Sabbath was truly a communal rest.

The Sabbath connected people with God in several ways. First, it reminded them that God rested on the seventh day of creation (Gen. 2:2-3). Created in God's image, we reflect God's image by resting on the seventh day. Second, the Sabbath commemorated the exodus—God's work of liberating the people from slavery in Egypt (5:15). Third, to live well, people and animals need a day of rest. God neither wants nor expects us to work seven days a week.

"Just give it a rest!" Such is our plea when someone keeps grinding away at a vexing issue or problem. Not even the most dedicated among us can toil without ceasing. And yet we need a commandment to help us rest! Although our way of life is much different from that of ancient Israel, the human need for rest continues. It is part of the God-given natural rhythm in which we are created.

God's commandment embraces everyone. It is not that weak people need a rest while the strong work without ceasing; this commandment shows God's mercy and care for all creatures. Sabbath rest gives us time to bask in God's grace as we remember God's saving deeds. Our resistance to this kindly commandment reveals pride: we live as though the world cannot possibly get along without us for one day. We simply must look busy! God's commandment deflates such vanity. There is only one position for God in the universe, and it has already been filled.

Even in biblical times, God's people often ignored the Sabbath. Using promises and threats, some prophets demanded stricter Sabbath observance (Jer. 17:19-27). At the other end of the spectrum, people could abuse the Sabbath by observing it so legalistically that its life-giving intent was lost. This is why Jesus found it necessary to challenge the Pharisees' approach (Mark 2:23–3:6). So there are different words to be spoken about the Sabbath, depending on which way people are running from God's command.

Those who preach on the first lesson from Deuteronomy, or on Mark's Gospel, or both, will need to ask themselves: What do my people most need to hear? Chances are that few people in congregations suffer from legalistic Sabbath-keeping. They are more likely to be overburdened by relentless demands that do not allow them to rest. The Sabbath gives us time to rest, express our commitment to God in public worship, and gather as a community of faith.

RESPONSIVE READING

PSALM 81

This psalm works well with the overall Sabbath theme. The first four verses call the faithful to worship and commemorate God's act of deliverance for Israel (vv. 4-5). The relief and rescue (vv. 6-7) clearly refer to Israel's time in the wilderness, but can be heard more generally as a testimony to God's mercy. The psalmist then admonishes Israel to stay true to God (vv. 8-10), and laments Israel's unfaithfulness (vv. 11-12). In vv. 13-16 the psalmist pleads with Israel to walk in God's ways, promising victory and abundance in return. We may hear verse 16 as God's desire to bless us when we gather for worship and to feed us on the Word.

2 CORINTHIANS 4:5-12

Interpreting the Text

The Corinthians had an ongoing problem of confusing the messenger with the message. In 1 Corinthians 1:12, Paul echoes Corinthian slogans: "I belong to Paul," or "I belong to Apollos," or "I belong to Cephas." Paul responds to these slogans by returning the people to the message of the cross, so central for faith and community life. Again in 2 Corinthians Paul tells the people to focus on the message, not on the preacher. He reminds them that Christ's ministers, whether ordained or lay, are fallible human beings who sometimes disappoint others—no matter how good their intentions. Paul compares all servants of Christ to clay jars that hold a treasure. The jar itself has a rough, unfinished exterior. What the jar bears, however, is of great value: the Word of God. The paradox of Christian witness is that God's power is most often made known through human weakness. God's love was most fully revealed through the death of Jesus of Nazareth, and continues to be made known through the service and witness of Jesus' followers.

> THE PARADOX OF CHRISTIAN WITNESS IS THAT GOD'S POWER IS MOST OFTEN MADE KNOWN THROUGH HUMAN WEAKNESS.

Responding to the Text

Fine china is used on special occasions. It can inspire compliments and make a meal more festive; but it has to be handled carefully lest it be scratched or chipped or broken. Most of the time it sits on a high shelf out of harm's way. In contrast, the everyday dishes are such a basic part of life that they seldom receive comment. These old dishes take a lot of hard use, but they are the ones that serve the good food, day after day. The "clay jars" that the apostle Paul wrote about are the everyday dishes. Unlike fine glass or polished gold, the clay jars were used constantly for serving. So too, Christians are ordinary human beings. Like jars we can be broken. We may look very ordinary, and we certainly have weaknesses, yet God chooses us to bear the good news of the Gospel. Those who serve Christ often do so in ways that are little noticed. The faithful are overlooked in the public eye as easily as a plain clay jar on a shelf.

Sometimes we "clay pots" get put to very hard use. Four times, in four distinctive ways (vv. 8-9), Paul says that we experience both hurt and hope, with God's love prevailing each time because Jesus has died for us. Verses 8 and 9 speak to us as we struggle with our "clay-ness" or vulnerability. First Paul tells the truth about human frailty, then he tells the greater truth of God's prevailing power and love. In relation to the other lessons for today, the Sabbath command tells us in effect that God knows we are made of "clay"; at the same time, we are fashioned to hold God's priceless love. Thus we need both rest and worship.

GOSPEL

MARK 2:23—3:6

Interpreting the Text

At first glance, the Pharisees' irritation with Jesus and his disciples seems petty. But in a world dominated by the Roman empire and infiltrated with Greek culture, Sabbath observance helped the Jewish people maintain their identity. David Rhoads and Donald Michie note: "In the ancient world, certain traditions and customs unified the Jews and distinguished them from other nationalities. The Sabbath was probably the most obvious of these observances; to disregard it threatened Jewish identity and the fabric of their society."[32]

The "boundary violations" which rumble like thunder through the opening chapters of Mark continue with the Sabbath controversies. By allowing his disciples to pluck grain on the Sabbath (technically a form of work), Jesus seems to ignore sacred laws and customs. So the Pharisees challenge him with a question: "Why are they doing what is not lawful on the Sabbath?" (v. 24). This is the latest in a string of questions expressing conflict between Jesus and the religious establishment (2:7, 16, 18).

Note that Mark 2:23—3:6 follows the same pattern as 2:3-11. Jesus' words violate a religious boundary (2:5; 27-28). Jesus' opponents challenge him (2:7; 24). Jesus performs an act of power demonstrating his authority as forgiver of sins (2:11-12) or as Lord of the Sabbath (3:5). In each scenario, a non-miraculous boundary violation is backed up by an act of power. In the presence of the man with the withered hand, the Pharisees choose regulations over mercy. And Jesus, angry at their hardness of heart, chooses mercy over rules—and heals the man.

The Pharisees have a definite point of view. To them, Jesus' disciples showed their lax attitude by plucking grain and defying the prohibition against harvesting on the Sabbath. When questioned by the Pharisees, Jesus tells how King David ate sacred bread which was reserved for priests alone (1 Sam. 2:1-6). The Pharisees think that Jesus, by connecting himself with David and placing himself over God's laws, is supremely arrogant. Jesus' words in verse 27 are the mirror opposite of the Pharisee's position. And the statement that "the Son of Man is lord even of the Sabbath" sounds as though Jesus puts himself in God's place. It more than hints at blasphemy.

This outrageous statement is dramatized by a controversial act of healing. True enough, it was lawful to save a life on the Sabbath in the event of an accident or emergency. But this man's withered hand was not an emergency. He could easily have waited a little while until the Sabbath was over. In his case, it would make little difference to wait a few more hours for healing. But Jesus makes a point of working on this "elective" case on the Sabbath, seemingly going out of his way to tweak the Pharisees.

The tension between Jesus and the religious authorities now blazes into anger so hot that Jesus' enemies conspire to destroy him (v. 6). The Pharisees think that Jesus cares for nothing but showing off his own power. And Jesus sees that the Pharisees disfigure the Sabbath so that God is not honored by it. For the Pharisees, the Sabbath was a day of regulations. For Jesus, it was a day of grace.

Responding to the Text

When it comes to the Sabbath observance, congregations probably have widely mixed ideas and experiences. Young adults and children may have no common memory that Sunday is, or ever was, much different from other days. North Americans in their mid-forties and older can remember when "blue laws" kept stores closed on Sundays. Older people can still recall prohibitions against working for pay or indulging in frivolous entertainment like movies or card-playing on Sunday. Still others have had recent vivid experiences of traveling to countries where restaurants and stores and even some forms of transportation cease for holy days. Americans who have come to expect access to everything seven days a week find these respites frustrating. And pastors are in the ironic situation of having their heaviest public workday at the very time they call their own congregations to worship and rest. So, compared with one hundred years ago, there is little common cultural and religious consensus for what it means to honor the Sabbath and keep it holy.

Yet at some level most people know that rest for body and soul makes life sweet, and that living without such rest makes life a grind. We may not be pharisaical in the keeping of religious rules, but we may at times be quite inhumane in denying rest to ourselves or withholding it from others. If our way of life is killing us, Sabbath tells us to "give it a rest." Sabbath opens up time for worship, for hearing God's word and praising God's name. It may even dawn

IF OUR WAY OF LIFE IS KILLING US, SABBATH TELLS US TO "GIVE IT A REST."

on us that we need to completely reorient our lives toward God. Pastors who model frenetic busyness and habitually hold committee meetings on Sundays are depriving themselves and their parishioners of a true Sabbath.

An exegetical sermon on this Gospel could retell the conflict between Jesus and the Pharisees in its historical context, then proclaim Jesus as "Lord of the Sabbath." The God who created heaven and earth has come to us in Christ, to be our Lord. In him we find our true peace and rest. A topical sermon about the Sabbath can move more quickly to contemporary concerns and issues. Lest such a sermon become merely a discourse on self-care, it needs to draw deeply from Jesus' claim to be Lord of the Sabbath. Jesus demonstrated that claim, not by resting himself, but by doing a work of healing. A topical sermon on Sabbath could give three reasons for keeping the Sabbath: rest, renewal, and reality check. *Rest* means that we do not need to prove ourselves by constantly looking busy. We can rest in being God's children, created and renewed by God. It is hard to imagine someone refusing a day off with pay. What except the sin of pride would make us resist such a gracious command?

Renewal comes when we are refreshed by God's word, especially through worship. Martin Luther said that keeping the Sabbath means "we are to fear and love God so that we do not neglect his Word and the preaching of it, but regard it as holy and gladly hear and learn it."[33] Sunday is not holier than any other day of the week, but there must be a time when Christians come together in Word and sacrament. It is not the column on the calendar, but the hearing of God's word that makes a Sabbath. Thus Luther emphasized what we should do on the Sabbath (hear God's Word) rather than what we should not do. People are hungry for spiritual renewal, for soul food, for refreshment on life's journey. The good news of the Sabbath is that God is ready and willing to give us all this: "I would feed you with the finest of the wheat, and with honey from the rock I would satisfy you" (Ps. 81:16). This is not about self-help, but about God's help.

Reality check is something that most people need on a regular basis. The Gospel reality check is that Jesus is Lord of the Sabbath and of all other days. The Sabbath call to worship restores us to our rightful place as creatures in God's creation. We are most truly ourselves as creatures praising the God who made us. People who do wilderness hiking or canoeing develop a habit of checking the map and compass regularly. The Sabbath gives us a chance to check our lives with God's own compass, God's Word. We may find that we've been heading the wrong way, as though we were lords of the universe. Worship repositions us to let God be God.

TRANSFIGURATION OF OUR LORD

LAST SUNDAY AFTER THE EPIPHANY

REVISED COMMON	EPISCOPAL (BCP)
2 Kings 2:1-12	1 Kings 19:9-18
Ps. 50:1-6	Ps. 27 or 27:5-11
2 Cor. 4:3-6	2 Peter 1:16-19, (20-21)
Mark 9:2-9	Mark 9:2-9

IN BLAZING LIGHT, JESUS' TRANSFIGURATION ENDS THE SEASON OF EPIPHANY. God's voice, which spoke with authority at Jesus' baptism, resounds again on the mountain: "Jesus is my beloved son! Listen to him." Transfiguration texts shine with God's glory. Jesus is the center of it all, yet in his presence we too reflect his glory. A vivid experience of God's power and presence is a rare thing; for most of us life can be mundane, overshadowed by worry and torn by conflict. Just one brilliant moment lights the way through all the valleys that lie ahead. "For it is the God who said, 'Let light shine out of darkness,' who has shone in our hearts to give the light of the knowledge of the glory of God in the face of Jesus Christ" (2 Cor. 4:6). A moment of revelation, transfiguration lights up the future by pointing us to Christ.

FIRST READING
2 KINGS 2:1-12

Interpreting the Text

After a career filled with drama and miracles, the prophet Elijah is about to be taken to heaven by God. His protégé Elisha insists on running alongside Elijah as far as he can go. Despite Elijah's repeated commands to "stay here" (vv. 2, 4, 6) and despite other prophets' admonitions (vv. 3, 5), Elisha will not leave Elijah's side. The two prophets cross the Jordan River in a water-parting scene intended to recall or reenact the Exodus. Then Elisha audaciously asks for a double portion of Elijah's spirit. Elijah makes no promises; such power is not his to give. But Elisha is allowed to see the fiery chariot and the whirlwind upon which Elijah ascends to heaven. Another parting of waters shows that God has indeed granted Elisha prophetic powers like Elijah's, and the other prophets recognized this. Royal succession comes through family inheritance (regardless of faithfulness, wisdom, or talent); but the office of prophet is given by God at will. God has even been known to choose a reluctant or unwilling prophet. Elisha's story is distinctive because he boldly asks for prophetic power (v. 9) and God gives it to him.

Responding to the Text

As a dramatic encounter with the holy—featuring the great Elijah—this text anticipates the Gospel story of transfiguration. But Elisha is a fascinating character in his own right. When Elijah is about to be carried away to heaven, all the other prophets have the good sense to keep their distance. No other prophet has the chutzpah to wedge himself into the picture with God and Elijah (two's company, three's a crowd). But Elisha sticks like a cocklebur, daring to ask for a double share of Elijah's power. The wonder is that God sometimes gives people just what they ask for. God allows Elisha to see the fiery chariot and whirlwind; God also gives him the prophetic power to lead others. Such an encounter with God changes relationships with human beings, too. For Elisha, the prophetic gift brings conflict, adventure, and danger.

As a model of leadership, Elisha has the following qualities: the desire to lead (v. 9), a holy vision (v. 11), the power to lead (v. 14), and the respect of others (v. 15). Most important, Elisha knew that the power came not from within himself or even from his predecessor Elijah, but from God.

1 KINGS 19:9-18 (BCP)

Interpreting the Text

The prophets of Baal have been slain in the great contest with Elijah at Mt. Carmel (1 Kings 18:17-40), and Queen Jezebel wants revenge. The fugitive Elijah runs to the wilderness, longing to die there and be done with the whole conflict. Instead of granting death, God sends an angel with food (19:4-7). Elijah journeys to Mt. Horeb, another name for Mt. Sinai, where Moses received the Ten Commandments. There he laments his hopeless situation (v. 10). God gives no sympathy or comfort. Instead, God sends wind, earthquake, and fire. Finally God appears to Elijah in "the sound of sheer silence" (v. 12). Elijah wraps his face to shield himself from God's dazzling holiness, which no one can see and live.

Like Jesus on the mount of transfiguration, Elijah does not tarry long in the glory. He must play his part in God's purposes down in the "real world." He must return to the turmoil that awaits him and work for God in the gritty conflict below. Elijah must help to install a rival government (anoint a new king). Old leaders will be killed and he himself will be replaced.

Responding to the Text

Elijah the fugitive prophet escaped from the battering conflict with Ahab and Jezebel only to be accosted by God's own wind, fire, and earthquake. Most terrifying of all was the sheer silence. Out of the silence God asks, "what are you doing here, Elijah?" People have sometimes been attracted to this text in which God speaks in silence or with "a still, small voice." The still small voice is easily sentimentalized. But Elijah's reply cuts through sentiment with a sharp lament: "God, I have suffered for you, everyone else has betrayed you and now your enemies want to kill me."

Instead of sympathy or a quick fix, God recommissions Elijah and sends him back to his life, back down the mountain, back to all the seething mess from which the prophet had fled. Elijah is not allowed to whine. God tells him: "You are not the lone wolf you think you are. There are seven thousand in Israel who are still faithful to me and who do not worship Baal." Responses to this text are to wait for the sound of sheer silence; to ponder how we would answer God's question, "What are you doing here?" and to return and face life again with God's help.

RESPONSIVE READING
PSALM 50:1-6

In this liturgy of divine judgment, the traits of holiness, majesty, and power place God above all human wisdom. The fire and tempest (v. 3) call to mind stories of Elijah and Elisha and also anticipate God's glory revealed on the mount of transfiguration. God commands the people to be gathered for judgment; the call goes out over heaven and earth. This psalm is a noble trumpet call to judgement, from which only God's mercy can save us. In an age that has tried hard to tame and make God "nice," this psalm reminds us that it is indeed a fearful thing to fall into the hands of the living God who is sovereign, holy, and free.

PSALM 27 (BCP)

At the climax of Epiphany, the psalm calls God our light and salvation (v. 1). The holy God is our advocate and defender. The lines, "your face, Lord, do I seek. Do not hide your face from me" (vv. 8-9), prepare the way for the Gospel in which the disciples glimpse God's glory in the face of Jesus. Peter, James, and John were terrified, yet God allowed them to live and to see Jesus fulfill his mission through death and resurrection. In Jesus we know that God loves us. If we "fear the Lord" we need fear nothing else.

As a preaching text in its own right, Psalm 27 meets human needs and fears with the promises of God. This psalm transforms anxiety into confidence, replaces fear with courage, and exchanges unbelief for faith. A luminous psalm for individual or corporate pastoral care, this text sheds light wherever it is heard.

SECOND READING
2 CORINTHIANS 4:3-6

Interpreting the Text

Paul defends the Gospel ministry not as his own work but as a gift from God. Paul's critics may have accused him of not making the Gospel clear enough. He acknowledges that for some people, the Gospel remains "veiled" or hidden. Paul insists, however, that this failure to "see"

THE GOSPEL IS NEVER PREACHED IN A NEUTRAL SETTING. IT ALWAYS COMPETES WITH OTHER "GODS" WHICH KEEP PEOPLE FROM SEEING THE TRUTH.

is neither the fault of the message nor the messenger, but results from unbelief. The Gospel is never preached in a neutral setting. It always competes with other "gods" which keep people from seeing the truth. Despite these conflicts, God's truth shines with the same light that burst forth at God's command (Gen. 1:3). In language reminiscent of the transfiguration, Paul refers to the light of glory shining from Jesus' face. When this light penetrates the human heart, God's new creation dawns.

Responding to the Text

This text addresses the conflict between faith and unbelief. Every person who comes to faith in Christ is God's fresh victory of light over darkness. In a culture of relativism, this is a provocative text. It does not say that any response to the gospel is OK as long as one is sincere. It does not say that unbelief is as good as faith. It does not say that we choose to believe the gospel if it "meets our needs." Rather, there is conflict between faith and unbelief, light and darkness. Not everyone who sees Jesus or hears about him believes, but only those into whose hearts the light of Christ shines.

While this text gives all the glory to God for Christ's saving work, it also holds us accountable for our response. Some of Paul's critics may have said, "I did not get anything out of that sermon—it must be the preacher's fault." It is true that preachers sometimes fail to preach God's word. But each of us, pastor or layperson, preacher or listener, is accountable for the message. Even the best sermon will not get through to someone who refuses to receive the word.

After conflict and accountability, the final theme of the text is the glorious light shining from the face of Jesus Christ. Like a storm followed by a sunburst, the text may evoke anxiety and then grateful worship.

2 PETER 1:16-19 (20-21) (BCP)

Interpreting the Text

The author of 2 Peter was deeply impressed by the eyewitness accounts about Jesus and looked forward to his return as judge of the world (3:10-12). Christ's return in glory is of a piece with the heavenly glory the disciples glimpsed during Jesus' transfiguration. Indeed, 2 Peter 1:16-18 testifies to the transfiguration: "We ourselves heard this voice come from heaven, while we were with him on the holy mountain" (v. 18). After the eyewitness testimony to the transfiguration comes an exhortation to remain faithful to the prophetic message (v. 19) since the testimony about Christ does not come from human will, but is inspired by the Holy Spirit (vv. 20-21).

Responding to the Text

In modern (or postmodern) times, the individual is thought to be the final authority for religious belief. The most authoritative a statement many can make about a particular religion is: "It works for me." In matters of religion, the individual is in the driver's seat. But 2 Peter 1:16-21 presents a completely different view of religious authority. Jesus Christ came in power and majesty, exercising God's own authority by God's approval. Christian faith in Jesus is based on eyewitness accounts, recorded in authoritative Scripture and further attested by the work of the Holy Spirit. Christians are not soloists improvising their own faith. Rather, we are part of an orchestra made up of other believers, inspired by a musical score that has already been given and is continually but faithfully transposed for new times and new cultures. The Holy Spirit conducts the music and each player has a part.

In other words, Christian faith works in and through community. The community extends not only across the globe, but backward in time to the apostles and forward to the return of Christ. It is, of course, a very good thing if we can say of Christianity "It works for me." But there may be times when what "works for me" is the exact opposite of what Christ calls us to do—as Peter found out. Individual commitment is very important, and yet the Christian faith is based on an authority much greater than personal, private choice: "no prophecy of scripture is a matter of one's own interpretation" (v. 20b). The apostles witnessed the glory of Jesus' transfiguration, and the Spirit entrusts their testimony to us. It is for us to keep the music playing, especially in dark and difficult places, until the day dawns and the morning star rises in our hearts.

GOSPEL

MARK 9:2-9

Interpreting the Text

The transfiguration was a brief glimpse of Jesus' destiny, approved by God, which led through suffering to death and resurrection glory. The heavenly voice at Jesus' baptism (Mark 1:11) was addressed only to Jesus, but at the transfiguration the voice spoke directly to the three disciples: "This is my Son, the Beloved; listen to him!" (v. 7). Jesus shone in dazzling brightness, like someone not of this world. For Peter, James, and John, and for all who hear the Gospel, this glimpse of glory helps us to follow Jesus all the way to the cross. This mysterious event was meant to inspire, not to explain. It was not a lecture but a direct encounter with the holy.

The word "transfiguration" (from the Greek *metamorphoô*) is rare in the New Testament. Don Juel notes that this passage "speaks about transformation into a heavenly being characterized by glory." The strange whiteness of Jesus' garments "confirms the unearthly character of his appearance," much like accounts of the angels at the tomb of the risen Jesus. The glory of his visage calls to mind both Jesus' glory with God from before all creation, and his glory as risen and ascended Lord. The Apostle Paul promises that Christians will also be transfigured (transformed) into Christ's image (2 Cor. 3:18).[34]

The mountain was a place to encounter God. Moses received the Ten Commandments from God on a mountain. God met Moses and later Elijah on a mountain. In Mark's Gospel, Jesus often retreats to mountains to pray. In Mark 9, it is on a mountain that Jesus is transfigured and three disciples see his glory (also Matt. 17:1-8; Luke 9:28-36; 2 Peter 1:16-18). Moses' and Elijah's return was promised long ago (Deut. 18:18; Mal. 4:5-6) and their appearance (v. 5) suggests that in Jesus, God's purposes are being fulfilled.

While the main focus is Jesus, the text also has important ties to Peter and his relationship with Jesus. Mark tells us that the transfiguration occurred "six days" after Peter's confession (8:29–9:2). The divine voice (v. 7) both rebukes Peter's equating Jesus with Moses and Elijah (v. 5) and confirms Peter's confession (8:29). Further, the words "listen to him" may recall that Peter refused to accept Jesus' passion prediction (8:31–33). Peter's suggestion "let us build three dwellings" (v. 5) referred to temporary shelters or booths like those used at pilgrimage festivals during the Jewish year. The precise meaning of the booths is unclear, but the larger point is that Peter, though terrified, wants to remain on the mountain and hold onto the glory. This was contrary to God's plan. Once again Mark shows that Peter, despite his deep devotion to Jesus, misreads what Jesus is about. Jesus' glory can only be fully revealed through his suffering, death, and resurrection.

Responding to the Text

In the church year, the transfiguration is a pivotal event between Epiphany (in which Jesus reveals God to us in word and deed) and Lent (in which we follow Jesus to the cross.) The day's Gospel text is a glorious high, framed on each side by predictions of suffering (8:31, 34–38; 9:9; 12). The Gospel text tells the story of Jesus' life and ministry with the conviction that Jesus is indeed

THE GOSPEL TEXT HIGHLIGHTS THE FACT THAT CONFLICT AND SUFFERING ARE COMMON AND GLIMPSES OF GOD'S GLORY ARE RARE.

God's beloved Son, through whom and in whom God's will is done. Its purpose is to reveal Jesus' heavenly glory. At the level of our own experience, the text highlights the fact that conflict and suffering are common and glimpses of God's glory are rare. But like lightning on a dark night, those bold flashes of glory illuminate the landscape. The text inspires us to follow Jesus through ordinary and hard times, times when glory is anywhere but here.

Many preachers have used this text as an occasion to consider our own "mountaintop" and "valley" experiences, in which we learn with Peter that we cannot hold onto the glory but must also follow Jesus and "listen to him" in the valley where life is lived most of the time. Though worn smooth from much use, this is still a good approach because it is informed by the text and speaks to the needs and experiences of God's people. Our basic need is to walk in God's presence and promise, whether our path be hard or easy. In particular, God's presence and promise are made known to us in Christ: we see only Jesus (v. 8).

A lesser used strategy works with God's glory and holiness. Like moths to flame, people are drawn to glory. We both pursue it and avoid it, desire it and fear it. Mid-twentieth-century pronouncements about the death of God still haunt used book shops, but God was never much impressed by these, nor are the millions of twenty-first-century people who continue trying, in many and various ways, to meet God. Even in popular entertainment, our fascination with special effects show our need to look beyond the ordinary and glimpse awe, wonder, and splendor larger than life. When the disciples saw Jesus in glory with Moses and Elijah, they were "terrified" (v. 6). The special effects were dazzling. No wonder that Peter, despite his fear, wanted to stay.

In his classic work, *The Idea of the Holy,* Rudolf Otto described natural human fear of, and fascination with, the Holy. He wrote that the "wholly other" is "quite beyond the sphere of the usual, the intelligible, and the familiar . . . filling the mind with blank wonder and astonishment."[35] Every once in a while, people have an encounter with God that reveals a dimension of reality not ordinarily open to us. Such was the transfiguration for the disciples. And there are many people of faith who report a sense of awe and wonder at being in the presence of God, particularly in near-death situations.

A sermon that works with Jesus' glory and holiness in Mark 9 could speak both to seekers and to those Christians for whom faith has grown dull. Using illustrations from current events, mass media, or local experience, the sermon could move from a general human quest to the specific glory of Christ. A three-part strategy might look like this: (1) Human beings search for the holy. (2) We look in the wrong places. (3) God shows us Jesus and says, "This is my Son, the Beloved; listen to him!" Such an approach would preach the text, observe an important moment in the church year, and speak directly to human needs and hopes. The goal is proclamation: Jesus reveals God's glory.

NOTES

1. Ronald A. Klug, "Rise, Shine, You People!" *Lutheran Book of Worship* (Minneapolis and Philadelphia: Augsburg and Board of Publication, Lutheran Church in America, 1978), 393.

2. Kathleen Thomerson, "I Want to Walk as a Child of the Light," *With One Voice* (Minneapolis: Augsburg Fortress, 1998), 649.

3. *The Apostle* (October Films, 1997); Robert Duvall, writer, director, and producer.

4. *The Birth of the Messiah: A Commentary on the Infancy Narratives in the Gospels of Matthew and Luke*, rev. ed., Anchor Bible Reference Library (Garden City, N.Y.: Doubleday, 1993).

5. Nikolai F. S. Grundvig, "Bright and Glorious Is the Sky," *Lutheran Book of Worship*, 75.

6. Richard Mouw, *Consulting the Faithful: What Christian Intellectuals Can Learn from Popular Religion* (Grand Rapids: Eerdmans, 1994).

7. Donald H. Juel, *Mark,* Augsburg Commentary on the New Testament (Minneapolis: Augsburg Books, 1990), 33.

8. Fred Pratt Green, "When Jesus Came to Jordan," *With One Voice*, 647.

9. Martin Luther, "The Freedom of a Christian," *The Career of the Reformer, I,* vol. 31 of *Luther's Works*, trans. W. A. Lambert and H. J. Grimm; ed. H. J.

Grimm (Philadelphia: Fortress Press, 1957), 344. This essay is also published
separately as *Christian Liberty* (Philadelphia: Fortress Press, 1957), 7.

10. Craig Koester, *Symbolism in the Fourth Gospel: Meaning, Mystery, Community* (Minneapolis: Fortress Press, 1995).

11. In his explanation of the first commandment in his *Larger Catechism*, Luther asks: "What is it to have a god? What is God? Answer: A god is that to which we look for all good and in which we find refuge in every time of need. To have a god is nothing else than to trust and believe him with our whole heart. As I have often said, the trust and faith of the heart alone make both God and an idol. If your faith and trust are right, then your god is the true God. On the other hand, if your trust is false and wrong, then you have not the true God. For these two things belong together, faith and God. That to which your heart clings and entrusts itself is, I say, really your God." Martin Luther, *The Book of Concord,* trans. and ed. T. G. Tappert (Philadelphia: Fortress Press, 1959), 365.

12. Charles Wesley, "Oh, For a Thousand Tongues to Sing," *Lutheran Book of Worship*, 559.

13. David Rhoads, Joanna Dewey, and Donald Michie, *Mark as Story: An Introduction to the Narrative of a Gospel,* 2d ed. (Minneapolis: Fortress Press, 1999), 67.

14. Christian Smith, *American Evangelicalism: Embattled and Thriving* (Chicago: Univ. of Chicago Press, 1998).

15. Bruce J. Malina and Richard L. Rohrbaugh, *Social-Science Commentary on the Synoptic Gospels* (Minneapolis: Fortress Press, 1993).

16. *Simon Birch* (Buena Vista, 1998); Mark Steven Johnson, writer and director; Laurence Mark and Roger Birnbaum, producers. This film is an adaptation of John Irving, *A Prayer for Owen Meany: A Novel* (New York: Morrow, 1989).

17. Michael Joncas, "You Who Dwell in the Shelter of the Lord (On Eagle's Wings)," *With One Voice*, 779.

18. Rhoads et al., *Mark as Story*, 67.

19. Paul J. Achtemeier, *Mark,* 2d ed., Proclamation Commentaries (Philadelphia: Fortress Press, 1986).

20. William Barclay, *Prayers for Help and Healing* (New York: Harper & Row, 1968); Alvin Rogness, *When You Are Suffering* (Minneapolis: Augsburg Books, 1999); and Morton T. Kelsey, *Healing and Christianity: A Classic Study,* 3d ed. (Minneapolis: Augsburg Books, 1995).

21. Martin Luther, "The Lord's Prayer," *The Large Catechism of Martin Luther,* trans. R. Fischer (Philadelphia: Fortress Press, 1959), 79–80. This is included as well in the larger work, *The Book of Concord,* ed. T. G. Tappert (Philadelphia: Fortress Press, 1959).

22. William Billings, "As the Hart Panteth," *A Land of Pure Delight: Anthems and Fuging Tunes,* Harmonia Mundi; compact disc #907048.

23. Juel, *Mark*, 43.

24. Achtemeier, *Mark*, 93–94.

25. For Jesus' running conflict with the scribes and other Judean authorities, see Rhoads et al., *Mark as Story*, 116–22.

26. Achtemeier, *Mark*, 89.

27. Ibid.

28. Malina and Rohrbaugh, *Social-Science Commentary on the Synoptic Gospels*, 189–94.

29. *Dead Man Walking* (Polygram, 1995); Tim Robbins, producer and director. This movie is based on the non-fiction book, Helen Prejean, *Dead Man Walking* (New York: Random House, 1993).

30. Juel, *Mark*, p. 53.

31. Christopher Wordsworth, "O Day of Rest and Gladness," *Lutheran Book of Worship*, 251.

32. Rhoads et al. *Mark as Story*, 81.

33. Martin Luther, *The Small Catechism: Explanation to the Third Commandment* (Philadelphia: Fortress Press, 1967).

34. Juel, *Mark*, p. 127.

35. Rudolf Otto, *The Idea of the Holy: An Inquiry Into the Non-rational Factor in the Idea of the Divine and Its Relation to the Rational,* 2d ed., trans. John W. Harvey (New York: Oxford Univ. Press, 1950), 26.

THE SEASON OF LENT

K. C. HANSON

L ENT IS THE SEASON OF REFLECTION, REPENTANCE, preparation, and renewal. It is a time to open our hearts anew and refresh our commitment to God. We confront our creatureliness before the Creator. We pray with twelfth-century monk Bernard of Clairvaux: "Lord, I am sad and poor, but boundless is your grace; give me the soul-transforming joy for which I seek your face."[1] Without false modesty, we face our limitations, our weakness, and our failures—not with the intention of humiliation, but to become who we really are—both individually and communally.

Since early in Christian history Lent has been a period of preparation for the baptism of catechumens. "Lent" comes from the Old English word *lencten* meaning springtime. The ancient names for Lent simply call it the "Forty Days" (Latin, *Quadregesima;* Greek, *Tessaronkoste*); but the forty days were calculated differently in the East and West and in different eras. For example, Sundays were not always counted as part of the forty.

Forty is an ancient symbolic number used throughout the Bible. It generally denotes a period of transition and preparation. It is leaving something behind and preparing to move on the next part of our lives; it is "in between" time:

- forty days and nights of rain during the great flood (Gen. 7:12)
- Moses' forty days on the mountain (Exod. 24:18; 34:28; Deut. 9:9)
- the Israelites' forty years in the wilderness (Exod. 16:35)
- forty years of Israel's "rest" (Judg. 3:11; 5:31; 8:28)
- forty years of Jerusalem's desolation before its rebuilding (Ezek. 29:11-13)
- forty days of warning before Nineveh's threatened destruction (Jonah 3:4)

- Jesus' forty days in the wilderness prior to beginning his ministry (Mark 1:13)
- forty days of Jesus' appearances prior to the bestowal of God's spirit (Acts 1:3)

This period of transition is what Arnold Van Gennep and Victor Turner have called the "liminal stage" or "liminality."[2] The Latin word *limen* means both "threshold" and "margin." So liminality refers to both the crossing of a threshold from one status (or stage) to another, as well as being on the "margins" of the rest of society during the period of transition. We stand in transition between Epiphany and Holy Week whether as catechumens preparing to become full members of the community or as members of the congregation reflecting on our creatureliness and sin. The English poet Edmund Waller wrote:

Leaving the old, both worlds at once they view,
That stand upon the threshold of the new.[3]

THE LATIN WORD *limen* MEANS BOTH "THRESHOLD" AND "MARGIN." SO LIMINALITY REFERS TO BOTH THE CROSSING OF A THRESHOLD FROM ONE STATUS (OR STAGE) TO ANOTHER, AS WELL AS BEING ON THE "MARGINS" OF THE REST OF SOCIETY DURING THE PERIOD OF TRANSITION.

Historically, this season has been characterized by prayer, fasting, penance, and special attention to spiritual exercises—all signposts of liminality. The mark of the ashes is an outward sign of accountability to the group, indicating that each of us has entered that wilderness and stands on that threshold. The disorientation of liminality is voiced by songwriter Leonard Cohen: "The blizzard of the world / has crossed the threshold / and it has overturned / the order of the soul / When they said REPENT / I wonder what they meant."[4]

During the Middle Ages, the use of this forty-day period as preparation for baptism declined. The emphasis shifted to repentance and reflection by the whole church, so that by the tenth century the whole parish participated in penitential rites, including ashing the forehead on Ash Wednesday. Marriages have been prohibited during the season of Lent since the fourth century in both the Eastern and Western churches[5]—an understandable custom since this is not a time of celebration and feasting, but of reflection and fasting.

When that "blizzard . . . has crossed the threshold," can we reorient our lives? Who are we in the face of the Wholly Other? What is our life in Christ? What are our responsibilities to our communities? In Lent there are no easy questions, and no facile answers will set right "the order of the soul." But a time in the desert may help us confront the questions more clearly, may provide a time to be re-created and transformed. Rilke writes:

Will transformation. Oh be inspired for the flame,
in which a thing disappears and bursts into something else;
that spirit of re-creation which masters this earthly form
loves in the soaring figure nothing like the pivot point.[6]

The desert, both literally and metaphorically, has long been the place of retreat, reflection, re-creation. Traveling with a group of my seminary students, we drove east of Jerusalem to the Palestinian village of Silwan. From the crest of the Judean hills in Silwan we looked eastward across the sharp drop-off down to the Jordan Valley and across the Judean wilderness to the Jordanian desert. From this vista the desert looked distant, forbidding, barren, vacant, and all the same.

But the desert should not be confused with a vacuum or mere emptiness. Anyone who has walked through a desert knows the diversity of the flora and fauna. The weather is unpredictable: sandstorms, thunderstorms, and flash floods in wadis can arise and subside in a moment. It is stark, quiet, and given to extremes of temperature.

After viewing the desert from the heights of Silwan, we drove across the Sinai desert to St. Catherine's Monastery and Jebel Musa (Mt. Moses). Every twenty minutes or so the landscape seemed to have completely changed: sand dunes, low hills, jutting cliffs, deep caverns, rocky terrain, high mountains—not typical surroundings for most of us. But it is because of its separateness from city and town life that so many have been drawn to the desert for shorter or longer periods of reflection. It brings respite from the noise and frantic pace of ordinary life. As the nineteenth-century priest and poet Gerard Manley Hopkins wrote:

> MANY HAVE BEEN DRAWN TO THE DESERT FOR SHORTER OR LONGER PERIODS OF REFLECTION. IT BRINGS RESPITE FROM THE NOISE AND FRANTIC PACE OF ORDINARY LIFE.

Elected Silence, sing to me
And beat upon my whorled ear,
Pipe me to pastures still and be
The music that I care to hear.[7]

The church has had a long tradition of desert "fathers" and "mothers"—both anchorites (solitary hermits) and coenobites (communal living monastics). St. Anthony of Egypt (c. 251–356), St. Pachomius (c. 290–346), St. Mary of Egypt (fifth century), and St. John Climacus (570–649) are early examples. But we have modern "desert teachers" as well, such as Thomas Merton and Kathleen Norris. What is striking to me about these teachers is that the desert (again, literally or figuratively) created a space within each of them for God to work, then for them to touch others. What is remarkable is their greatness of soul. As Roberta Bondi has observed, it is love and humility that run through the lives and writings of the early desert teachers. "But humility for them did not mean a continuous cringing, cultivating a low self-image . . . . Instead, humility meant to them a way of seeing other people as being as valuable in God's eyes as ourselves. It was for them a relational term having to do precisely with learning to value others, whoever they were."[8]

May God work that sort of humility in us all during this Lenten season.

ASH WEDNESDAY

MARCH 8, 2000

REVISED COMMON	EPISCOPAL (BCP)	ROMAN CATHOLIC
Joel 2:1-2, 12-17 or Isa 58:1-12	Joel 2:1-2, 12-17	Joel 2:12-18
Ps. 51:1-17	Ps. 103 or 103:8-14	Ps. 51:3-6, 12-14, 17
2 Cor. 5:20b—6:10	2 Cor. 5:20b—6:10	2 Cor. 5:20—6:2
Matt. 6:1-6, 16-21	Matt. 6:1-6, 16-21	Matt. 6:1-6, 16-18

THE SEASON OF LENT BEGINS WITH Ash Wednesday, a day of prayer, fasting, repentance, and contrition. During the Reformation, Pope Leo X issued a bull (*Exsurge, Domine*; June 15, 1520) attacking Martin Luther for his critique of acts of contrition as practiced in the Middle Ages. This disagreement cuts to the core of the Church's ongoing balancing of form in liturgy and internalization in practice. In the wake of the Reformation, the Council of Trent called for changes in the Roman Church, specifically advocating a deeply experienced sense of contrition as "sorrow of heart and detestation of sin committed, with the purpose of not sinning in future."[9] The biblical passages for this day speak to the need for our integration of form and internal spirit.

FIRST READING
JOEL 2:1-2, 12-18

Interpreting the Text

The prophet Joel (whose name means "Yahweh is God") proclaims in this passage a message of judgment generating fear and havoc. Note that the invading army described is not mentioned by name. In fact, we do not know precisely when Joel prophesied—probably during the Persian Period (539–331 B.C.E.). But the concluding verses speak of Yahweh's people repenting, participating in a liturgy of petition, and culminating in Yahweh's pity on the land.

While the prophet adapted images from earlier prophets, his sense of poetry and image in these verses immediately catch our attention: the blowing of the trumpet in alarm (v. 1a); Zion as Yahweh's holy mountain (v. 1b); the day of

Yahweh as judgment (v. 1c-d); dark and ominous clouds (v. 2a-c); an incomparably powerful people (v. 2d-f), indicating an overpowering invading army; earthquakes (v. 10); fasting, weeping, and mourning (v. 12); the bride and groom emerging from their chambers (v. 16); and the priests crying out in anguished petition (v. 17). The passage moves, then, from fear and judgment, to devastation, to repentance and prayer, to deliverance. But note that the deliverance is not a foregone conclusion. Because of the I-Thou relationship between Yahweh and Israel, the future is open: "Who knows whether he will not turn and relent, and leave a blessing behind him?" (v. 14, NRSV).

The prophet alerts the people that the outcome is not predetermined. What is clear is everything was *personal*. That is to say, cause and effect are always answered by a "who" not a "what" to the peoples in the ancient Mediterranean.

Responding to the Text

This passage in Joel highlights the communal sense of responsibility. It is the whole community that is called to repentance. It is in the liturgy that the group meets God. But the future is open. Is that openness that Joel mentions a promise or a threat? What God will do in the future must remain open—despite our desire to know.

Like the blowing of the ram's horn in ancient Judah, Ash Wednesday brings the church up short and calls us to pay attention. In the church year this day calls us to repentance, reflection, and recollection of who we are. Speaking of repentance, John Climacus, the great Orthodox theologian and Abbot of Sinai, advises us: "Let your prayer be very simple. For the tax collector and the prodigal son just one word was enough to reconcile them to God."[10]

RESPONSIVE READING
PSALM 51:1-17

This psalm is an individual complaint (or petition) song; that is, it articulates the call of an individual to God *for change*. Though commentators often have called this type of psalm a "lament," that misses the message and intent; there is very little trace of laments in the book of Psalms (but see below in the fourth Sunday of Lent under Psalm 137, p. 201). Laments cry out in pain over something that cannot change (death, destruction, loss). They are part of the grief process; for example, David's lament over the deaths of Saul and Jonathan (2 Sam. 1:17-27), or the poet's lament over the destruction of Jerusalem by the Babylonians (Lam. 1). Complaints and petitions, on the other hand, call out in pain for God to intervene and bring about needed change: relief, help, deliverance, sustenance, healing, or forgiveness. "Israel enacted and trusted liturgical practices that made the transformation of pain vivid, powerful, and credible. It did its singing and praying and praising in ways that shaped pain into hope, and grief into possibility."[11]

This song has been used by ancient Israel, Judaism, and Christianity because it voices an earnest sense of need and urgency as well as being cast generally enough to apply in a variety of circumstances. In it we hear a desperate cry for help coupled with an acknowledgement of responsibility and culpability: sin, iniquity, transgression. "The removal of this intolerable thing cannot be [the psalmist's] own work but only God's: a divine blotting out, cleansing, and washing away."[12] Note all the imperative verbs calling for help:

- have mercy (v. 1a)
- blot out (v. 1b)
- wash (v. 2a)
- cleanse (v. 2b)
- teach (v. 6b)
- purge (v. 7a)
- wash (v. 7a)
- fill (v. 8a)
- let rejoice (v. 8b)
- hide (v. 9a)
- blot out (v. 9b)
- create (v. 10a)
- put (v. 10b)
- do not cast (v. 11a)
- do not take (v. 11b)
- restore (v. 12a)
- uphold (v. 12b)
- deliver (v. 14a)
- open (v. 15a)

Perhaps more than any other psalm, this song provides us a rationale for not only praying our own prayers, but *praying with the psalmists,* those who give voice to our deepest experiences. In discussing the role the psalms play in Benedictine communities, Kathleen Norris observes:

> The communal recitation of the psalms works against this form of narcissism, the tendency in America to insist that everything be self-discovery. . . . The [Benedictine] vow of "conversion of life," . . . means that you commit yourself to being changed by the words of the psalms, allowing them to work on you, and sometimes to work you over.[13]

PSALM 103 (B C P)

While Psalm 51 (discussed above) is an individual complaint song, Psalm 103 represents the flipside: an individual thanksgiving song. Thanksgivings are songs that celebrate God's deliverance, healing, and rescue (see, for example, Pss. 30, 40, 92, 138). The introduction (vv. 1-5) and conclusion (vv. 19-22) praise

Yahweh for forgiveness, redemption, and renewal. The lines that appear in Joel 2:13 are repeated here in verse 8:

> Yahweh is merciful and gracious,
> slow to anger, and abounding in loyalty. (my trans.)

This is an ancient liturgical formula that appears, with variations, throughout the Old Testament (Exod. 34:6; Num. 14:18; 2 Chron. 30:9b; Neh. 9:17b, 31b; Pss. 86:15; 111:4b; Jonah 4:2; Sir. 2:11). It expresses a fundamental theological proposition about the character of God.

The great joy in this song is a function of proclaiming Yahweh's character, a God who "works vindication and justice for the oppressed" (v. 6), is "merciful and gracious" (v. 8), and "does not deal with us according to our iniquities" (v. 10). In contrast, we humans are "like grass" and "a flower of the field" over which "the wind passes. . . . and it is gone" (vv. 15-16). In these images we are majestically, starkly, and irrefutably confronted with our fragility as creatures. It is God who meets us in our weakness, who meets us in the desert.

> IN THESE IMAGES WE ARE MAJESTICALLY, STARKLY, AND IRREFUTABLY CONFRONTED WITH OUR FRAGILITY AS CREATURES. IT IS GOD WHO MEETS US IN OUR WEAKNESS, WHO MEETS US IN THE DESERT.

SECOND READING
2 CORINTHIANS 5:20—6:10

Interpreting the Text

We know that many communications passed between Paul and the church at Corinth after he had left the city, and that he visited them repeatedly (2 Cor. 13:1). Already in 1 Corinthians 5:9 and 11, Paul mentions an earlier letter he had written them. And we know that he had received letters from Corinth (1 Cor. 7:1) as well as messages from Chloe's people (1 Cor. 1:11). But while 1 Corinthians seems to be a single letter, written in about 53 C.E., many scholars have come to the conclusion that 2 Corinthians is a collection of fragments of Paul's letters to the Corinthians, written about 55–56 C.E. (probably from Ephesus and Macedonia), which have been stitched together perhaps in the following manner:[14]

2 Corinthians 2:14—6:13; 7:2-4: A letter of defense against Paul's opponents in the Corinthian church (2:5; 7:12). Relations were deteriorating, and Paul had previously made "a painful visit" (2 Cor. 2:1; 12:14, 21; 13:1).

2 Corinthians 10–13: The "tearful letter" (see references in 2:3-4; 7:8), evidently delivered by Titus (see 12:18). Paul defends himself.

2 Corinthians 1:1—2:13; 7:5-16: A letter of reconciliation (see especially 7:5). Evidently the "tearful letter" had a positive effect.

2 Corinthians 8: A fragmentary letter of recommendation for Titus concerning "the collection" for the Jerusalem church (see Rom. 15:25-26; 1 Cor. 16:1-4; Gal. 2:10).

2 Corinthians 9: Another letter fragment concerning the collection for the Jerusalem church.

2 Corinthians 6:14—7:1: A non-Pauline fragment inserted into the final version of 2 Corinthians.

The passage of 5:20—6:10, then, is part of Paul's letter of defense against his detractors. They have evidently arrived in Corinth with letters of recommendation (2 Cor. 3:1). But Paul calls them "peddlers of God's word" (2:17). He implies that these other leaders use "disgraceful, underhanded ways," "practice cunning," and "tamper with God's word" (4:2).

But at the heart of Paul's appeal in this section are forms of the word "reconcile" (Greek: *katallagē* [noun]; *katallassō* [verb]). This word has the sense of restoring relationship, and Paul repeats it in describing the broader context of God's relationship to humanity:

- "God, who through Christ *reconciled* us to himself" (5:18a)
- "and gave us the *ministry of reconciliation*" (5:18b)
- "in Christ, God was *reconciling* the world to himself" (5:19a)
- "entrusting to us the *message of reconciliation*" (5:19b)
- "*be reconciled* to God" (5:20b)

Thus, Paul sums up what the church is about as communicating the reconciliation that God has already enacted. The trouble Paul sees is that the Corinthians were tacitly living as if unreconciled.

In the ancient world, one of the most pervasive relationships was that between patron and client, and the Bible often uses patron-client terminology to portray the divine-human relationship. Furthermore, intermediaries were often necessary to communicate with the most powerful patrons. In the New Testament, Jesus is portrayed as the "broker" of God's reign. In this passage, Paul portrays himself as the "ambassador" (broker) for Christ. Thus, God made his appeal *through* Paul (v. 20). Shortly after this passage, Paul strings together several phrases from the Old Testament, culminating in a metaphor of kinship that identifies God as the patron of the community: "I will be a father to you, and you shall be my sons and daughters, says the Lord Almighty" (2 Cor. 6:18).

Relative to the Lenten season, Paul portrays the hardships he has suffered in the course of his ministry on behalf of the community: "in afflictions, hardships, calamities, beatings, imprisonments, tumults, labors, watching, hunger" (v. 4b-5). But keep in mind that he is not simply telling his story—he is establishing his defense against those who would demean his apostleship, call his spirituality into question, or dispute his importance to the Corinthian church. He brings up these "hardships" repeatedly to this church (1 Cor. 4:8-13; 2 Cor. 4:7-12; 6:3-10; 11:23-30). He had to come back to this again in the "tearful letter," and prefaces it with the remark that he is "talking like a madman" (11:23).

Responding to the Text

It is difficult for us to hear Paul's letters with the same freshness that the early churches did. They are now "Scripture" for us rather than part of a dialogue. But receiving a letter from Paul must have been quite an experience. One never knew quite what to expect. Would it be "I thank my God in all my remembrance of you" (Phil. 1:3), or "O you foolish Galatians, who has cast the evil eye on you? Having begun with the Spirit, are you now ending with the flesh?" (Gal. 3:1, 3).

Some in the Corinthian congregation must have been excited in anticipation of Paul's response, while others rolled their eyes thinking, "Won't this guy ever leave us alone?" As Buechner describes Paul's letter-writing: "He bullied. He coaxed. He comforted. He cursed. He bared his soul. He reminisced. He complained. He theologized. He inspired. He exulted. Punch-drunk and Christ-drunk, he kept in touch with everybody."[15]

Gospel
MATTHEW 6:1-6, 16-21

Interpreting the Text

The Gospel of Matthew includes five major speeches by Jesus, the first of which contains this lection:

- 5–7   Sermon on the Mount
- 10   Mission of the Twelve
- 13   Parables Discourse
- 18   Group Order and Discipline
- 24–25   Apocalyptic Discourse

The Sermon on the Mountain is also cast as one of the Gospel's five mountain scenes:[16]

- 4:1-11   mountain of testing and initiation
- 5–7   mountain of instruction
- 15:29-31   mountain of healing
- 17:1-13   mountain of epiphany
- 28:16-20   mountain of commissioning

So Matthew 6 is part of the second mountain scene in the Gospel. Mountains are important throughout the ancient Mediterranean and Middle Eastern world as locations of altars, temples, and other types of divine/human encounter. Like the desert, mountains are liminal areas where transformation takes place. Mt. Sinai and Mt. Zion are especially significant mountains in Israelite and Judahite tradition as the place where the Law is received by Moses and where Solomon builds the central Yahweh temple.

Mountains are the highest points, thus connecting earth and sky—the realms of the humans and God respectively. They take on symbolic significance as sacred meeting places and cosmic centers. Their height is a multivalent symbol of reaching up toward the sky (and thus the divine realm); prominence and honor symbolized as "above," "high," or "over"; center of attention; distance from daily existence; danger (especially when volcanic); and inaccessibility (see Exod. 19: 16-18). Isaiah captured these elements with reference to the Zion traditions:

> It shall happen in the latter days that the mountain of Yahweh's house shall be established as the highest of the mountains, and shall be raised above the hills; and all the foreigners shall flow to it, and many peoples shall come and say: "Come, let us go up to Yahweh's mountain, to the house of Jacob's God." (Isa. 2:2-3, my trans.)

The symbolic significance of mountains is developed further in the *Book of Jubilees* (part of the Judean Pseudepigrapha; second century B.C.E.), which articulates the cosmic significance and relationship of Eden, Sinai, and Zion:

> And he knew that the garden of Eden was the holy of holies and the dwelling of the LORD. And Mount Sinai (was) in the midst of the desert and Mount Zion (was) in the midst of the navel of the earth. The three of these were created as holy places, one facing the other. (Jub. 8:19)[17]

And in *1 Enoch* (also in the Pseudepigrapha; second century B.C.E. to first century C.E.) one finds the connection of the navel of the earth, the cosmic tree, and the holy mountain (26:1).

What the evangelist signals to the audience is that something extraordinary will happen when Jesus goes "to the mountain" (his formulaic phrase). This extraordinary phenomenon is ritual transformation. The evangelist does not name any of the five mountains, so the significance is not placed on a particular location but on the symbolic significance of the mountain. This is where the divine and humans meet; this is where transformation will take place. In each of these passages Jesus and those accompanying him are separated from the rest of society.

Here in Matthew 5 the mountain scene begins with Jesus' separation and ascent of the mountain, followed by the crowds and his disciples (Matt. 4:25—5:1). The crowds come from the major regions of Palestine: Galilee (north), Decapolis (northeast), Jerusalem and Judea (south), and "beyond the Jordan" (southeast). This crowd-gathering speaks to two issues: Jesus' increasing honor, and his increased honor as a source of envy by the Judean leaders (see Matt. 26:3-5). Jesus then went "to the mountain" (the identifying formula in these mountain passages; see 4:8; 15:29; 17:1; 28:16). While on the mountain, Jesus teaches them (5:3—7:27; see 5:2). Here he establishes his foundation teachings, and the result is the response from the crowds: "And when Jesus finished these sayings, the crowds were astonished at his teaching, for he taught them as one who had authority, and not as their scribes" (7:28-29, RSV). When he is finished teaching, he descends the mountain, completing the scene (8:1).

Much of the Sermon on the Mount is Matthew's combination of Jesus-sayings taken from Mark or Q (the Sayings Source). The sayings in verses 19-21 are also in Luke (therefore from Q): Matthew 6:19-20/Luke 12:33 and Matthew 6:21/ Luke 12:34. But the sayings in Matthew 6:1-6 are unique in the New Testament; they do have some parallels outside the canon: Matthew 6:3b/*Gospel of Thomas* 62, and Matthew 6:5a/*Didache* 8:2a.

Responding to the Text

The sequence of the mountains scenes in Matthew takes the audience through developmental stages of discipleship: initiation, teaching, healing, epiphany, and commissioning. So Matthew's mountain passages form a model of discipleship, one of the structuring principles of the Gospel, and a five-act ritual drama of Jesus' transforming presence. Whenever Jesus goes up the mountain, nothing will remain the same.

A FRIEND TELLS THE STORY OF HEARING AN ENGLISH VICAR PRAY IN THE MOST GRANDIOSE OF TONES, "O GOD, DELIVER US FROM POMPOSITY."

If prayer, almsgiving, and fasting, as examples of "piety," are fundamentally ways of connecting to God, then what Jesus is exposing are wrongly focused and wrongly motivated acts of self-aggrandizement. The road of discipleship is one of maturing in Christ, not building a personal reputation. When we are focused upon ourselves, we lose track of the relationship at the core of the act itself. A friend tells the story of hearing an English vicar pray in the most grandiose of tones, "O God, deliver us from pomposity." For me, a large part of the humor in that story is recognizing something of myself in that vicar. As humans we seem to find the most intriguing ways of shooting ourselves in the foot.

But Jesus' sayings here also expose how complex our motivations are. Just as we think we know why we are doing something, it becomes clear to us that our own deeper reasons may not be so obvious nor so clean. It is part of the Lenten experience to reflect on exactly those motivations—not with a spirit of self-mutilation, but of honesty. Honest to God.

FIRST SUNDAY IN LENT

REVISED COMMON	EPISCOPAL (BCP)	ROMAN CATHOLIC
Gen. 9:8-17	Gen. 9:8-17	Gen. 9:8-15
Ps. 25:1-10	Ps. 25 or 25:3-9	Ps. 25:4-10
1 Peter 3:18-22	1 Peter 3:18-22	1 Peter 3:18-22
Mark 1:9-15	Mark 1:9-13	Mark 1:12-15

EXCEPT FOR THE PSALM READING, THESE PASSAGES juxtapose sin and water. In Genesis 9 the sins of humanity grow so great that God sends a deluge to "wash" the whole earth and begin a "new creation." First Peter connects the great flood with baptism as the sign of deliverance. And in Mark 1 the baptism of John is described in terms of repentance and forgiveness of sin, in which Jesus then participates. Baptism is thus also tied to new creation. Chaos and creation, cleansing and deliverance, death and resurrection—water can get you coming and going. It is a potent symbol of change. And frankly, for most of us, change is an unsettling—even disturbing—notion.

FIRST READING
GENESIS 9:8-17

Interpreting the Text

All of Genesis 9:1-17 is cast as a speech of God to Noah and his family. It is a speech punctuated by a repeated blessing—"Be fruitful and multiply" (vv. 1, 7)—and it proceeds to the establishment of a covenant (vv. 8-17). This parallels God's speech to the primal male and female in Genesis 1:28-30. In the covenant speech God promises never again to destroy the earth with a flood (9:11). We tend to reserve the word "covenant" in English for religious usage; but the term in Hebrew (*berith*) is a general word for contracts of various types.

The story of the great flood and the surviving "boatman" and family is an ancient one in the Mediterranean and Near East. It is also pervasive. The people in Mesopotamia (Sumer and Babylon) had been telling versions of the flood story for at least 2,000 years before there were any Israelites; and the Israelites and Neo-Assyrians continued the tradition for centuries more. In the "Sumerian

King List" and "Sumerian Flood Story," Ziusudra (whose name means "Ancient of Days") is the hero who survives the great flood. In the "Gilgamesh Epic," Gilgamesh (the king of Uruk) longed for immortality; he searches out Utnapishtim (also called Athra-Hasis, meaning "The Exceedingly Wise One"), the flood hero who had been granted immortality by the gods for his faithfulness. In the later Neo-Assyrian "Athra-Hasis Epic," Athra-Hasis is the hero and head of the surviving family after the gods used the flood in their attempt at population control. In an ancient Persian work, *The Avesta,* the flood hero was Yima (or Yama); in Indian literature, Manu is saved from the world flood; and in Roman literature, Ovid (in *Metamorphoses*) wrote about the righteous Deucalian and his pious wife, Pyrrha, who were the sole survivors of the flood.[18] One of the things these stories from the ancient world share is that the hero of the flood and his family mark the transition between the old era before the flood (antediluvian) and the following era (postdiluvian).

Responding to the Text

In United States law, contracts "in perpetuity" are generally invalid. The problem with such contracts is that they cannot reasonably be carried out because people die, things change. As humans, we have a hard enough time keeping a promise to the end of the week. But it is precisely God's constancy that backs up "an everlasting covenant" as described in this passage. We don't really have much to compare that sort of faithfulness to in our experience of human relations.

I have heard it said that "we experience all change as loss." The truth in that aphorism is that with every transition we leave something behind. Moving to a new house means leaving behind the old house (with all its memories) and neighborhood (with all our friends). Getting a promotion—even though it includes a raise in pay—means losing the comfort of a job well practiced. This new covenant between God and "all flesh" means no more total destruction by flood. Noah and his wife become the new Adam and Eve. But it also means leaving the antediluvian era behind, when Yahweh walked in the garden in the cool of the day, when the heroes lived to be hundreds of years old, and when the Nephilim walked the earth. These were the "olden days" par excellence, gone for good.

Think of all the eras that we have left behind. Economists, for example, speak of "the Great Transformation" when discussing the move from the pre-industrial era to the Industrial Revolution of the nineteenth century with it mass production, engine-driven machinery, and railroads. In 1950 the first kidney transplant was performed by Dr. Richard Lawler in Chicago; and in 1967 the first heart transplant was performed by Dr. Christaan Barnard in South Africa—issues of life and death would never be discussed in the same light. In 1903 the Wright brothers flew the first power-driven airplane; in 1969 Armstrong and Aldrin walked on the moon—the world shrinks to smaller proportions. But for all these great achievements, we have also brought in a new era in our capabilities to destroy: toxic waste dumping (e.g., the Love Canal); atomic explosions (Hiroshima and Nagasaki) and meltdowns (Chernobyl); the deterioration of the ozone layer; and the destruction of thousands of animal species on land, in the sea, and in the air.

The new day that Noah witnessed could only be lived in hope and on a promise. As Buechner expresses it: "'Never again,' God had said, and Noah clung on to those words like a raft in a high sea."[19]

RESPONSIVE READING
PSALM 25

Psalm 25 is an alphabetic acrostic poem (compare Pss. 9; 10; 34; 37; 111; 112; 119; 145; Lam. 1–4; Nahum 1; Prov. 31:10-31; and Sir. 51:13-30; and see Ps. 119 below, under "The Fifth Sunday in Lent"). This means that the twenty-two verses follow the sequence of the Hebrew alphabet, but in this case with some irregularities (for example, it includes two *resh*-lines, verses 18 and 19). This alphabetic stylistic device—which explains the somewhat awkward progression of the psalm—is employed here with the genre of the individual complaint song (see Ps. 51 above under "Ash Wednesday").

The recurring themes developed here are: the fear of shame before the community (vv. 2-3, 20), Yahweh's forgiveness (vv. 6-7, 11, 18), Yahweh as "teacher" (vv. 4-5, 8-9), and Yahweh's deliverance from enemies (vv. 2-3, 15, 19-20). One might take verse 20 as the thematic summary: "O protect my life, and deliver me; do not let me be shamed, for I take refuge in you" (my trans.). This is something like the feeling one imagines Noah and his family would have had.

SECOND READING
1 PETER 3:18-22

Interpreting the Text

In this lection we are back to Noah again, but in an unusual way. The passage describes the waters of the great flood as *saving* Noah and his family (v. 20). Rather than the flood as a symbol of death, destruction, and chaos, the author of 1 Peter uses it as the means of rescue for Noah's family. This provides a (somewhat strained) analogy, then, to baptism as the means of deliverance. Compare this to the focus on the wood in the book of the Wisdom of Solomon:

> The hope of the world took refuge on a raft;
> and, guided by your hand, left to the world the seed of a new generation.
> For blessed is the wood by which righteousness comes. (Wis. 14:6-7,
> NRSV)

Baptism is described as a pledge (not "appeal" as in the RSV and NRSV) to God for a clear conscience.

Note the oppositions this passage develops:

Christ died (v. 18)	resurrection (v. 21)
unrighteous (v. 18)	righteous (v. 18)
put to death in the flesh (v. 18)	made alive in the spirit (v. 18)
spirits in prison (v. 19)	Noah and family (v. 20)
removal of dirt (v. 21)	pledge to God (v. 21)

But these oppositions are not repetitions of the same idea; they articulate the distinctions of past and present (dead/raised), humans and Christ (unrighteous/righteous), groups who chose different paths (spirits in prison/Noah's family), different modes of existence (flesh/spirit), and wrong and right understandings of baptism (washing/pledge).

Responding to the Text

Noah was a popular figure in the literatures of the ancient Judeans and the early church. The great flood, the ark, and Noah come up often as examples in the Old Testament, Apocrypha, Pseudepigrapha, and New Testament (see, for example, Isa. 54:9; Ezek. 14:14, 20; 2 Esd. 3:9-11; Tobit 4:12; Wis. 10:4; Sir. 40:10-11; 44:17; 3 Macc. 2:4; 4 Macc. 15:31-32; Bar. 3:26-27; *1 Enoch* 65–67; 106:17—107:3; *2 Enoch* 70:5-10; 73:1-9; *4 Ezra* 3:8-11; *Jubilees* 5; 9:14—10:17; *Apocalypse of Adam* 3; Matt 24:37-39; Luke 17:26-27; Heb. 11:7; and 2 Peter 2:5). He is an example of faithfulness, obedience, and righteousness.

But the emphasis in this passage is christological. Christ is the ultimate mediator/broker whose "once for all" death "brings us to God" (v. 18). The victorious Christ, under whom the powers have been subjected, makes the life of the baptized believer rich with possibilities. It is the freedom that Christ brings that frees us to live with hope and confidence.

THE VICTORIOUS CHRIST, UNDER WHOM THE POWERS HAVE BEEN SUBJECTED, MAKES THE LIFE OF THE BAPTIZED BELIEVER RICH WITH POSSIBILITIES.

GOSPEL READING

MARK 1:9-15

Interpreting the Text

No dialogue, and only short snippets of narrative—this is a passage that assumes a lot and moves at lightning speed. Following an extremely brief description of John's ministry and proclamation, the reader is taken rapidly from Jesus' baptism by John, the descent of the Spirit, the voice from heaven, forty days in the wilderness, John's arrest, and the summary of Jesus' message. Mark 1:1-15 functions as the prologue, leading into the main section of the Gospel.

But these are necessary establishing elements for Mark, not footnotes. The quotations from Malachi 3:1 (Mark 1:2) and Isaiah 40:3 (Mark 1:3) establish John's connection with Israel's long chain of prophets. Nazareth in Galilee indicates Jesus' home and social setting. Jesus' baptism connects him with John's ministry. The Spirit and voice establish God's choosing of Jesus as "son." The forty days of testing in the wilderness by "the satan" (note the parallel to the satan [an adversary] in the story of Job; Job 1:6—2:8) function as Jesus' liminal period in preparation for his ministry (see the introduction to the Lenten Season, above). John's arrest provides a closure to his ministry and a beginning for the ministry of Jesus. The note of Jesus' entry into Galilee provides the geographic landscape of his ministry. And the summary of his message signals the reign of God as the central metaphor of what Jesus is up to.

Mark makes it clear that it is *Jesus* who experienced the dove-like descent of the Spirit; and it is *Jesus* who heard the voice—not John and not the crowd. This is important because it indicates that these were visionary and auditory "altered states of consciousness" experienced by Jesus. And this altered state of consciousness connects Jesus with the great prophets of Israel's and Judah's past. Isaiah, for example, describes his "call" experience in a similar way: "In the year that King Uzziah died, I saw the Lord sitting upon a throne, high and lofty; and the hem of his robed filled the temple" (Isa. 6:1, NRSV). And the book of Ezekiel begins "In the thirtieth year, in the fourth month, on the fifth day of the month, as I was among the exiles by the river Chebar, the heavens were opened, and I saw visions of God" (Ezek. 1:1).

But besides the prophetic connections that John the Baptizer and the altered state of consciousness indicate, the declaration of Jesus' sonship by God calls up Davidic-royal connections, even if faintly. In Nathan's prophecy to David, Yahweh declares about David's heir "I will be his father, and he shall be my son" (2 Sam. 7:14); when his son is born to Bathsheba, David names him Yedidiah, "Beloved of Yahweh," because "Yahweh loved him" (2 Sam. 12:24-25). And

Psalms 2 and 89 seem to indicate that the Judahite king was "adopted" by Yahweh at his enthronement: "I will proclaim Yahweh's decree; he said to me, 'You are my son; today I have begotten you'" (2:7; see 89:26-27).

Responding to the Text

This amazing good news that God has planned is off to a peculiar start. John the baptizer eats locusts and is dressed in camel skins—let's not confuse this with a camel hair sportcoat! Jesus comes from Nazareth in Galilee—talk about a backwater, Nazareth was *it*—and returns to Galilee to begin his ministry. It would take a fairly large imagination to picture anything of importance coming out of this beginning.

But this "reign of God" proclaimed by, and manifested in, Jesus obviously envisions a different sort of kingdom. Rather than heavy tribute and taxes, it has debt relief as its agenda (Matt. 6:12; 18:23-34). Rather than royal banquets, it practices open table fellowship (Mark 2:15-17). Rather than war, it brings healing (Mark 1:32-34). In the words of Frederick Buechner:

> Insofar as here and there, and now and then, God's kingly will is being done in various odd ways among us even at this moment, the kingdom has come already.
>
> Insofar as all the odd ways we do his will at this moment are at best half-baked and halfhearted, the kingdom is still a long way off—a hell of a long way off, to be more precise and theological. . . .
>
> When the kingdom really comes, it's as if the thing you lost and thought you'd never find again is you.[20]

SECOND SUNDAY IN LENT

MARCH 19, 2000

REVISED COMMON	EPISCOPAL (BCP)	ROMAN CATHOLIC
Gen. 17:1-7, 15-16	Gen. 22:1-14	Gen. 22:1-14
Ps. 22:23-31	Ps. 16 or 16:5-11	Ps. 116:9-10, 15-19
Rom. 4:13-25	Rom. 8:31-39	Rom. 8:31-34
Mark 8:31-38 or 9:2-9	Mark 8:31-38	Mark 9:2-10

FIRST READING

GENESIS 17:1-7, 15-16

Interpreting the Text

The Abraham saga encompasses Genesis 11:10—25:26. The genealogy from Shem to Abram and his two brothers, Nahor and Haran (11:10–30), provides the introduction to the saga and a transition from the primeval saga (1:1—11:9). In terms of the traditional sources, the Yahwist material (J, or a combination with the Elohist [E]: JE) dominates. But this passage in Genesis 17 is one of the few in the Abraham saga from the Priestly writers (P).

Notice that this covenant-making narrative begins as if the covenant-making narrative in Genesis 15 (J) had not taken place. Genesis 15 emphasizes the animal slaughter and ritual; but 17 emphasizes circumcision—no sacrifice takes place because P reserves all sacrifices for the period after the divine instructions for them on Mt. Sinai. The deity is called "El Shaddai" here—the first such reference in the Bible. And the connection is made between Israel's deity, Yahweh, and this more ancient name in God's speech to Moses: "I appeared to Abraham, to Isaac, and to Jacob as El Shaddai, but by my name, Yahweh, I did not make myself known to them" (Exod. 6:3, my trans.). The meaning of the name Shaddai has been disputed, but probably refers to the "god of the wilderness mountains." The translation of "Almighty" (RSV and NRSV) is based on the mistaken Greek rendering *pantokratōr* ("all powerful").[21]

The change of names for Abram to Abraham (v. 5) and Sarai to Sarah (v. 15) is a traditional act of sovereignty—kings rename their vassals. Examples of this are: the pharaoh changes Joseph's name to Zaphenath-paneah (Gen. 41:45); Pharaoh

Neco changes Eliakim's name to Jehoiakim (2 Kings 23:34); Nebuchadnezzar renames Mattaniah "Zedekiah" (2 Kings 24:17); and the Babylonian chief eunuch renames Daniel "Belteshazar," Hananiah "Shadrach," Mishael "Meshach," and Azariah "Abednego" (Dan. 1:7). God also renamed Jacob "Israel" (Gen. 32:28), and Jesus renamed Simon "Peter" (Mark 3:16).

Though the land is gift and sign of the covenant in Genesis 15, in Genesis 17 it recedes into the background and is primarily the geographical context for the promised descendants. Here the children are central, highlighted by the interpretation of the name Abraham as "father of a multitude" (v. 5). This story is also told looking forward to Israel's kings (v. 6). The contract articulated here is complex: numerous descendants (vv. 2, 5-6, 16); an everlasting covenant (v. 7); the land of Canaan (v. 8a); the identification of God with Abraham's descendants (v. 8b); and the birth of a son to the renamed Abraham and Sarah (v. 16).[22]

Responding to the Text

To name something or someone can be an act of grace or an act of domination and control: power is involved in both instances. Our names are not simply labels, but speak of who we are and to whom we belong, our heritage. Jim Croce's song "I've Got a Name" emphasizes the importance of our names. And Frederick Buechner brings this home:

> Buechner. It is my name. It is pronounced Beekner. If somebody mispronounces it in some foolish way, I have the feeling that what's foolish is me. If somebody forgets it, I feel that it's I who am forgotten. . . . If my name were different, I would be different. When I tell somebody my name, I have given him a hold over me that he didn't have before. If he calls it out, I stop, look, and listen whether I want to or not.[23]

God changing the names of Abram and Sarai is part of their long and complex relationship. Their new names mean the relationship has taken a new turn. Our lives of faith will hopefully keep our names written in the "Book of Life" (Rev. 17:18; 20:15).

GENESIS 22:1-14 (BCP/RC)

Interpreting the Text

In this section of the Abraham saga (see above), the Elohist (E) narrator tells a horrifying story of God's outrageous test of Abraham's faithfulness (v. 1). Keep in mind that this story follows on the heels of Abraham losing Hagar and Ishmael on Sarah's demand and God's affirmation (21:8-14). How much can God ask of him? God requires that Abraham offer his son Isaac as a whole burnt offering (Hebrew *'olah*). This is a sacrifice that is entirely consumed in flames (see Lev. 1:3-17).

The instructions from God, along with the explanation to the reader of the "test," appear in verses 1-2. Verses 3-10 are the "compliance report"—the description of how Abraham carries out God's instructions. But the story takes a turn in verses 11-14: Yahweh's angel intervenes, explains the test, and provides the ram caught in the thicket as a substitute.

The speech of the angel in verses 15-18 concludes the story. Here the promises of descendants and land are reiterated, parallel to Genesis 12:1-3; 15:5, 18-21; 17:4-8, 16. What begins as a story fraught with danger ends triumphantly with this affirmation of the promises.

Responding to the Text

This story is something like a "second call" for Abraham. It has numerous parallels with the beginning of the Abraham saga in Genesis 12:1-9. In both stories God calls Abraham to leave and go to an unknown place (12:1; 22:2); God calls him to leave his clan (12:1) and his future family (22:2); Abraham responds immediately and without comment in both stories (12:4; 22:3).[24] God calls him into the unknown, and Abraham responds with obedience.

But this is a fundamentally unsettling story. God tests his servant Abraham by seeing if he will physically sacrifice his son in a fiery blaze. Like reading about the tests Job endured (see Job 1–2), we can go along with the ancient storyteller's game: we know that it is God at work, and that everything will turn out OK. Job will have his fortunes restored and Abraham will go home with his arm around Isaac. But Job and Abraham do not know that a test is going in, or obviously the test would not work. One could say, "With friends like this, who needs enemies?" Job says:

> I loathe my life; I would not live forever.
>> Let me alone, for my days are a breath.
> What are human beings, that you make so much of them,
>> that you set your mind on them,
> visit them every morning,
>> test them every moment? (Job 7:16-18)

This "testing by God" motif comes up fairly often in the biblical tradition (for example, Deut. 6:16; 13:3; Judg. 2:22; Ps. 11:5; 26:2; 66:10; 2 Cor. 8:2; 1 Thess. 2:4; James 1:3). Most of these instances, however, are quite general statements rather than specific incidents.

But tough questions come to mind:

1. Is the God we worship outrageously capricious?
2. Who was the bigger fool: God for trumping up this test, or Abraham for going along with it?
3. What are we supposed to imagine Sarah's response was to this situation—screaming in agony in the tent, or watching quietly?
4. Why is Isaac's response to the binding not described?

Whatever we make of this story, one must imagine that Isaac never slept really easily after that early morning awakening. It is no wonder that this story has produced a wealth of Jewish literature and art (ancient and modern) reflecting on its implications. Jews have traditionally called this story the *'Aqedah* (the Binding).

Two modern Jewish writers have dealt with it in different ways. Woody Allen tells this story in an ironic and poignant way in his comedic piece, "The Scrolls." In the conversation, when Abraham tells Isaac that God had instructed him to sacrifice his son, Isaac retorts with shock and outrage: "So what did you say? I mean when He brought this whole thing up?"[25] The poet/songwriter Leonard Cohen explores it eloquently in "The Story of Isaac": "He said, 'I've had a vision / and you know I'm strong and holy, / I must do what I've been told.' . . . Then my father built an altar, / He looked once behind his shoulder, / but he knew I would not hide."[26]

One approach to take with this story is to pursue the issue of God testing people. Isn't it only on later reflection that we may perceive or interpret something as a test? What would identify something in our lives as a testing by God? Are we more likely to interpret our own experiences or the experiences of others as tests? Are we more likely to interpret something as a test if we feel we have "passed"?

Another approach might be to focus on the repetition of the verb "see" (Hebrew root, *r'h*) in the story. Abraham "lifted up his eyes and saw (*wayyare'*)" from afar the place God intended for the sacrifice (v. 4). When Isaac pointed out that they had fire and wood but no animal for the sacrifice, Abraham replied "God himself will see (*yir'eh*) to it" (v. 8). And after having been prevented from sacrificing Isaac, "Abraham lifted his eyes and looked (*wayyare'*)" seeing a ram in the thicket (v. 13). Then Abraham called the place "Yahweh will see" (*Yhwh yir'eh*), and the proverbial Israelite saying became "On the mount of Yahweh it shall be seen (*yērā'eh*)" (v. 14). Throughout, God's "seeing" has the double meaning of watching and providing. What do the "eyes of faith" see? How are we blinded by the immediate circumstances from seeing the most important things? Did Abraham ever really see Isaac?

RESPONSIVE READING

PSALM 22:23-31

This psalm is composed of two corresponding halves. Verses 1-21 are a complaint/petition song of the individual (see Psalm 51 under Ash Wednesday pp. 164–65). The psalmist expresses the anguish of separation from God, the scorn of enemies, physical pain, and the immanence of death. The poet cries out for protection, healing, and God's care.

Verses 22-31 form the complement; they comprise a thanksgiving song of the individual whom God has delivered from the brink of death. The text conveys the joy and relief at God's intervention on the poet's behalf. The praise takes place in the congregation (vv. 22, 25). Its exuberance is overwhelming: "Those who seek him shall praise Yahweh! May your hearts live for ever!" (v. 26). And the result of deliverance is sharing and proclaiming the experience: "Future generations will be told about the Lord, and proclaim his deliverance to a people yet unborn, saying that he has done it" (v. 31).

PSALM 16 (BCP)

The psalm begins like a complaint/petition song of the individual (see "Ash Wednesday" under Psalm 51, pp. 164–65): "Protect me, O God, for in you I take refuge" (v. 1), a brief line which includes the petition, invocation, and motivation. But the psalm immediately shifts gears in favor of the individual thanksgiving song form. The tone is joyful for deliverance from death (Sheol, the Pit; v. 10). James Luther Mayes keenly highlights the development of the theme of trust throughout the poem. "Trust is first of all the relationship that determines all else about a person [vv. 1-2]. Trust is monotheistic, not pluralistic [vv. 3-4]. Trust takes the very relation to God itself as the greatest benefit of the LORD's way with the servants of God [vv. 5-6]. Trust concentrates the mind on the LORD [vv. 7-8] Trust is confidence of life in the face of death [vv. 9-11]."[27]

PSALM 116:9-10, 15-19 (RC)

This powerful text is in the form of an individual thanksgiving song (see "Ash Wednesday" under Psalm 103, pp. 165–66). It recalls the threat of death (v. 3), the call to Yahweh for help (v. 4), and Yahweh's response with deliverance (vv. 6-7). It even quotes the painful cries (vv. 4b, 10b, 11b).

Verses 12-19 focus on the joyful response. This response takes place within the community, but not just any community; this is one of the few psalms that mentions the Jerusalem temple. But it saves that for the culminating punch line (vv. 14, 18, 19). It also mentions the "thanksgiving [better: acknowledgement] sacrifice," highlighting one of the three meanings of the Hebrew *tôdah:* the giving of acknowledgment, the acknowledgment song, and the acknowledgment sacrifice.

One of the most poignant lines is v. 15: "Precious in the sight of Yahweh is the death of his faithful ones." This theme is developed further in the passage traditionally read in funeral liturgies: Wisdom 3:1-9.

Second Reading
ROMANS 4:13-25

Abraham plays a major role in two of Paul's letters: Romans and Galatians. In this section of Romans (3:21—4:25), Paul lays out the basics of his understanding of the law, God's grace, faith justification, and righteousness. In this last section, he explains how God's promises to Abraham of children and land (see Gen. 15) were rooted in a faithful relationship rather than a legal arrangement.

But Paul does not recount the story of Abraham and Sarah for its own sake. The conclusion makes his intention clear: our faithfulness should mirror that of Abraham. Our faithfulness is manifested in both belief and loyalty. And the epithet for God Paul uses here is fundamental to his theology: "the one who raised from the dead Jesus our Lord" (v. 24).

Abraham's faithful response is also a way for Paul to again raise the fundamental point that both Judeans and gentiles are heirs of Abraham. Paul makes this point through these interconnected notions: Abraham was reckoned righteous before his circumcision (4:10), Abraham is "the father of all who believe without being circumcised . . . and likewise of the circumcised," and Abraham is the father of "all those who share Abraham's faith, for he is the father of us all" (v. 16).

ROMANS 8:31-39 (BCP/RC)

This passage provides the conclusion the whole section of Romans 5–8, in which Paul articulates the relationship between hope and faithful behavior. He develops his argument in three sections, each with a rhetorical question followed by affirmations.

The first section (vv. 31-32) begins with Paul's rhetorical question: "If God is for us, who can be against us?" The expected answer: "No one." It is not that no one can oppose us, but that no one can be victorious over us with God on our side. Paul's own life demonstrates that this means taking the long view, since he certainly had his share of opponents as well as setbacks.

The second section (vv. 33-34) begins with: "Who shall bring a charge against God's elect?" God's justification—putting things right—and Jesus' intercession make the attacks by others seem laughable. No one has the "legal standing" to indict the faithful whom God has chosen.

The third section (vv. 35-39) begins with: "Who shall separate us from the love of Christ?" This question elicits a litany of life's extremes, none of which could result in this separation: death/life, angels/principalities, present/future, powers, height/depth, anything in creation. The upshot of all this is to comfort the believing community. The fears of inadequacies, opponents, and alienation are all issues that God's power, faithfulness, and love allays. Our hope lies in God, not ourselves. To summarize his logic: God is for us, God justifies us, Christ is for us.

> THE FEARS OF INADEQUACIES, OPPONENTS, AND ALIENATION ARE ALL ISSUES THAT GOD'S POWER, FAITHFULNESS, AND LOVE ALLAYS. OUR HOPE LIES IN GOD, NOT OURSELVES.

GOSPEL
MARK 8:31-38

Interpreting the Text

The Gospel of Mark emphasizes Jesus' own predictions of his Passion in this section (8:31; 9:31; 10:32-33). But the evangelist prepares the reader for the Passion narrative already in Mark 3:6: "The Pharisees went out, and immediately held counsel with the Herodians against him, how to destroy him." This is a Gospel that points us, from beginning to end, in the direction of the cross. The cross is where Jesus is headed; but the cross becomes a symbol of where the disciple/audience is headed as well.

In the first section of this passage, describing Jesus with the Twelve, the exchange between Jesus and Peter highlights the misunderstanding of the disciples—another of Mark's themes. They do not understand the parables (4:13), the loaves (6:52), the saying about defilement (7:17), the lack of bread (8:17, 21), Jesus' prediction of his Passion and Resurrection (9:32), or what they themselves ask (10:35-38). This theme may be the evangelist's way of criticizing the apostolic leadership of his day, or a more general comment on how disciples need to pay close attention since it is easy to misunderstand Jesus. Here Peter does not take seriously enough the opposition of the Jerusalem leaders or the grave consequences of Jesus' message and ministry.

The sequence of sayings in Mark 8:34-38, addressed to the Twelve and the multitude, all highlight the commitment involved in following Jesus: take up the cross (v. 34), lose one's life (v. 35), gaining the world (vv. 36-37), and being ashamed of Jesus (v. 38). Jesus casts all of these as either/or statements (or rhetorical questions). This is a call to decision.

Responding to the Text

The call to discipleship is a serious one in which Jesus engages our whole selves. In this passage Jesus clarifies the cost of discipleship. He was not headed to Wall Street or Hollywood, he was headed to the cross. The outrageousness of this prospect elicited a rebuke from Peter and a counter-rebuke from Jesus. Peter just didn't get it. But he did continue to follow. As Buechner describes the Twelve:

> There is no evidence that Jesus chose them because they were brighter or nicer than other people. In fact the New Testament record suggests that they were continually missing the point, jockeying for position and, when the chips were down, interested in nothing so much as saving their own skins. Their sole qualification seems to have been their initial willingness to rise to their feet when Jesus said, "Follow me." As St. Paul put it later, "God chose what is foolish in the world to shame the wise, God chose what is weak in the world to shame the strong." (1 Corinthians 1:27)[28]

The disciples in Mark's Gospel are both a warning and a message of hope. The warning is: do not make the same foolish mistakes they did. The message of hope is: despite their plodding, self-serving, and thickheaded responses, they kept following—however imperfectly. That should make us take heart. We do not have to understand it all; but we do need to "rise to our feet."

MARK 9:2-10 (RC)

Interpreting the Text

Jesus' sonship is a critical issue throughout Mark's Gospel. He begins with "The beginning of the gospel of Jesus Christ, the Son of God" (1:1). Then at Jesus' baptism, a voice from heaven declares "You are my beloved son" (1:11). The unclean spirits declare "You are the Son of God" (3:11). The Gerasene demoniac cries out "What have you to do with me, Jesus, Son of the Most High God?" (5:7). And at the crucifixion, the Roman centurion declares "Truly this is the Son of God" (15:39). From start to finish, Jesus is acclaimed as God's son. For Mark, Jesus' sonship is an important—if not the most important—indicator of his honor. It identifies the closeness of his relationship with God, his being chosen, and his high rank.

Here in the story of the Transfiguration, Jesus is again singled out—this time from Moses and Elijah—as God's beloved son (v. 7). His role and status are unique and dominant, even over these great figures of Israel's past, Moses and Elijah, who here may embody the "Law and the Prophets."

Some scholars have interpreted this passage as a resurrection story that the evangelist retrojected into the time period of Jesus' ministry. It certainly shares common elements with stories of the resurrected Lord. But it also rings true as a story about an "altered state of consciousness" experience, a vision.

Responding to the Text

The response of Peter in this story is one of excitement. And in his excitement he wants to build lasting monuments or shrines in the wake of this experience of the holy. But the disappearance of Moses and Elijah, followed by the divine proclamation, seems to indicate that Peter had missed the point.

Rudolph Otto, in his groundbreaking work *The Idea of the Holy*, identified the encounter with the sacred/holy as *mysterium tremendum et fascinans*: the sense of tremendous and fascinating mystery. It moves us deeply; it changes our perceptions. As Kathleen Norris observes:

Prayer is not doing, but being. It is not words but the beyond-words experience of coming into the presence of something much greater than oneself. It is an invitation to recognize holiness, and to utter simple words—"Holy, Holy, Holy"—in response. Attentiveness is all.[29]

THIRD SUNDAY IN LENT

MARCH 26, 2000

REVISED COMMON	EPISCOPAL (BCP)	ROMAN CATHOLIC
Exod. 20:1-17	Exod. 20:1-17	Exod. 20:1-17
		or 20:1-3, 7-8, 12-17
Ps. 19	Ps 19:7-14	Ps 19:8-11
1 Cor. 1:18-25	Rom. 7:13-25	1 Cor. 1:22-25
John 2:13-22	John 2:13-22	John 2:13-25

FIRST READING
EXODUS 20:1-17

Interpreting the Text

The Decalogue (literally "Ten Words"; see Exod. 34:28; Deut. 4:13; 10:4) is perhaps the best known and most often cited part of the Old Testament. It is set within the larger framework of the revelation on Sinai (Exod. 19–34) in which Moses goes up and down the mountain. Exodus 20:2-17 itself is cast as a self-contained Yahweh-speech. The people react with fear to the thunder and lightning on the mountain (20:18-19), but Moses reassures them of Yahweh's beneficent intent (20:20).

However old it may have been in its original form (a highly debated issue), the Decalogue has clearly been edited in later periods. The first hint is the switch from references to God in the first person in verses 1-6 to the third person in verses 7-17. It also assumes, for example, a settled life, a time when the Israelites had slaves (v. 10), houses (v. 17), and servants (v. 17), and there were resident aliens in the land (v. 10). The "neatness" of the series has also been disrupted by editorial digressions that provide explanations and motivations (vv. 2, 5b-6, 7b, 9-11, 12b). The final form of the series also comes from a period that assumes the central importance of the sabbath and the Priestly account of creation (v. 11; Gen. 1:1—2:4a); but these both derive from the period of the Babylonian exile.

The other thing we know is that a very similar decalogue appears in Deuteronomy 5:6-21, which includes a variety of minor variations. And we find another type of decalogue in Exodus 34:11-26, emphasizing cultic matters: altars, sacrifices, idols, festivals, the sabbath, etc. The series in Leviticus 19 may originally have been a decalogue, and it overlaps with the issues covered in Exodus 20. And in Deuteronomy 27:15-26 one finds a curse ritual with a dodecalogue (series of twelve) of curses; four items in that series overlap with Exodus 20.

One of the most important observations to make about the decalogue in Exodus 20 is that it is a list composed of prohibitions (negative formulations) and commands (positive formulations) that are not formally law. A law includes a *violation* (for example, murder) followed by a *sanction* (for example, the death penalty). But the items in this series are phrased in the second person masculine singular ("you") and include no sanctions. In other words, the consequences of these behaviors are not articulated. Furthermore, this series constitutes a list of *fundamental challenges to honor:* to Yahweh (vv. 3-7) and other members of the local community (vv. 8-17). That is to say, this list of behaviors identifies critical challenges to honor that require retaliation.[30] For Yahweh this includes diminished priority (v. 3), manufacture and veneration of idols (vv. 4-5), abuse of the divine name (v. 7), and profaning the sabbath (vv. 8-11). For family and community members this means shaming parents, murder, adultery, kidnapping ("stealing [a person]"; v. 15, see 21:16), perjury, and theft ("coveting"; v. 17). These are all issues that cannot be simply apologized for; reparations are required. And most of them constitute capital crimes.

The theological foundation for this list as a whole is found in verses 1-2. In form, 20:1-17 is cast as the report of a Yahweh-speech: "God spoke all theses words" (v. 1). The rationale is that the relationship derives from Yahweh's deliverance of Israel from Egyptian bondage (v. 2). But rationales are found in the individual items as well. The prohibition of idol making and veneration includes a description of Yahweh's character: "for I Yahweh your God am a jealous God" (vv. 5-6). And the sanctity of the Sabbath is justified on the basis of creation and Yahweh's rest (v. 11).

Responding to the Text

All relationships have boundaries. Most of those are unstated and implicit. But the relationship between God and the Israelites articulated in the Decalogue identifies boundaries both vertically (God-humans) and horizontally (between humans). This is how Jesus can summarize the Law (Matt. 22:34-40) as love of God (Deut. 6:5) and love of neighbor (Lev. 19:18). One cannot avoid taking caring of both dimensions. Martin Buber comments on the complementarity of these relationships: "God carries his absoluteness into his relationship with man. Hence the man who turns toward him need not turn his back on any other I-You relationship: quite legitimately he brings them all to God and allows

When detached from these relationships, the Decalogue may sound like a lot finger-wagging. As Kathleen Norris comments:

> For years I dreaded hearing the Ten Commandments read aloud in church. They seemed overwhelmingly negative, and for me were haunted by the family ghosts. . . .
>
> Tobacco, banjo playing, and dominoes do not figure in the Decalogue as recorded in the Book of Exodus. But particularly in nineteenth- and twentieth-century America, Christians have been adept, and remarkably inventive, at interpreting God's commandments to cover just about anything they don't approve of. The effect, of course, is to make the surpassingly large God of the scriptures into a petty Cosmic Patrolman.[32]

An approach one might take to preaching on the Decalogue is to ask the congregation to reflect on what they might include if they were to write their own Decalogue. What should be included in our boundaries with God and our community? What is "beyond the pale" in our relationships? Do these boundaries create fear in us? Can we find any sense of security in knowing what is expected of us? And as Christians, how might we reformulate the theological foundation of the boundaries to replace the Exodus from Egypt?

The day I wrote this the U.S. House of Representatives passed the "Juvenile Justice Bill," stipulating that the Decalogue should be posted in schools and government buildings (commentators think it unlikely that the Senate will pass it). This came up in the context of the Columbine High School shootings and related school violence, and it was evidently meant to renew a moral foundation for children. Would this likely have the desired effect? Out of context, what would children make of the references to the Exodus from Egypt, worshipping other gods than Yahweh, or the sanctification of the sabbath? How does the separation of church and state affect the way we would use such a text in a multi-cultural context outside the church or synagogue?

RESPONSIVE READING
PSALM 19

The two halves of this psalm are quite different, though complementary. Verses 1-6 (commonly referred to as 19A) focus on the praise of God in creation. Verses 7-14 (19B) focus on Yahweh's law. 19A uses the Hebrew *'elohim* (God), while 19B uses the divine name Yahweh. 19A is flowing and evocative, 19B is aphoristic and reads more like lines from Proverbs. Theologically, 19A speaks to the wordless witness to God by the created order, and 19B focuses on the verbal communication of the law as the mediator of the divine human relation. Kathleen Norris writes: "The best description I know of the Dakota sky came from a little girl at an elementary school on the Minot Air Force Base, a shy black girl who had recently moved from Louisiana and seemed overwhelmed by her new environment. She wrote: 'The sky is full of blue / and full of the mind of God.'"[33]

Keep in mind that the Hebrew word *torah* is a broader concept than the English word "law." Besides law and legislation, it encompasses the notions of instruction, teaching, and direction. This explains why the book of Genesis, which contains no legislation, is included in the Torah/Pentateuch. As Hans-Joachim Kraus points out, "The *torah*-understanding of Psalm 19B has nothing to do with nomism; rather, this psalm should always provide a new impetus to think about the mystery and the wonder of the revelation of God in his word, that is, about the word that contains both encouragement and demand."[34]

SECOND READING
1 CORINTHIANS 1:18-25

Interpreting the Text

(On the Corinthian correspondence as a whole, see above, "Ash Wednesday," pp. 166–68).

The epistle of 1 Corinthians is structured along the lines of the classic Greek letter:[35]

I. Introduction (1:1-9)
  A. Salutation (1:1-3)
    1. Senders: Paul and Sosthenes (1:1)
    2. Recipient: "the church of God at Corinth" (1:2)
    3. Greeting: "Grace and peace . . ." (1:3)
  B. Thanksgiving: "I give thanks to God always" (1:4-9)
II. Central Section (1:10—15:58)
  A. Body: Factions in the community (1:10—4:21)
  B. Ethical Exhortations and Instruction (5:1—15:58)
    1. Incest and sexual morality (5:1-13)
    2. Litigation (6:1-11)
    3. Sexual morality (6:12-20)
    4. Marriage and celibacy (7:1-4)
    5. Christian freedom and love (8:1—11:1)

6. Christian worship (11:2-34)
7. Spiritual gifts (12:1—14:40)
8. Resurrection of the dead (15:1-58)
III. Conclusion (16:1-18)
   A. Miscellaneous business matters and exhortations (16:1-18)
   B. Greetings (16:19-20a)
   C. Kiss (16:20b)
   D. Author's authentication (16:21)
   E. Curse (16:22)
   F. Benediction (16:23-24)

This epistle structure is important to keep in mind here so that one sees where an individual part fits in the larger whole. It is also important to remind ourselves that these letters were occasioned by very specific circumstances; they are not theological tracts, but real letters from and to people in very real life settings. The passage of 1:18-25, then, is part of the opening of the "body"—the main issue addressed in the letter. And in 1 Corinthians, the key issue for this body is factions, dissension, quarreling (1:10-13). In other words, Paul's comments about "folly" and "wisdom" are not simply didactic lessons on the nature of intellectual activity, both divine and human. Rather, they are part of his polemic against a congregation torn apart with quarreling.

The factions had evidently divided along the lines of affiliation with leaders in the church: Paul, Apollo, Cephas (Peter), and Christ (1:12; see 3:4-5)! Paul ironically points out how ludicrous this is. Later he points to divisions between the "haves" and "have-nots" that are keeping them from sharing at their agape-feasts (11:17-34).

One should not take Paul's polemic, then, as an attack on common sense, education, or thoughtfulness. Rather, he is making an ironic point here against a sense of a superiority among certain members of the Corinthian church who had failed to understand the message of the cross.

Responding to the Text

Things are not always as they appear, Paul chides the Corinthians. And the "wise" of this world may not be able to see what God is up to. How difficult it is to penetrate beneath appearances—it takes both insight and time. An antique dealer may see the beautiful crafting beneath layers of paint and varnish where others see only a piece of junk. A skilled and sensitive teacher may see the potential of a student where others see only attitude and rebellion. Or a pastor may see opportunities for growth and ministry in a congregation others thought was near death.

A fundamental message of the cross is that God can work even in the context of humiliation, torture, loss, and death. When society at large sees the cross, it sees nothing but shame. When "those who are being saved" see the cross, they know more is at work than degradation. In fact, God may find the best opportunity for growth, meaning, and connection right at the point of brokenness. Beuchner notes how different this is from many other religious traditions: "A six-pointed star, a crescent moon, a lotus—the symbols of other religions suggest beauty and light. The symbol of Christianity is an instrument of death. It suggests, at the very least, hope."[36]

ROMANS 7:13-25 (BCP)

Interpreting the Text

Paul's letter to the Romans is a complex document. It is more densely written, more conceptual, less personal, in general, than his other letters. Paul did not found the congregation(s) in Rome; indeed he had not previously been there and had no firsthand knowledge of these congregations (Rom. 1:10-15; 15:22-23)—though we can deduce that they were composed primarily of gentiles (1:13-14; 11:13-16; 15:15-21). He probably wrote from Corinth (Rom 15:24-26), but his reason for writing has been disputed. The main suggestions have been:

> A FUNDAMENTAL MESSAGE OF THE CROSS IS THAT GOD CAN WORK EVEN IN THE CONTEXT OF HUMILIATION, TORTURE, LOSS, AND DEATH.

1. It was a circulating letter that went to several congregations, and eventually to Rome.
2. Paul was seeking the support of the gentile church in Rome to present a unified front of gentile churches prior to his trip to Jerusalem.
3. Paul was seeking to introduce himself to the congregation at Rome before asking for their support.
4. It was Paul's "last will and testament," abstracting and summarizing his major themes before his fateful trip to Jerusalem.

The epistle is structured like the classic Greek letters of the period. But it has some unusual elements as well:[37]

I. Introduction (1:1-17)
   A. Salutation (1:1-7)
      1. Sender: Paul (1:1-6)
      2. Recipients: "God's beloved in Rome . . . saints" (1:7a)
      3. Greeting: "Grace . . . and peace" (1:7b)
   B. Thanksgiving: "I thank my God . . . for all of you (1:8-17)

II. Central Section (1:18—15:32)

    A. Body (1:18—11:36)

        1. Justification by faith (1:18—4:25)

        2. New life in Christ (5:1—8:39)

        3. Israel in God's plan (9:1—11:36)

    B. Ethical Exhortations and Instructions (12:1—15:13)

III. Conclusion (15:14—16:20)

    A. Travel plans and parenesis (15:14-32)

    B. Peace wish (15:33)

    C. Recommendation of Phoebe (16:1-2)

    D. Greetings (16:3-15)

    E. Kiss (16:16)

    F. Parenesis (16:17-20a)

    G. Benediction (16:20b)

    H. Additional greetings (16:21-24)

    I. Doxology (16:25-27)

Several points concerning the structure are worth making. First, note the unusually extended self-identification of the sender (1:1-6). Normally, this would cite only the sender's name, or perhaps an additional phrase or two. Here, Paul extends his identification into a virtual summary of not only his apostleship but his understanding of the gospel. This may be explained by the fact that Paul needed to introduce himself more fully to people he had never met. Second, many scholars believe Romans 16 is a separate letter that has been "tacked on" to the end of Romans 1–15. As it stands, the letter's conclusion (Rom. 16) is more complex than those in Paul's other letters: it includes a recommendation (vv. 1-2), two sets of greetings (vv. 3-15, 21-23), and an extensive doxology (vv. 25-27). Paul's own greeting (vv. 3-15) is separated from the greetings of his companions and scribe (vv. 21-23). The recommendation of Phoebe is unique in Paul's letter (compare 3 John), as is the doxology as a letter's conclusion. But brief doxologies do appear in both the Pauline and deutero-Pauline letters (Rom. 11:36; Gal. 1:5; Eph. 3:20-21; Phil. 4:20; 1 Tim. 1:17; 6:15b-16; 2 Tim. 4:18b). A further "problem" with the doxology is its status in the earliest Greek manuscripts: in some it appears at the end of chapter 16; in others, at the end of 14 or 15; in still others, not at all.

In this particular passage, 17:13-25, Paul reveals his agonized relationships between himself, sin, death, the law, and God. The law is fundamentally good because it is given by God. But the law also makes him think of things he never would have otherwise considered. He struggles with his own motivations, the disparity between his intentions and his behavior.

The contrasts Paul plays upon here are familiar from other parts of Romans, as well as his other letters—especially Galatians. Those contrasts include:

good (v. 13a)	sin (v. 13b)
spiritual (v. 14a)	carnal (v. 14b)
what I want (vv. 15b, 19a)	what I hate (vv. 15c, 19b)
right (v. 21a)	evil (v. 21b)
law of God (vv. 22, 25)	law of sin (v. 23, 25)
inmost self (v. 22)	body of death (v. 24)

As James D. G. Dunn points out so elegantly, both the individual and the law are "conflicted":

> How does this help defend the law? What has been too little appreciated at this point is that in the second part of this argument (7.18-23), Paul maintains in effect that the law shares the same plight as the "I." As the "I" is divided, so also is the law. There is "the law of God" cherished by the "I" (7.22), approved by the mind (7.23, 25), even when sin conspires with human weakness to prevent compliance. And there is the law used by sin (in the way described in 7.7-13) to bind the "I" ever more tightly to death. This must be what Paul means by "the law of sin" (7.23, 25) and the "law of sin and death" (8.2). The weakness of the flesh means that the law on its own is unable to counteract the power of sin (8.3). . . . The defense of the law is clear, therefore. It is not the law that is at fault. Its role in defining and measuring sin remains unaffected. . . . The weakness of the flesh gives the power of sin such scope and so disables the law."[38]

Responding to the Text

Paul's struggle with his inner urges, his sense of sin and the demonic, and his relationship to the law and to God are all encapsulated here. His conflict may not be exactly ours, but if we are honest with ourselves, eventually we have to face our own inadequacies, our own inconsistencies of behavior, and our own demons. We may have to confront our own shame for "what we have done" and for "what we have left undone."[39]

The United States was recently dragged through a tabloid exposé of the President, the process of his impeachment, the exposing of his sexual behavior, and his confession of sin before a national audience. Whatever one makes of all that, one man's inadequacies were displayed for all to see in glaring detail. He had to confront—obviously unwillingly—his own demons, and it wasn't a pretty sight. For all the hand-wringing, rock-throwing, and moral outrage over President Clinton's behavior, the exposure of his sin should have made each of us reflect on how great our own failures have been.

But for Paul, the issue is not simply struggle, hand-wringing, or self-mutilation. The "punch line" to the whole section is an overwhelming sense of God's grace—only *that* will do, and nothing else: "Who will deliver me from this body of death? Thanks be to God through Jesus Christ our Lord!" (vv. 24b-25). That is the essence of the gospel message: we cannot deny, obscure, or dismiss our failures, our sins, our inconsistencies; but God's love and acceptance is so overwhelming that God extends grace toward us all—no exceptions, no footnotes, no small print.

This unspeakable gift may seem too good to be true. Or we may be completely incapable of encountering God because that means looking honestly at ourselves. Thomas Merton put it so well:

> Perhaps the reason why so few men believe in God is that they have ceased to believe that even a God can love them. The man who is not afraid to admit everything that he sees to be wrong with himself, and yet recognizes that he may be the object of God's love precisely because of his shortcomings, can begin to be sincere. His sincerity is based on confidence, not in his illusions about himself, but in the endless, unfailing mercy of God.[40]

GOSPEL
JOHN 2:13-25

Interpreting the Text

This story, traditionally called "The Cleansing of the Temple," is a compressed and exciting one. The scene is the Passover, and Jesus is among the pilgrims who go to Jerusalem for the great festival in the spring. The temple courtyard is filled with sellers of animals and money changers (v. 14). Jesus takes cords and drives them out of the temple area and overturns the money changers' tables. Havoc prevails. A thrilling, and simultaneously disturbing, scene.

John's narrative is paralleled in Matthew 21:12-17; Mark 11:15-19; and Luke 19:45-48. The basic plotline is the same in all four Gospels. But John is different in four significant ways:

1. John's Gospel includes three Passovers (2:13; 6:4; 11:55), with Jesus' ministry covering, then, approximately two to three years; the synoptic Gospels include only one Passover, and Jesus' ministry seemingly covers less than one year. Because the synoptics all place the temple-cleansing immediately prior to

Jesus' arrest, they emphasize the importance of this event as leading to his arrest and crucifixion. John places the story during the first Passover, two years before Jesus' arrest.

2. John adds the oxen and sheep to the scene (v. 14).

3. The synoptics have Jesus juxtaposing quotations from Isaiah 56:7 ("house of prayer") and Jeremiah 7:11 ("cave of bandits"); in John's Gospel Jesus does not quote Scripture, but his disciples make the connection (v. 17) to Psalm 69:9 ("zeal for your house").

4. John adds the conversation between Jesus and the Judeans (presumably Judean leaders) about destroying and rebuilding the temple, and the commentary about the connection to Jesus' resurrection (vv. 18-22; see Mark 13:2; 14:58). This has the effect, consequently, of connecting the story to the Passion even though the evangelist situates the narrative in an earlier time.

This story has sometimes been interpreted in the Christian tradition to mean that Jesus is taking a stand against the temple traditions of sacrifice as a whole. He therefore chases the animal sellers and money changers out of the temple, signaling the end of the need for sacrifices. But several issues speak against this. First, Jesus came to Jerusalem to participate in the festival, and elsewhere demonstrated support of the sacrificial system (Matt 5:23; Mark 1:44). Second, nothing in what Jesus says or does within the story indicates an anti-sacrificial stance. Third, Jesus refers to the temple as "my Father's house" (v. 16). And fourth, this stance has often derived from a Christian bias against "ritual"—as if Christianity did not include rituals!

My own understanding of this passage within the historical setting of Jesus' ministry is that it is a prophetic-political act of outrage directed, not only against the sellers, but also the Jerusalem priesthood. Victor Eppstein has argued that rabbinic sayings from a variety of eras reflect on a peculiar phenomenon: during Joseph Caiaphas' high priesthood (c. 30 C.E.), the sellers of sacrificial animals were invited into the temple courtyard proper. What was unusual about this is that these financial transactions were traditionally handled outside the temple courts—on the Mount of Olives. The high priest, during this one year, was in conflict with the Sanhedrin, and the animal sellers on the Mount of Olives had given the Sanhedrin a place to meet. So Caiaphas' actions were his way of getting back at them—using other animal sellers and money changers, thus undercutting their sales.[41]

If this was the case, then Jesus' temple-action was not about stopping sacrifices, but about protesting the trade going on in the sacred space where the community was supposed to be singing, praying, and sacrificing (v. 16)! As Eppstein notes, the public awareness of the unusual situation would explain why Jesus was not arrested on the spot, despite the fact that there were temple police inside and Roman guards in the Antonia fortress next door.

Within the Gospel of John, the story takes on further connotations. It helps to frame the conflict between the Jerusalem leadership and Jesus, which is what runs throughout the Gospel—for example, 5:16, 18; 6:41; 7:1, 13, 35; 8:48; 10:19-21, 31; 19:7. (Note that the translation of the Greek *ioudaioi* as "Jews" in the RSV and NRSV is misleading in most Johannine passages, and the New Testament in general. The Gospel of John uses it primarily to distinguish the Judeans—and especially the Judean leaders—from Galileans [for example, Jesus and his followers].) It is also one of the cases of misunderstanding (vv. 19-20), where Jesus' audience takes him literally and the evangelist tells the reader that Jesus is speaking metaphorically or about something else—for example, 3:3-4; 4:13-15, 31-34; 6:51-52; 7:32-36. Lastly, it is an opportunity for the evangelist to prepare the reader for the Passion and resurrection (vv. 18-22).

> THE TRANSLATION OF THE GREEK *IOUDAIOI* AS "JEWS" IN THE RSV AND NRSV IS MISLEADING IN MOST JOHANNINE PASSAGES, AND THE NEW TESTAMENT IN GENERAL. THE GOSPEL OF JOHN USES IT PRIMARILY TO DISTINGUISH THE JUDEANS—AND ESPECIALLY THE JUDEAN LEADERS—FROM GALILEANS (FOR EXAMPLE, JESUS AND HIS FOLLOWERS).

Responding to the Text

It is likely that those who organized the lectionary readings chose this passage to accompany the Decalogue in Exodus and Paul's struggle with the law in Romans because of the traditional "law-gospel" dichotomy. The "Jews" in John 2 represent the law, and Jesus represents the gospel. But I would suggest that better approaches to preaching this passage would be to focus on Jesus' prophetic stand against the power structures, or on the resurrection.

We are not all prophets. We will not all make dramatic public gestures of protest. But that does not prevent us from standing with what is right. Jesus spoke the truth in the midst of a cacophony. What he put his finger on was an abuse of the people by those in power and a breaking of faith with the spirit of worship. John will raise this issue again in Jesus' encounter with the Samaritan woman at the well: "But the hour is coming, and now is, when the true worshippers will worship the Father in spirit and truth, for such the Father seeks to worship him. God is spirit, and those who worship him must worship in spirit and truth" (4:24).

FOURTH SUNDAY IN LENT

APRIL 2, 2000

REVISED COMMON	EPISCOPAL (BCP)	ROMAN CATHOLIC
Num. 21:4-9	2 Chron. 36:14-23	2 Chron. 36:14-17, 19-23
Ps. 107:1-3, 17-22	Ps. 122	Ps. 137:1-6
Eph. 2:1-10	Eph. 2:4-10	Eph. 2:4-10
John 3:14-21	John 6:4-15	John 3:14-21

THE PASSAGES FOR THIS FOURTH WEEK OF Lent center around danger and God's deliverance: snakebites and healing (Num. 21), destruction and rebuilding (2 Chron. 36), hunger and sustenance (Ps. 107; John 6), death and rebirth (Eph. 2), darkness and light (John 3). Ephesians describes this as God's gift: "For by grace you have been saved through faith; and this is not your own doing, it is the gift of God" (2:8).

FIRST READING
NUMBERS 21:4-9

Interpreting the Text

A magical story about snakebites and an apotropaic image of a snake on a pole is very unusual in the Old Testament. The Decalogue prohibits making cult images of "anything that is in heaven, or in the earth below, or in the water under the earth" (Exod. 20:4). And certainly the Israelites incurred Yahweh's wrath when they built the golden calf (Exod. 32). But this is an odd situation for another reason: Yahweh personally commissions the making of the snake image!

This story is recalled in 2 Kings 18:4: Hezekiah "removed the high places, broke down the pillars, and cut down the sacred pole. He broke in pieces the bronze serpent that Moses had made, for until those days the people of Israel had made offerings to it; it was called Nehushtan." But as Ronald S. Hendel points out, the snake may have long been a symbol of Yahweh's power to heal.[42]

The plot line is familiar from many other stories in the "Wilderness Wandering" stories of the Pentateuch. The Israelites cry out, Yahweh sends a judgment against them, the people request Moses to intercede, and Yahweh provides relief. We find this, for example, in Numbers 11:1-34 and 25:1-13.

One of the things that becomes clear throughout the Bible is that everything is personal. Things don't "just happen." Someone makes things happen; someone is always responsible. In this story the people of Israel are responsible for their impatience. But Yahweh is also responsible for sending the fiery serpents. In our contemporary setting we are continuously made aware that a single cause resulting in a single effect seldom occurs. Things are more complex than that.

The recent shootings at high schools around the United States have made parents, educators, politicians, and television pundits all scramble for answers. Is it television? Rock and roll? Movies? Bad parenting? A culture of violence? Easy accessibility of firearms? Societal pressure on teens? We would like to be able to control everything that happens to us. We would like to protect all the children. The proliferation of "psychic hotlines" and the popularity of magical amulets are two manifestations in contemporary culture that speak to our yearning for control. But Buechner issues a warning about what we are up to:

> Magic is the technique of controlling unseen powers and will always work if you do it by the book. Magic is manipulation and says, My will be done. Religion is propitiation and says, Thy will be done. . . . Religion is praying, and maybe the prayer will be answered and maybe it won't, at least not the way you want or when you want and maybe not at all. . . . If security is what you're after, try magic. If adventure is what you're after, try religion. The line between them is notoriously fuzzy.[43]

2 CHRONICLES 36:14-23 (BCP/RC)

The Chronicler's History is a narrative adapting the Deuteronomistic History—Joshua, Judges, Samuel, and Kings—and other sources reflecting on the histories of Israel and Judah. It is an account that has a specific agenda: to enhance the Judahite monarchy, beginning with David, and the centrality of the Jerusalem temple. Everything prior to David is just prologue (1 Chron. 1–9); David is the hero responsible for all the good things grounding the monarchy and worship in Jerusalem. But unlike the Deuteronomistic History, the Chronicler's History extends the story past the Babylonian exile to the restoration of Judah by Cyrus, king of the Medes and Persians.

> "IF SECURITY IS WHAT YOU'RE AFTER, TRY MAGIC. IF ADVENTURE IS WHAT YOU'RE AFTER, TRY RELIGION. THE LINE BETWEEN THEM IS NOTORIOUSLY FUZZY."
> —FREDERICK BUECHNER

This final passage of the Chronicler's History summarizes approximately fifty years of Judah's history. It begins with a summary of how the Judahites were led in their unfaithfulness by the leading priests (1 Chron. 36:14), followed by a summary of Yahweh's repeated attempts to turn the people around by way of the prophets (vv. 15-16). Next comes a brief description of the Babylonians' invasion, destruction of the temple, and taking captives into exile (vv. 17-21). The conclusion is Cyrus' proclamation of rebuilding the temple and releasing the Judahites who want to return (vv. 22-23).

Theologically, this passage emphasizes Yahweh's compassion on the people (v. 15) and judgment in the wake of Judah's rejection: "Yahweh's wrath rose up against his people until there was no remedy" (v. 16). And like Deutero-Isaiah (Isa. 44:28; 45:1), the Chronicler identifies Cyrus as Yahweh's instrument. But the culmination of story for the Chronicler is Cyrus' grant to rebuild the Jerusalem temple at the commissioning of "Yahweh, the God of the heavens" (v. 23).

RESPONSIVE READING
PSALM 107:1-3, 17-22

Psalm 107 is a psalm of communal thanksgiving, singing Yahweh's praises for Israel's deliverance. Each group who owes Yahweh acknowledgement for his great deeds is called upon to respond appropriately with sacrifice and gratitude: thirsty and hungry desert wanderers (vv. 4-9), prisoners who were released (vv. 10-16), the sick who were healed (vv. 17-22), and the seafarers caught in a storm and brought safely back to port (vv. 23-32). Verse 1b was a doxological refrain used throughout the canon: "for his steadfast love endures forever" (see 1 Chron. 16:34, 41; 2 Chron. 5:13; 7:3, 6; Ezra 3:11; Pss. 106:1; 118:1, 2, 3, 4, 29; 138:8; and most notably, its repeated use in every verse of Psalm 136).

PSALM 122 (BCP)

The superscription of this song, like all of Psalms 120 to 134, is "A song of ascents." This is a pilgrim liturgy celebrating Jerusalem; the "ascent" is from the lowlands to the heights of Jerusalem. While Jerusalem is not located on a huge mountain compared to the great ranges of the world, it is significantly higher than anything else in the immediate vicinity. When driving from Tel Aviv to Jerusalem, one is struck by the steep slope of the highway. But unlike many of these other more general pilgrimage songs, Psalm 122 may also be classed as a "song of Zion" (compare Pss. 48; 69:34-36; 76; 84; 87). Verses 1-2 provide the introduction and the beginning of the pilgrimage, verses 3-5 extol the greatness of Zion, and verses 6-9 offer prayers for the peace of Jerusalem.

This psalm begins with a sad lament about the destruction of Jerusalem and the exile into Babylon. It is the pitiful flip side of Psalm 122 (see above). Rather than pilgrimage, this song reflects on the tragedy of being torn from Zion by Babylonian invaders in 598 B.C.E. and the destruction of the city in 587 B.C.E. The cry for revenge in verses 7-9 is usually omitted when this psalm is used in Christian worship. The community weeps together, remembers together, mourns together.

SECOND READING
EPHESIANS 2:1-10

Interpreting the Text

The book of Ephesians was most likely not written by Paul himself, but perhaps by an associate after his death. This conclusion is based on vocabulary, style, theology, and missing elements compared to Paul's letters. Regarding the last point, this book includes no addressees: "who are in Ephesus" (v. 1) is not in the oldest manuscripts. It is also rather impersonal, and it includes no greetings to or from individuals. Ephesians also seems to reflect knowledge of all of Paul's letters, and seems to draw explicitly from Colossians. The conclusion that Paul did not write this letter does not diminish its importance; it simply puts it in a somewhat different social context, and we need not try to reconcile it with Paul's other letters.[44]

This passage picks up numerous themes found throughout the Pauline and deutero-Pauline epistles. A few samples will make the point: dead in sin/alive in Christ (vv. 1-5; see Rom. 8:9-11); passions of the flesh (v. 3; see Gal. 5:24); raised with Christ (v. 6; see Col. 3:1-3); and works/grace (vv. 8-9; see Rom. 11:6). But it also includes phrases quite unlike Paul: "prince of the power of the air" (v. 2); "sons of disobedience" (v. 2); "we were by nature children of wrath" (v. 3); "heavenly places" (v. 6); "his workmanship" (v. 10).

Responding to the Text

In this passage the message that cries out is acceptance: God's acceptance of us. Despite what we have done, despite our attitudes, God has included us, God has reached out to us, God has lifted us up. All of this is the result of a transformation that has happened in Christ. The Ephesian passage articulates this in a variety of ways: "he made you alive" (vv. 1, 5), "God . . . loved us" (v. 4), "raised us up" (v. 6), "by grace you have been saved" (v. 8), and "we are his workman-ship" (v. 10).

For many in our society, self-acceptance may be one of the hardest things to come to. At the heart of the gospel, though, is God's acceptance of us—as individuals and as communities of faith. The author's appeal in this passage is that God's acceptance of us should have an impact on how we view ourselves, how we act, how we relate to God, and how we view the world. We cannot achieve this, we cannot earn it, we cannot manufacture it, and we cannot connive it—we can only receive it, accept it, believe it. It is fundamentally a relationship; what we are, what we are becoming, is a function of *whose* we are and what we have received. Our world, our selves, cannot be the same when we are loved with a love that will not let us go.

WHAT WE ARE, WHAT WE ARE BECOMING, IS A FUNCTION OF WHOSE WE ARE AND WHAT WE HAVE RECEIVED. OUR WORLD, OUR SELVES, CANNOT BE THE SAME WHEN WE ARE LOVED WITH A LOVE THAT WILL NOT LET US GO.

A friend of mine once had the opportunity to spend a day with the renowned psychologist, Carl Rogers. I asked her if he had been a daunting figure. She said that quite the opposite was true. She described an experience of unconditional acceptance, one like she had never experienced from any other person. He listened, responded, received, and was not distracted. One imagines that this is a glimmer of what it means to experience God's acceptance and love. Referring to his father, a fifth-grader wrote:

> I remember him
>   like God in my heart,
> I remember him in my heart
>   like the clouds overhead,
>   and strawberry ice cream and bananas
>   when I was a little kid.
> But the most I remember
>   is his love,
>   as big as Texas
>   when I was born.[45]

JOHN 3:14-21

Interpreting the Text

Jesus' encounter with Nicodemus has always been an intriguing story. Nicodemus comes to Jesus under the cover of darkness to question Jesus. He is a Pharisee, a "ruler of the Judeans" (v. 1), and a "teacher of Israel" (v. 10). But the evangelist blurs the lines of where this story ends and where his miniature christological essay begins: does the story end in verse 12, or 13, 14, or 15? Does the evangelist intend for us to think Jesus continues speaking from 3:10 through 3:21? Given John's style, this ambiguity is probably intentional. The reference to Moses lifting up the serpent provides the transition to the evangelist's referring to Jesus' death and its significance for humanity.

This passage incorporates the repeated motifs and themes of the Fourth Gospel: life (Greek: *zōē*) and death (*thanatos*) (vv. 15-16; see, for example, 5:24), God vis-à-vis the world (*kosmos*) (vv. 16-17; 1:10), the Son as the means of deliverance (v. 17; 5:19-23), believing/being loyal (*pisteuō*) (v. 18), condemning (*krinō*) and delivering (*sōzō*) (vv. 18-19; 16:8-11), darkness (*skótos*) and light (*phōs*) (vv. 19-20; 1:4-5), love (*agapaō*) and hate (*miseō*) (vv. 19-20), and truth (*alētheia*) (v. 21; 8:32). But the emphasis in this passage is on the Son as the means of grace. The whole function of the Son is to deliver.

But Jesus' presence and ministry also creates a crisis-point of decision. This is the import of verse 19. The view of the Fourth Gospel has often been called "realized eschatology." But eschatology in the New Testament has certainly been a controversial issue for the past century. The point, however, is that the evangelist understands the encounter with Jesus as the critical point, not some unknown future event. It is in Jesus and his ministry that one is confronted with God's grace as well as the decision about how one will respond to it.

Responding to the Text

Nicodemus was searching. But the story does not clarify exactly what he was searching for. Eavan Boland writes, "Exile, like memory, may be a place of hope and delusion. But there are rules of light there and principles of darkness. . . . The expatriate is in search of a country, the exile in search of a self."[46] By Boland's definition, Nicodemus is an exile, evidently in search of something more in his life. The homily might well focus on the human search for meaning, for understanding, for our true selves.

The Gospel of John speaks in this passage of being loved, being delivered, being in the light, and doing what is true. The level of metaphor is intense. It reads more like prose poetry rather than discourse. It is as if the evangelist keeps coming at the same issues from different angles. As you read the passage and as you preach it, keep a few things in mind: (1) the focus and complexity of each metaphor (2) the constellation of metaphors (3) and the overall effect and intention of the metaphors. Metaphors are a fundamentally different mode of communication than discourse or argumentation, and they elicit different emotive as well as cognitive responses. What emotions do these metaphors raise in us? Would these be the same responses as a first-century audience?

JOHN 6:4-15 (BCP)

This feeding story is reminiscent of those found in the synoptic Gospels, especially Mark 6:31-44//Matt 14:13-21//Luke 9:10-17; but see Mark 8:1-10//Matt 15:32-39 as well. Compare these parallel motifs:

	John	Mark
Going across the Sea of Galilee	6:1	6:32
The multitude follows Jesus	6: 2	6:33-34
The hungry people	6:5	6:35-36
Two hundred denarii worth of bread	6:7	6:37
Five loaves and two fish	6:9	6:38
Jesus' command to sit	6:10a	6:39
Five thousand men	6:10b	6:44
Jesus gives thanks/blesses	6:11a	6:41a
Distribution of the loaves and fish	6:11b	6:41b
The people are filled/satisfied	6:12	6:42
Gathering twelve baskets of leftovers	6:13	6:43

Note the unique elements of John's story as well. The geographical setting is a mountain (6:3) rather than Mark's "lonely place." The temporal setting is just prior to the Passover (6:4). Jesus tests Philip (6:5-7). Andrew brings the boy with food (6:8) rather than "the disciples" in Mark. And the people declare Jesus a prophet at the climax of the story (6:14). The unique singling out of Philip and Andrew is characteristic of the Fourth Gospel's emphasis on one-to-one encounters and dialogues with Jesus.

Gerd Theissen comments on the wondrous feeding stories:

These miracles can be understood only if the longing they express is taken seriously, the longing for unlimited quantities of bread, fish and wine, in short for food for a multitude; they can be understood only if we do not feel ourselves above the longing for the goods of this world to be available without toil and in sufficient quantity. The gift miracles also particularise the experience of a boundary: situations of material want are transcended and a particular negativity is overcome.[47]

But we can go beyond this and say that this story speaks of Jesus' care for people, the addressing of real need, and the inclusivity and intimacy of Jesus eating with a crowd without the tight strictures normally expected. And these stories clearly take us beyond the immediacy of one meal. Frederick Buechner remarks: "Man does not live by bread alone, but he also does not live long without it. To eat is to acknowledge our dependence—both on food and on each other. It also reminds us of other kinds of emptiness that not even the Blue Plate Special can touch."[48]

FIFTH SUNDAY IN LENT

APRIL 9, 2000

REVISED COMMON	EPISCOPAL (BCP)	ROMAN CATHOLIC
Jer. 31:31-34	Jer. 31:31-34	Jer. 31:31-34
Ps. 51:1-12 or 119:9-19	Ps 51 or 51:11-16	Ps 51:3-4, 12-15
Eph. 2:1-10	Heb. 5:(1-4), 5-10	Heb. 5:7-9
John 3:14-21	John 12:20-33	John 12:20-33

THE FEAST OF MARY OF EGYPT IS CELEBRATED in the Eastern tradition on the fifth Sunday of Lent, and in the Western tradition on April 2, 3, or 9. She was a fifth-century actress and courtesan in Alexandria, Egypt. Her story was committed to legend by Cyril of Scythopolis in the sixth century and Sophronius of Jerusalem in the seventh century. The story goes that out of curiosity she joined pilgrims on their way to Jerusalem when she was twenty-nine. While at the Holy Sepulchre she had a conversion experience, and a voice told her that rest awaited her if she crossed the Jordan River. She spent the remainder of her life as a hermit, but one who shared hospitality with strangers who came to meet her there in the Judean wilderness. Her story has been important for the church because it witnesses to the possibility of change, that openness to God is the crack that lets in the light. In our brokenness and despair, choosing life may be the hardest thing—but it is where God leads.

FIRST READING
JEREMIAH 31:31-34

Interpreting the Text

The prophet Jeremiah had a tough job. First, he had to proclaim the Yahweh-word of judgment and repentance in a period of optimism during King Josiah's reign (640-609 B.C.E.; see 2 Kings 22:12—23:30). Later, he had to proclaim the Yahweh-word to Judahites who had been invaded (598 B.C.E.; see 2 Kings 24:1-17) and then decimated (587 B.C.E.; see 2 Kings 25:1-21) by the Babylonians led by King Nebuchadnezzar.

If this prophecy in 31:31-34 envisions an ideal situation of total commitment to Yahweh's law—a covenant written on the heart—then it is also one of "hopeful imagination"[49] in the midst of brokenness, alienation, and death. That is to say, the Yahweh-word intrudes here in a space where it looks as if there is no room for hope and invites the audience to imagine something completely different. Scholars have come to call Jeremiah 30–31 "The Little Book of Hope" because the editors of the book have organized and concentrated Jeremiah's prophecies of hope in these chapters.

Notice that the emphasis in this proclamation is on what Yahweh *does,* mostly in the future, but also in the past: "I *will make* a new covenant" (v. 31), "I *took* them by the hand" (v. 32), "the covenant I *will make*" (v. 33a), "I *will put* my law" (v. 33b), "I *will write*" (v. 33c), "I *will be* their God" (v. 33d), "I *will forgive*" (v. 34), and "I *will remember* no longer" (v. 34). What Jeremiah describes here is not human achievement, but gift. But note too that it is *Yahweh* who does these things.

Responding to the Text

The message of hope that Jeremiah brings to the Judahites in exile comes to them in the "desert" of their loss of home: land, temple, king, and independence. When we are at a loss, it is difficult to fight the pull of despair, to believe that in the midst of the pain God might meet us there. Holding fast to hope—against all onslaughts—can be a struggle with death. As Gerard Manley Hopkins describes this battle:

> Not, I'll not, carrion comfort, Despair, not feast on thee;
> Not untwist—slack they may be—these last strands of man
> In me or, most weary, cry *I can no more.* I can;
> Can something, hope, wish day come, not choose not to be.[50]

Jeremiah speaks of "tattooed" hearts and a forgetful God—strange images indeed. But the hope that the prophet holds out to the community of faith is that it is time to move on, to process the loss and look ahead. But what of God's anger? What of our inability to keep the law with complete faithfulness? The image of a law "written on the heart" is one of a relationship fully realized and internalized. And the "forgetful God" image speaks to the fear and shame of standing before the creator of the world and the "Ground of all being" with all our inadequacies exposed. God is ready to move on—are we?

THE IMAGE OF A LAW "WRITTEN ON THE HEART" IS ONE OF A RELATIONSHIP FULLY REALIZED AND INTERNALIZED.

But this "new covenant," what does it entail? Hans Walter Wolff comments:

We have seen that the first element that is totally new in the new covenant is the heart on which God himself has written; that is to say, the complete renewal of our conscience, our will, and our passions through God himself. In Jesus we see this newest-of-the-new realized and present in our midst. With him, therefore, the time which Jeremiah 31 announces as the coming time has actually arrived. In him, the new covenant is present. With him, the end of time has begun. For ourselves, for the church of Jews and gentiles, we perceive it fragmentarily, as an advance payment. Along with Israel we are waiting for its completion. And yet through Jesus we are all now, in the present, already actually called to be God's new people—called again or called for the first time.[51]

RESPONSIVE READING
PSALM 51

See above under the comments under Ash Wednesday (pp. 164–65).

PSALM 119:9-19 (RCL)

Psalm 119 is an alphabetic acrostic poem (see also Pss. 9; 10; 25; 34; 37; 111; 112; 145; Lam. 1–4; Nahum 1; Prov. 31:10-31; Sir. 51:13-30; as well as the comments on Psalm 25 under the first Sunday in Lent, p. 174). It is also the longest poem in the Psalter (176 verses). Each of the twenty-two stanzas (one for each of the letters in the Hebrew alphabet) begins each line with the same Hebrew letter (eight lines beginning with 'aleph, eight with beth, and so forth). Thus, verses 9-16 all begin with the second letter in the Hebrew alphabet, beth (pronounced "bait"). Furthermore, almost every line in the psalm includes a word related to law. In this stanza they are: word (v. 9), commandments (v. 10), word (v. 11), statutes (v. 12), ordinances (v. 13), testimonies (v. 14), precepts (v. 15), statutes (v. 16). As a poem, Psalm 119 reads rather mechanically with all these clever devices. But the individual lines still have life. Especially moving in this Lenten season is verse 15: "I will meditate on your precepts, and fix my eyes on your ways." The heart and the eye are connected. Meditation and keeping a keen focus on God are what the Lenten desert is all about.

HEBREWS 5:1-10 (BCP/RC)

Interpreting the Text

This passage is the conclusion of the larger unit of Hebrews 3:1—5:10, which develops the theme of Christ as faithful and merciful. Hebrew 5:1-10 is composed of two smaller units: a description of Israelite high priests in general (vv. 1-4), and Christ as a priest in Melchizedek's order (vv. 5-10).

The author begins by making several observations about the nature of the high priesthood:

- The high priest is a member of the Israelite community, acting on its behalf as a mediator to God (v. 1a).
- The office entails the performance of rituals (v. 1b).
- The high priest's own weakness makes him empathetic to human weakness (v. 2), but also requires sacrifices for himself (v. 3).
- The high priesthood is divinely appointed rather than self-appointed (v. 4).

Verses 5-10 stand as both comparison and contrast to the general picture of verses 1-4. Like other high priests, Christ was divinely appointed (vv. 5-6, 10). But while the others are described in terms of their weakness, Christ is devout (v. 7), obedient (v. 8), and perfect (v. 9). While their priesthood is of Aaron (v. 4), his is of Melchizedek (vv. 6, 10).

The English translations give the impression that Christ's "learning through suffering" stands in contradiction to his "sonship" (v. 8), indicated by the introductory "although." But I suggest that this phrase should be translated "Since he was a son . . . ," for the Judean raising and training of sons expected obedience to be learned through harsh discipline.[52] Another Jesus—Jesus Ben Sira—advised fathers c. 200 B.C.E.:

> He who loves his son will whip him often
> so that he may rejoice when he matures. . . .
> Pamper your child, and he will terrorize you;
> indulge him, and he will bring you grief. . . .
> Bend him to the yoke when he is young;
> thrash his sides while he is still small,
> lest he become stubborn, disobey you,
> and your spirit be disconsolate. (Sir 30:1, 9, 12, my trans.)

One finds similar sentiments in Proverbs (3:11-12; 13:24; 23:13-14; 29:15). And see Hebrews 12:5-8 for the quotation and discussion of Proverbs 3:11-12 on this topic.

Thus Christ's obedience is framed as the result of precisely the type of paternal discipline that an ancient Mediterranean audience would expect. As the author develops his theme later in terms of the audience's own discipleship, any son who is not disciplined would be counted as a bastard (Heb. 12:8)!

Responding to the Text

Few of the images in this passage are likely to resonate very deeply with modern U.S. audiences in a positive sense. For us today, the distinctions between Aaronide and Melchizedekian high priests have little of the significance they had for the original audience. And the depiction of Jesus' death as a form of divine "discipline" parallel to the beatings fathers were expected to give their sons is more than a little horrifying in a time when we have become painfully aware of the effects of child abuse.

But preaching on this passage might focus on the positive attributes exhibited by Jesus: not claiming status for himself (v. 5); prayer and supplication (v. 7); "reverence" (NRSV: "godly fear"; Greek *eulabēs;* v. 7); and obedience (v. 8). If Christ is the "pioneer and perfecter of our faith" (Heb. 12:2), then these attributes are worthy of our meditation and practice.

GOSPEL

JOHN 12:20-33 (BCP/RC)

Interpreting the Text

Each of the four Gospels interprets Jesus' death differently. In the Gospel of John Jesus' death is continually referred to as the point at which Jesus is glorified, as well as the means of glorifying God's name. One of the key issues to recognize is that honor and shame are the foundational values of the Mediterranean world.[53] To say that Jesus' death is "glory" (Greek *doxa*) or "honor" is to view it from a very odd angle indeed. Crucifixion was the most shaming, excruciatingly painful, and prolonged form of torture and execution that the ancient world could come up with—the Romans did not invent it, they just perfected it. Cicero, the Roman orator, quotes the ancient execution formula that demonstrates the role of shame in crucifixion: "Lictor, go bind his hands, veil his head, hang him on the tree of shame."[54] Yet in John's portrayal of Jesus, his crucifixion was where one could really see God's honor at work. This John relates as the confluence of Jesus' obedience and God having the last word.

This passage in John is composed of an interesting assortment of narrative elements alongside Jesus' sayings. The "Greeks" who have come for the "feast"

(Passover) were in all likelihood Greek-speaking Israelites from somewhere in the hellenistic world (v. 20). They make their roundabout way to Jesus through Philip and then Andrew. Jesus gives these "outsiders" (since they are not from Jesus' inner circle of Galilean disciples) a summary of what is going to come: death (v. 24), loss (v. 25), trouble (v. 27), and judgment (v. 31). But the proclamation is that in this brokenness lies the seed of life: glory (v. 23), fruit (v. 24), eternal life (v. 25), honor (v. 26), and nearness (v. 32). The evangelist does not so much explain all this as he does ring the changes on it.

The sayings in this passage are reworkings of various aphorisms (short, pithy sayings) from the Jesus tradition, modified in John's style and worked into a larger monologue—a common Johannine strategy. Note the parallels in the synoptic Gospels:

12:25: "For whoever would save his life will lose it; and whoever loses his life for my sake and the gospel's will save it." (Mark 8:35/Matt. 10:39/Matt. 16:25/Luke 9:24/Luke 17:33, RSV)

12:26: "For the Son of man also came not be served but to serve, and to give his life as a ransom for many." (Mark 10:45/Matt. 20:28, RSV)

12:27: "My soul is anguished, even to death . . . Abba, Father, . . . remove this cup from me; yet not what I want, but what you want." (Mark 14:34, 36/Matt. 26:38-39, my trans.)

12:28: "And a voice came from the heavens, 'You are my beloved son; I am very pleased with you.'" (Mark 1:11/Matt. 3:17/Luke 3:22, my trans.)

12:31: "I saw Satan fall like lightning from the sky." (Luke 10:18, my trans.)

The sayings in this passage speak to the danger which lies ahead for both Jesus and his disciples. It may mean honor, but it is not a road of tranquility.

Responding to the Text

The hope in this passage is that the disciples' lives are linked to Jesus. The lesson is not that we can escape suffering or avoid the cross, but rather that in letting go of the safe grip we have on our lives, we will live. "We think of Eternal Life, if we think of it at all, as what happens when life ends. We would do better to think of it as what happens when life begins."[55] If we "wish to see Jesus," as the Greeks did, then we necessarily have to learn the lesson of the

> THE LESSON IS NOT THAT WE CAN ESCAPE SUFFERING OR AVOID THE CROSS, BUT RATHER THAT IN LETTING GO OF THE SAFE GRIP WE HAVE ON OUR LIVES, WE WILL LIVE.

grain of wheat. Otherwise the picture we get of Jesus is a saccharine, plastic, bloodless Jesus who does not look death in the face. This comes through in George Matheson's lines:

> O Cross that liftest up my head,
> I dare not ask to fly from thee;
> I lay in dust life's glory dead,
> And from the ground there blossoms red
> Life that shall endless be.[56]

Notes

The Lenten Season

1. Bernard of Clairvaux (1090–1153), "Wide Open Are Your Hands," trans. C. P. Krauth (1823–1883) quoted in Judith Mattison, *The Seven Last Words of Christ: The Message of the Cross for Today* (Minneapolis: Augsburg, 1992), 29.

2. Arnold Van Gennep, *The Rites of Passage*, trans. M. B. Vizedom and G. L. Caffee (Chicago: Univ. of Chicago Press, 1960); Victor Turner, *The Ritual Process: Structure and Anti-Structure* (Ithaca, N.Y.: Cornell Univ. Press, 1969).

3. Edmund Waller (1606–1687) from "On the Foregoing Divine Poems."

4. Leonard Cohen, "The Future," in *Stranger Music: Selected Poems and Songs* (New York: Random House, 1993), 370.

5. Council of Laodicea, canon 54. See Peter G. Cobb, "The History of the Christian Year," in *The Study of the Liturgy*, ed. C. Jones, G. Wainwright, and E. Yarnold (New York: Oxford Univ. Press, 1976), 403-19 (see 413). The Council of Laodicea took place c. 364.

6. Translation adapted from Rainer Maria Rilke, *The Sonnets to Orpheus*, trans. S. Mitchell (New York: Simon & Schuster, 1985), 94-95.

7. Gerard Manley Hopkins (1844-–1889), "The Habitat of Perfection."

8. Roberta Bondi, *To Love as God Loves: Conversations with the Early Church* (Philadelphia: Fortress Press, 1987), 18.

Ash Wednesday

9. Council of Trent, sess. 14, cap. 4. Quoted in *The Oxford Dictionary of the Christian Church* (Oxford: Oxford Univ. Press, 1983), s.v. "Contrition."

10. St. John Climacus (c. 570-–649), *The Divine Ladder*, quoted in Kathleen Norris, *Amazing Grace: A Vocabulary of Faith* (New York: Riverhead Books, 1998), 69.

11. Walter Brueggemann, *Israel's Praise: Doxology against Idolatry and Ideology* (Minneapolis: Fortress Press, 1988), 136.

12. Karl Barth, *Church Dogmatics*, vol. 4/1, trans. G. Bromiley (Edinburgh: T. & T. Clark, 1975), 459.

13. Kathleen Norris, *The Cloister Walk* (New York: Riverhead Books, 1996) 101.

14. Adapted from Dennis C. Duling and Norman Perrin, *The New Testament: Proclamation and Parenesis, Myth and History*, 3d ed. (Fort Worth: Harcourt Brace College Publishers, 1994), 180-83, 230-32.

15. Frederick Buechner, *Peculiar Treasures: A Biblical Who's Who* (San Francisco: Harper & Row, 1979), 129.

16. K. C. Hanson, "Transformed on the Mountain: Ritual Analysis and the Gospel of Matthew," *Semeia* 67 (1994):147-70. [http://www.stolaf.edu/people/kchanson/mountain.html]

17. Translation by O. S. Wintermute, "Jubilees," in *The Old Testament Pseudepigrapha*, ed. J. H. Charlesworth (Garden City, N.Y.: Doubleday, 1985), 2:73.

First Sunday in Lent

18. See Isaac M. Kikawada, "Noah and the Ark," in *Anchor Bible Dictionary* vol. 4 (New York: Doubleday, 1992), 1123-31.

19. Buechner, *Peculiar Treasures*, 124.

20. Buechner, *Wishful Thinking: A Theological ABC* (New York: Harper & Row, 1973), 50.

Second Sunday in Lent

21. Ernest Axel Knauf, "Shadday," in *Deities and Demons in the Bible*, ed. K. van der Toorn et al., 2d ed. (Leiden: Brill, 1999), 749-53.

22. George W. Coats, *Genesis*, Forms of the Old Testament Literature 1 (Grand Rapids: Eerdmans, 1983), 134.

23. Buechner, *Wishful Thinking*, 12.

24. David M. Carr, *Reading the Fractures of Genesis: Historical and Literary Approaches* (Louisville: Westminster John Knox, 1996), 197.

25. Woody Allen, "The Scrolls," in *The Complete Prose of Woody Allen* (New York: Random House, 1991), 35-36. Originally in *Without Feathers* (New York: Random House, 1975).

26. Leonard Cohen, "The Story of Isaac," in *Stranger Music*, 139-40.

27. James Luther Mays, *Psalms* (Louisville: John Knox, 1994), 86-87.

28. Buechner, *Wishful Thinking*, 62.

29. Norris, *Amazing Grace*, 350.

Third Sunday in Lent

30. Bruce J. Malina, *The New Testament World: Insights from Cultural Anthropology*, rev. ed. (Louisville: Westminster John Knox, 1993), 46.

31. Martin Buber, *I and Thou*, trans. W. Kaufmann (New York: Scribners, 1970), 182.

32. Norris, *Amazing Grace*, 85-86.

33. Kathleen Norris, *Dakota: A Spiritual Geography* (Boston: Houghton Mifflin, 1993), 21.

34. Hans-Joachim Kraus, *Psalms 1-59* (Minneapolis: Augsburg, 1988), 276.

35. Adapted from Duling and Perrin, *The New Testament*, 211, 220-30.

36. Buechner, *Wishful Thinking*, 19.

37. Adapted from Duling and Perrin, *The New Testament*, 211, 241-48.

38. James D. G. Dunn, *The Theology of Paul the Apostle* (Grand Rapids: Eerdmans, 1998), 157-58.

39. From "The Confession of Sin," in *The Book of Common Prayer* (New York: The Episcopal Church, 1979), 360.

40. Thomas Merton, *A Thomas Merton Reader*, rev. ed., ed. T. P. McDonnell (New York: Doubleday, 1996), 126.

41. Victor Eppstein, "The Historicity of the Gospel Account of the Cleansing of the Temple," *Zeitschrift für die neutestamentliche Wissenschaft* 55 (1964):42-58. See also K. C. Hanson and Douglas E. Oakman, *Palestine in the Time of Jesus: Social Structures and Social Conflicts* (Minneapolis: Fortress Press, 1998), 155-56. [http://www.stolaf.edu/people/kchanson/ptj.html]

Fourth Sunday In Lent

42. Ronald S. Hendel, "Nehushtan," in *Deities and Demons in the Bible*, ed. K. van der Toorn et al., 2d ed. (Leiden: Brill, 1999), 615-16.

43. Buechner, *Wishful Thinking*, 55.

44. Buechner, *Wishful Thinking*, 12.

45. Quoted from Norris, *Cloister Walk*, 54.

46. Eavan Boland, *Object Lesson*, quoted in Norris, *Cloister Walk*, 53.

47. Gerd Theissen, *The Miracle Stories of the Early Christian Tradition*, trans. F. McDonagh, ed. J. Riches (Philadelphia: Fortress Press, 1983), 106.

48. Buechner, *Wishful Thinking*, 12.

Fifth Sunday In Lent

49. Walter Brueggemann, *Hopeful Imagination: Prophetic Voices in Exile* (Philadelphia: Fortress Press, 1986).

50. Gerard Manley Hopkins, from "Carrion Comfort."

51. Hans Walter Wolff, *Confrontations with Prophets: Discovering the Old Testament's New and Contemporary Significance* (Philadelphia: Fortress Press, 1983), 57.

52. John J. Pilch, "'Beat His Ribs While He Is Young' (Sir 30:12): A Window on the Mediterranean World," *Biblical Theology Bulletin* 23 (1993):101-13.

53. Malina, *New Testament World*, 28-62.

54. Quoted in Martin Hengel, *Crucifixion in the Ancient World and the Folly of the Message of the Cross*, trans. J. Bowden (Philadelphia: Fortress Press, 1977), 43-44.

55. Buechner, *Wishful Thinking*, 22.

56. George Matheson (1842–1906), " O Love That Will Not Let Me Go."

For Further Reading

Auden, W. H. *W. H. Auden: Collected Poems*. Edited by E. Mendelson. Franklin Center, Penn.: Franklin Library, 1976.

Brueggemann, Walter. *Hopeful Imagination: Prophetic Voices in Exile*. Philadelphia: Fortress Press, 1986.

_____. *Israel's Praise: Doxology against Idolatry and Ideology*. Minneapolis: Fortress Press, 1988.

_____. *The Message of the Psalms: A Theological Commentary*. Augsburg Old Testament Studies. Minneapolis: Augsburg, 1984.

Buber, Martin. *On the Bible: Eighteen Studies*. Edited by N. N. Glatzer. New York: Schocken, 1968.

Buechner, Frederick. *Peculiar Treasures: A Biblical Who's Who*. San Francisco: Harper & Row, 1979.

_____. *Whistling in the Dark: An ABC Theologized*. San Francisco: Harper & Row, 1988.

_____. *Wishful Thinking: A Theological ABC*. New York: Harper & Row, 1973.

Duling, Dennis C., and Norman Perrin. *The New Testament: Proclamation and Parenesis, Myth and History*. 3d ed. Fort Worth: Harcourt Brace College Publishers, 1994.

Elliott, John H. "1 Peter." In R. A. Martin and John H. Elliott, *James; I–II Peter/Jude*, 53-116. Augsburg Commentary on the New Testament. Minneapolis: Augsburg, 1982.

_____. *What Is Social-Science Criticism?* Guides to Biblical Scholarship. Minneapolis: Fortress Press, 1993.

Hanson, K. C. "Jesus on the Mountain: Ritual Transformation and the Gospel of Matthew." *Semeia* 67 (1994):147-70.
[http://www.stolaf.edu/people/kchanson/mountain.html]

_____, and Douglas E. Oakman. *Palestine in the Time of Jesus: Social Structures and Social Conflicts.* Minneapolis: Fortress Press, 1998.
[http://www.stolaf.edu/people/kchanson/ptj.html]

Jones, Cheslyn, Geoffrey Wainwright, and Edward Yarnold, eds. *The Study of Liturgy.* New York: Oxford Univ. Press, 1978.

Kraus, Hans-Joachim. *Psalms 1–59.* Translated by H. C. Oswald. Continental Commentaries. Minneapolis: Augsburg, 1988.

_____. *Psalms 60-150.* Translated by H. C. Oswald. Continental Commentaries. Minneapolis: Augsburg, 1989.

Malina, Bruce J. *Christian Origins and Cultural Anthropology: Models for Interpreters.* Atlanta: John Knox, 1986.

_____. *The New Testament World: Insights from Cultural Anthropology.* Rev. ed. Louisville: Westminster John Knox, 1993.

_____, and Jerome H. Neyrey, *Portraits of Paul: An Archaeology of Ancient Personality.* Louisville: Westminster John Knox, 1996.

_____, and John J. Pilch, eds. *Handbook of Biblical Values.* 2d ed. Peabody, Mass.: Hendrickson, 1998.

_____, and Richard L. Rohrbaugh, *A Social-Science Commentary on the Gospel of John.* Minneapolis: Fortress Press, 1998.

_____, and Richard L. Rohrbaugh, *A Social-Science Commentary on the Synoptic Gospels.* Minneapolis: Fortress Press, 1992.

Mays, James Luther. *Psalms.* Interpretation. Louisville: John Knox, 1994.

Merton, Thomas. *A Thomas Merton Reader.* Rev. ed. Edited by T. P. McDonnell. Introduction by M. S. Peck. New York: Doubleday, 1996.

Miller, Patrick D. *They Cried to the Lord: The Form and Theology of Biblical Prayer.* Minneapolis: Fortress Press, 1994.

Newsom, Carol A. and Sharon H. Ringe, eds. *The Women's Bible Commentary.* Expanded ed. Louisville: Westminster John Knox, 1998.

Neyrey, Jerome H. *Paul in Other Words: A Cultural Reading of His Letters.* Louisville: Westminster John Knox, 1990.

Norris, Kathleen. *Amazing Grace: A Vocabulary of Faith.* New York: Riverhead Books, 1998.

_____. *The Cloister Walk.* New York: Riverhead Books, 1996.

_____. *Dakota: A Spiritual Geography.* Boston: Houghton Mifflin, 1993.

Rohrbaugh, Richard L., ed. *The Social Sciences and New Testament Interpretation.* Peabody, Mass.: Hendrickson, 1996.

HOLY WEEK

GERARD S. SLOYAN

IN WHAT CIRCUMSTANCES DID HOLY WEEK, CALLED *Hebdomada Major* in the pre-Reformation service books, first come to birth? It is not easy to discover. J. W. Tyrer wrote a history of the week, but even he had to piece together scattered data on the earliest celebration of the various feasts.[1] We know that Sunday observance came early in the Greek-speaking diaspora, after the Sabbath day gathering in Palestine of the first believers in Jesus Christ Risen. Was it because God raised him up from the dead on that day? There is no early evidence to tell us so. It is likely that the day was first chosen for assembly to distinguish the Jesus believers from other Jews. This was a sorting-out problem the Roman Empire did not solve for some time, since its harassment of Christians for not worshiping the gods of Rome was as a sect of Jews. St. Paul proposed the Roman *dies solis,* the day of the sun which occurred first in the week, as the day the Corinthians should take up a collection for the Jerusalem believers (1 Cor. 16:1–2). Acts 20:7 names the evening of the first day of the week in Troas as the occasion for a bread breaking (*klasis tou artou*), an early designation of the Eucharist. A certain John writes that "on the Lordish [or Dominical] day" he experienced a loud voice like a trumpet enjoining him to write what he saw while he was detained on the island of Patmos "because of the word of God and the testimony of Jesus" (Rev. 1:10). The silence of these three New Testament passages on whether Sunday was already agreed on as the day of Christian worship accounts for the existence of Christian Sabbatarians. There is considerable evidence from the first two centuries that in Asia Minor, Syria, and Egypt, Sabbath rest was observed, but modern seventh-day Christians came upon this evidence well after the fact.

Witness to the emergence of "Queen Sunday," as a medieval Jewish hymn hailed the Sabbath, began to multiply in the second century. "Those, then, who lived by ancient practices arrived at a new hope," wrote St. Ignatius of Antioch. "They ceased to keep the Sabbath, and lived by the Lord's day, on which our life as well as theirs shone forth, thanks to Him and his death."[2] Perhaps shortly after this the *Didachē,* a compact catechism of moral conduct and sacramental practice, spoke of "every Lord's Day—his special day" as the day on which you must "come together and break bread and give thanks [celebrate the Eucharist], first confessing your sins so that your sacrifice may be pure."[3] St. Justin, writing in his *First Apology,* a defense of the faith, around 155 described the prayers and thanksgivings offered by the presider over bread and wine and water, then their distribution and the reception of the consecrated elements by each one. A collection was taken and deposited with the presider for distribution to widows, orphans, and the sick, to prisoners and travelers. "We all hold this common gathering on Sunday, since it is the first day, on which God, transforming matter and darkness, made the universe; and Jesus Christ our Savior rose on the same day."[4] By the year 200, that day was taken for granted as the Christian holy day. The *Apostolic Tradition* of about that date, attributed to Hippolytus of Rome, says matter-of-factly: "When [the bishop] has been named and shall please all, let him, with the presbytery and such bishops as may be present, assemble with the people on Sunday."[5]

In 321, Constantine made Sunday an official day of rest. This not only enabled Christians to worship by day rather than by night after a day of work, it introduced the possibility of enjoying a day of leisurely non-activity in emulation of the Sabbath. By this time, Sunday was regularly being described eschatologically as "the eighth day," the day on which the sacrifice is offered that fulfills the promise of the completed creation (St. Clement of Alexandria in his Stromata ["Quiltings"]).[6]

If Sunday was the first Christian feast, when did Easter emerge as first among the Sundays? An apocryphal *Epistle of the Apostles,* otherwise known as *The Testament of Our Lord in Galilee* (140–60 C.E.), appears to contain the earliest mention of it, although it might have become the premier Sunday some time before. "But you, see that you commemorate my death. When the Pascha [Easter] comes, one of you shall be cast into prison for my name's sake; and he will be in grief and sorrow because you keep the Pascha while he is separated from you, for he will be sorrowful because he does not keep the Pascha with you. . . . When you have accomplished the memorial that is made of me, and the *Agapē,* he shall again be cast into prison."[7]

Apollinaris, bishop of Hierapolis, wrote much during the time of Marcus Aurelius (161–80) but none of it is extant. One of his treatises testified to in a Chronicon, however, is titled *On the Pascha.* Melito, bishop of Sardis, wrote the better known homily of that title about the same time, which may have been the germ for the hymn to the Christ-candle that begins *exsultet* (of St. Ambrose authorship?) and almost certainly of the regrettable Good Friday Improperia ("Reproaches"), a much later composition.[8]

The observance of Easter on a Sunday rather than on the first day of Passover, fourteenth Nisan, which could fall on any day of the week, was the result of a struggle between East and West. It tells us most of what we know about the observance of Easter. Bishops of Asia Minor with Polycrates at their head, including the martyred Polycarp of Smyrna and Syria, held out for the date in the Jewish lunar calendar, while Roman bishops including Anicetus and Victor maintained that the nearest Sunday was the better tradition.[9] Pope Victor somewhat high-handedly attempted an excommunication procedure against the Asian bishops, for which Irenaeus reprimanded him but strove to act as peacemaker. Eventually Victor's view prevailed in the West in the form of observing Easter on the Sunday after the first full moon after the vernal equinox. The East held out for this Sunday only if it fell after Passover. This means that to this day Orthodoxy and the West can in some years celebrate Easter a month apart, the full phases of the moon in twenty-eight days.

Since the Passover occurred by the computation of the Palestinian rabbis as they sighted the new moon four weeks before, and since Christians outside that land were following the solar Julian calendar, they needed a fixed date for the death of Jesus. At first, March 25 was chosen, the date of the spring equinox in the Julian calendar. This led to the placing of Jesus' conception on the day of Gabriel's tidings brought to Mary—in Greek *Euaggelismos,* the West's feast of the Annunciation and England's Lady Day. Hence Christmas came exactly nine months later because the Nativity was seen as the earthly beginning of human redemption.

The tradition of celebrating Easter on the Great Sunday, meanwhile, had won out. It was confirmed by the growing practice of celebrating baptisms on that day or, more accurately, on the vigil of that Sunday kept through the night. Saturday had been preceded by a fast in preparation for this paschal initiation, from which the last two days, Thursday and Friday, were separated and given a special character.

Holy Week seems to have been a development in the Christian East, coming out of the practice of pilgrimages to Jerusalem. The earliest account of a visit to Jesus' tomb by a European can be dated to 333 by the writer's naming the Roman consuls in office at the time. The anonymous writer is known simply as "the pilgrim of Bordeaux." The account

HOLY WEEK SEEMS TO HAVE BEEN A DEVELOPMENT IN THE CHRISTIAN EAST, COMING OUT OF THE PRACTICE OF PILGRIMAGES TO JERUSALEM.

is largely a listing of stopping places along the way, distances in leagues and miles and changed modes of transportation. In the land of Israel itself, sites are identified by incidents attached to them in the Bible. The pilgrim mentions the place where the high priest Caiaphas' house had stood and writes that "the column at which they fell on Christ and scourged him still remains there."[10] Mention is made of some walls that were once either part of Pilate's residence or the praetorium of Jesus' trial, which is identified in this way: "On the left is the hillock Golgotha where the Lord was crucified, and about a stone's throw from it the crypt in which his body was laid and [from which] he rose on the third day." The account speaks of a basilica that it calls the *dominicum* built on the site by order of Constantine; but of any liturgical observance nothing is said. Neither do we know in what season the pilgrim was present, whether the one commemorating Christ's death and resurrection or another.

Eusebius, the Arian-leaning bishop of Caesarea who let himself be convinced of orthodox Christology at Nicaea, is credited with *A Life of Constantine,* written between the emperor's death in 337 and his own two years later. It described the cave where Jesus' tomb was situated, upon which had stood a temple of Aphrodite, demolished by Constantine's order. Numerous layers of soil were removed to reveal the cave that Eusebius called "the holy of holies." There is no mention of anything resembling Golgotha, only the fact that the emperor ordered a house of prayer to be built in the vicinity of the cave. This was evidently not a church, or if it was it was a small chapel. Fifty years later we are told of "the Great Church, the *Martyrium*" on the site.

A certain Cyril was a presbyter in the Jerusalem church in 347–48 under Bishop John when, after delivering a preliminary charge to the candidates enrolled for baptism, he preached a series of eighteen catechetical sermons on the Creed and the Our Father. These were part of their final instruction before the Great Night of the Pascha, an Aramaic but then a Greek word for the Christian Passover. Upon becoming bishop in 351, an office he held for thirty-four years, Cyril delivered the five post-baptismal *Mystagogic Catecheses* that led the neophytes deeper into the church's sacramental life.[11] These grace-bearing symbols were called the *mysteria,* a term from pagan Greek religions. Nowhere does Cyril describe the liturgical rite with which Easter was celebrated or even how he thought to extend the celebration from the Easter Vigil back to the later termed "paschal three days." By replicating Jesus' entry into Jerusalem accompanied by other pilgrims, Cyril invented Holy Week.

For our knowledge of the prayer of the Jerusalem church in that week we depend on a pilgrim's description of it some thirty years later.[12] Her name was Aetheria, although various manuscripts spell it differently (notably Egeria who was a Latin goddess; some scribe must have substituted this for her name). She came from Spain or Gaul, in any case a place where the sea was in view. She probably was a nun who kept a careful diary of her travels to bring back to her "reverend ladies," sometimes addressed as "sisters." The travels took place between 381 and 383 and were extensive: through Egypt, Palestine, Syria, and many other provinces of Asia Minor. Everywhere her party encountered churches and monasteries where they were hosted by monks and bishops. She gives an extended account of the daily prayer led by the bishop in Jerusalem's "holy places," the *Anastasis* which houses a cave and the cross. On "the seventh day, the Lord's day, there gather in the courtyard before cock-crow all the people, as many as can get in [the Great Church on Golgotha built by Constantine] as if it were Easter" (*Egeria's Travels,* 24.8). The actual Lord's day (Sunday) liturgy is described in detail as a matter of regular occurrence. Egeria is most impressed by the singing of psalms and antiphons, the preaching, and the people's evident familiarity with the rite. A designated person translates the rite into Syriac for those who do not understand the Greek and helpful monks do the same for her in Latin.

Coming to our matter of special interest, there is first the assembly of Christians on the day before Palm Sunday at the church near Bethany (Lazarium) where Mary met Jesus, having been summoned to it by her sister (John 11:29). There a presbyter mounts the platform from which he reads John 11:55—12:11 and at the dismissal (*missa*) announces Easter.

The next day, Sunday, is the beginning of the Great Week, as Jerusalemites call it. The lengthy morning liturgy is as usual, but as the people break up and start home for a quick meal they are told to assemble at 1:00 P.M. at the Eleona Church ("of the olive tree") on the Mount so named. Hymns and readings follow until 3:00 P.M. and then the people sit down on the Hillock from which the Lord ascended into heaven (Acts 1:12) for more hymns and readings. At 5:00 P.M. the passage is read from the Gospel about the children who met the Lord with palm branches, saying, "Blessed is he who comes in the name of the Lord" (Matt. 21:6-10). Then the people go down through the city bearing olive or palm branches. On Monday and Tuesday they do the same as in the rest of Lent, namely, keep a fast, which Egeria describes in her familiar terms from home as "The Fortieth" and "The Forty Days" when she refers to the ongoing instruction of catechumens. In Jerusalem there are forty-one fast days in eight weeks but not on Saturday or Sunday. One difference she notes is that on Tuesday the people return late at night to the church on the Mount of Olives. Once inside, they hear the bishop proclaim the lengthy discourse of Jesus on the final days, followed by two parables and the last judgment scene (Matt. 24:1—26:2). On Wednesday things are much the same except that the bishop's reading is Matthew 26:3-16, the Temple priests' plot, the woman's pouring costly ointment on Jesus' head, and Judas's bargain to hand Jesus over. Thursday is taken up with the familiar assemblies and prayers, but the Eucharist, called the Offering or *Anaphora,* is celebrated in a unique place on this day of the year, and all the people receive Communion.

They then eat a quick evening meal at home and go up to Mount Olivet for the night service of four hours of psalmody by the light of lamps and candles (the *Lychnicon; Lucernare* in the West). But the night is not over, for at 11:00 P.M. or so, they set off to the place of Jesus' agony, then down the mountainside to Gethsemane, and back to the city to hear the Gospel passage describing Jesus before Pilate (John 18:28—19:22). By this time, dawn has arrived and some repair to their beds. But the hardy stay awake for a gathering at 8:00 A.M. Friday for the veneration of the cross. Its remnant is produced from a gold and silver box, and also the title that Pilate ordered written. A three-hour office begins at midday consisting of readings from the Psalms, then the Epistles or Acts, and finally the Gospel passages that describe Jesus' sufferings culminating in John 19:19-37. After the interval of an afternoon spent in prayer, the people hear the short passage that describes Joseph's asking Pilate for Jesus' body and the entombment (Matt. 27:57-61) and are dismissed.

Saturday witnesses the regular services at nine and noon but there is no Eucharist on this day, to observe Jesus' lying in the tomb. Egeria is brief in describing prayer through Saturday night until dawn on Sunday: "They keep their paschal vigil like us, but there is one addition. As soon as the "infants" [viz., adults] have been baptized and clothed . . . the bishop . . . says a prayer for them behind the screen . . . and returns with them to the church"[13]. All else is just as at home for Egeria, reaching its peak in the eucharistic offering.

When she indicates a place in the Bible from which a reading is taken she does not cite chapter and verse because they had not yet been devised. These are deduced from the earliest actual lectionary we have of the season, an early fifth-century Armenian codex.[14] Cyril's liturgy made its way to the West some time around 450, but in the pontificate of Leo I (440–61) the mystery of Jesus' supper with his disciples, his sufferings and death, and his resurrection had not yet been celebrated on separate days in Rome. The *mysterium fidei* was conceived sacramentally as a single event, although the passion narrative was already being read on the Sunday before Easter. A century later, in that city there appears to have been a strict fast throughout the next week, a gathering with no Eucharist celebrated on Wednesday and Friday, the Easter Vigil on Saturday night including the baptism and anointing of new Christians, and the Eucharist as culmination at midnight.

The Christian East, both in Jerusalem and Constantinople, fixed its rites early. When they were adopted by the West they tended to be austere in the Roman manner. Gradually Hispano-Gallic influences entered in, then Frankish, contributing a regional flavor to what began as something Jewish-Greek. There is a fourth-century Sicilian sarcophagus that shows Jesus riding on an ass while people wave fronds around him. The Gelasian and Gregorian sacramentaries,

both from the eighth century, refer to "Palm Sunday," even though such a procession with palms was introduced only in the twelfth. The liturgical books were
calling it, by the early Middle Ages, the "Second Sunday of the Passion." This was
part of a tendency to view the Great Week in its entirety as a commemoration of
Jesus' sufferings and death. But the actual week in history began and ended in triumph. This means that the Sundays at either end should be celebrated joyously, if
solemnly, the day of palms no less than the day of resurrection. There is one day
devoted to reflection on Jesus' passion and atoning death. It is nestled between
the anticipation of coming glory and the full measure of that glory. St. John's
Gospel presents the historical happenings well, so well that its chapters 13–21
have been termed accurately both "the Book of the Passion" and "the Book of
Glory."

SUNDAY OF THE PASSION
PALM SUNDAY

APRIL 16, 2000

REVISED COMMON	EPISCOPAL (BCP)	ROMAN CATHOLIC
Ps. 118:1-2, 19-29	Ps. 118:19-29	(LECTIONARY FOR MASS)
Mark 11:1-11	Mark 11:1-11a	Mark 11:1-10
or John 12:12-16		or John 12:12-16

THE LITURGY OF THE PALMS SEEMS TO HAVE its origins in Constantinople, if Thomas Talley is correct in his research.[15] He relies on evidence from the fourth-century *Apostolic Constitutions* stating that, in the church, the observance of Lent was distinct from that of the six days of the paschal feast, and that the two were separated by a Saturday and a Sunday that looked to neither. The former was a feast of Lazarus' resuscitation, the latter of Jesus' triumphal entry into Jerusalem. John's Gospel was read on Sunday because it alone relates that entry chronologically to the passion. The Jerusalem observance, on the other hand, was rooted in the Gospel of Matthew and introduced a procession on Sunday as an embellishment of a tradition that came from outside the city, perhaps influenced by the numerous pilgrims from Constantinople. When the practice of a procession with palms reached the West, it was already joined to the paschal days that lay ahead more than to the waning days of Lent amidst which it was situated. The modern reading of the passion narratives at this Sunday's liturgy, a practice of long standing, tends to obscure the event in Jesus' life it is meant to commemorate. It will be suggested below that either of the following readings be the Gospel reading for today, in relation to Isaiah and Philippians, leaving time for adequate homiletic treatment.

GOSPEL
MARK 11:1-11

Mark has Jesus approach two villages east and at the base of the Mount of Olives on the Jericho road. He sends two disciples into Bethany to appropriate a colt they will find tethered in the open street. Challenged by the onlookers, the two explain what Jesus has said and the animal is released to them. Matthew has been following Mark faithfully, correcting or supplementing him when he feels the need. He adds an ass to the colt, perhaps unhappy at the description of Jesus coming on festal pilgrimage on such a small beast but more likely to make the citation conform to Zechariah 9:9c. Leafy branches and cloaks are spread out on the path before Jesus (Mark 11:8). This is not any pilgrim. This pilgrim is a uniquely blessed one who comes in the name of the Lord. The reign of "our ancestor David" is hailed on the same terms—as "blessed"—by the enthusiastic crowds. Mark thus reports a specific enthusiasm, namely, that this teacher from the north may be the one to fulfill all messianic hopes. Jesus surveys the temple scene, then returns to Bethany, from which he will return to the city on successive days. The passage as proclaimed by the reader must convey something of the excitement in the crowd on that day—not read overdramatically but with a restrained intensity.

JOHN 12:12-16 (RCL/RC)

John is briefer than Mark but adds one important detail. He says that the people of the time could not have known the significance of what they had done (v. 16). John has written the same with respect to Jesus' saying about "this temple" being his body to be raised up in three days (2:22); also, the slow dawning on Peter and the beloved disciple as to what "the Scripture . . . that Jesus had to rise from the dead" might mean (20:9). In each of the three cases it would be the Advocate, the Holy Spirit who would remind the disciples of all that Jesus had said to them (14:26).

Christian believers have had the resurrection revealed to them, and so they can hear of Jesus' brief entry in triumph on Passion/Palm Sunday only as a foreshadowing of his final triumph. They have been Spirit-enlightened since their baptisms. Hence they hear these Scriptures and go in procession with palms, secure in the knowledge of who Jesus is, the Crucified who is the Risen One.

Some churches have a blessing of palms, others simply a prayer of dedication said over them respecting the use to which they will be put. It is wise to have congregants go in procession with the palms borne on their shoulders. This may have to be inside the church for reasons of weather but outside is better and if possible in the public streets—optimally, two or three neighboring congregations joined in an ecumenical unity that may not yet be achievable in the Lord's Supper to follow. "All Glory, Laud and Honor," and "Ride On, Ride On" are perhaps the best known hymns sung during the procession, while J. B. Faure's "The Palms" is far too somber. The mood is joyful because this is a people on pilgrimage with its Lord. They know well the pain both he and they must endure before resurrection but there is no reason not to anticipate it with joy.

RESPONSIVE READING
PSALM 118:1-2,19-29

This psalm introduces the Gospel fittingly with its verses about opening the gates (vv. 19-20), its translation of "Hosanna" (v. 25a), and procession with branches (v. 27b). Some essays in the journal *Liturgy* on how Palm Sunday should be celebrated, especially those of Harms and Madigan, should prove helpful to congregations as transmitted through their worship committee and pastor.[16]

THE EUCHARIST OR LORD'S SUPPER

REVISED COMMON	EPISCOPAL (BCP)	ROMAN CATHOLIC
Isa. 50:4-9a	Isa. 45:21-25	Isa. 50:4-7
	or 52:13—53:12	
Ps. 31:9-16	Ps. 22:1-21 or 22:1-11	Ps. 22:2, 8-9, 17-20, 23-24
Phil. 2:5-11	Phil. 2:5-11	Phil. 2:6-11
Mark 14:1—15:47	Mark (14:32-72);	Mark 14:1—15:47
or 15:1-39, (40-47)	15:1-39 (40-47)	or 15:1-39

GOSPEL
MARK 14:1—15:47, 15:1-39, (40-47)

As to the lengthy passage proposed for today, including the optional verses from chapter 15, some pastors will favor reading it all but not, it is hoped, with roles distributed. It may well be asked why it has been retained in all the revised liturgies. To be sure, Jesus was welcomed into the city joyfully by fellow pilgrims—there to suffer and die. But the anticipation of his sufferings and death five days before their liturgical observance seems all wrong. If his death, why not his resurrection? St. Mark, in alerting his hearers to the way his Gospel would end, proclaimed death and resurrection as the one mystery not once but three times (8:31; 9:31; 10:33). The church does the same at each Sunday eucharist. Why not at this one? The Passover supper of Jesus with the Twelve will be commemorated on Maundy Thursday so there is no need to recount it all on the previous Sunday. A Gospel passage that might profitably be proclaimed to prepare a congregation for the Great Night of Easter is Mark 14:26-51 followed by 16:1-8.

What?! Mention Easter before its time? By all means. The mystery of our redemption is one undivided mystery and should always be proclaimed as such.

To separate the two, however long-standing the tradition, is to do violence to all the ancient eucharistic prayers (canons, anaphoras) and to Christian faith itself, which knows the two to be inseparable. For the evangelists there were no chapter divisions. Shame led directly into glory in their recounting of events. So should it be with us.

The shorter reading suggested immediately above will leave time for a much needed homiletic exposition: of Jesus' desertion by his friends, of the rehabilitation of one of them, and above all the charge delivered to the holy women which they did not obey out of fear. All four gospels reflect the shock still felt decades later at the enormity of Peter's denial of Jesus and Judas's handing him over. The women's failure to proclaim the resurrection is used by Mark to make a similar powerful point. If Jesus' closest friends could desert him and fear to announce him as risen, how much more the possibility among later believers.

The Hallel had been sung at the close of the meal (Pss. 113–118, the "hymn" of Mark 14:26). Mark finds Zechariah 13 fitting to describe what will come next: a shepherd struck, a flock scattered. There then follows a prediction. Jesus whom death cannot hold proposes Galilee as a muster point for his disciples after he is raised up.

> WHAT?! MENTION EASTER BEFORE ITS TIME? BY ALL MEANS. THE MYSTERY OF OUR REDEMPTION IS ONE UNDIVIDED MYSTERY AND SHOULD ALWAYS BE PROCLAIMED AS SUCH.

The young man at the tomb will say the very same to the holy women, that Jesus who was crucified has been raised up and will meet them (16:7). But for now Jesus foretells Peter's denial of him before cockcrow and is met with a blustery denial that it could ever happen (Mark 14:29-31). Jesus goes up the slope to Gethsemane ("olive press") and prays in a state of agitation, lying prostrate. He calls on God as "Father" to deliver him but is open to God's will in his regard rather than his own. The three accompanying disciples, meanwhile, aided by the Passover draughts of wine have fallen asleep. Jesus charges their spirit with being no match for weak flesh and calls the chapter closed with a brusque "Enough!"—the impatient *basta* you hear all over Italy, or *halaz* in Arab lands. The betrayer is at hand and does his deed.

Jesus challenges his captors who are evidently part of the Temple guard ("from the chief priests"): "Have you come out . . . to arrest me as though I were a bandit?" (v. 48), one of the highwaymen who infested Palestine's roads, or perhaps an insurrectionist. He then allows the Scriptures to be fulfilled and submits, but his close associates these many months desert him and flee (v. 50). There is one who attempts it and succeeds only by leaving behind the linen cloth in which he was clad. What kind of dress was this for a chilly spring night? The detail is highly improbable until we see what Mark is up to. The young man's naked flight into the night is a figure of the fearful believer of Mark's day who, in deserting Jesus under pressure, is stripped of the protective garment of faith.

But there is hope. Just as the epilogue to John restores Peter to the company of believers by an elicited threefold affirmation of love, canceling out his three-fold denial (John 21:15-17), so Mark rehabilitates the anonymous disciple by having him seated calmly on the right side of the tomb dressed in a white robe (Mark 16:5; cf. 5:15; 9:26-27). In these three narratives and that of Jesus' transfiguration itself, Mark teaches the possibility of restoration to a grace-filled, even a risen life after figurative death. He likewise employs the women's fear to tell a cautionary tale. Instructed to tell the other disciples and Peter of the marvel of a risen Christ, they do not. There the original text abruptly ends. "Do not hesitate to proclaim the resurrection out of fear," Mark tells his church and the church tells us the same. The women's terror and amazement may not grip us but the unbelief all around us may overwhelm us. Speak up boldly, we are told, whether in our actions or in our words, about the Risen One.

A sermon on these two portions of Mark's passion which make a unity should dispel any mystification over the choice of the reading. It should prepare worshipers to consider the seriousness of their participation in the upcoming paschal mystery. True, many are present only on this day in great numbers and will be here again on Easter Day. But they will not be deprived of a reminder of Jesus, the innocent sufferer for our sins, so much as motivated to enter into his death and resurrection as members of his body. A spirited homily including an invitation to come celebrate the mysteries on Maundy Thursday and Good Friday if people are able to, will surely induce some.

Isaiah 50:4-9a is the third "song of the servant of the Lord" to occur in sequence (see Isa. 42:1-9; 49:1-7; 52:13—53:12). Like the others it prefigures Jesus' passion admirably. The humiliated figure may be an individual, some even suppose the poet author of chapters 40–55 himself. Most, however, conclude that the subject intended is the people of Judah. Brought low in Babylonian exile, the Jews there are a teacher to others within their ranks but even more to their Chaldean oppressors (Isa. 50:4a). They have not rebelled against the hardships God has asked of them (Isa. 50:5). Instead they have reacted passively but determinedly to blows and insults and spitting. In all this they experience no shame because the one who will vindicate them is near (Isa. 50:8); the Hebrew verb is "justifies." They are ready to take on any contender, no matter who their adversary. The God who is Lord stands ready to help them (Isa. 50:9a).

THE SUFFERING CHRIST OF THE COMING WEEK'S LITURGY SHOULD BE A REPROACH TO CHRISTIANS WHO MAKE OTHER CHRISTIANS SUFFER, AS THEY SUPPOSE IN HIS NAME.

This besieged condition is a grim reality for Christians of various churches and of no church but the Bible who are a minority in various parts of the world. There are even diaspora situations in this country and Canada where one's Christian Communion will be sneered at and ridiculed by others who profess the "true faith," namely theirs. The suffering Christ of the coming Week's liturgy should be a reproach to Christians who make other Christians suffer, as they suppose in his name. The Bible passages are especially meaningful to the Christians being persecuted in Egypt, Algeria, Malaysia, and Indonesia. Psalm 31:9-16 responds to the Isaiah 50 passage perfectly as the psalmist describes himself wasting away in misery, a pariah to all around him. He nonetheless trusts in God's steadfast love. The same fittingness is true of Psalm 22 (BCP and RC), on which see Good Friday below.

First Reading
ISAIAH 45:21-25 (bcp)

Here the righteous God and Savior ("there is no other besides me" [v. 21d]) is, alone, the righteousness and strength of all "who were incensed against him." The Israelites will triumph and glory while their adversaries shall come to God in shame. An oblique reference to the completely reversed fortunes of the humiliated Jesus is evident, but the chief reason for the selection is the phrase, "To me every knee shall bow, every tongue shall swear" (v. 23b). The Philippians hymn of this same Passion Sunday concludes with it in expanded paraphrase (Phil. 2:10-11). The alternate for the BCP, Isaiah 52:13—53:12, is commented on under Good Friday.

Second Reading
PHILIPPIANS 2:5-11

Philippians 2:5-11 gives every evidence of being a hymn known to Paul into which he apparently inserted the phrase "death on a cross" for emphasis (v. 8; there is no "even" in the Greek). The apostle does not contribute a Christology of his own, relying on a quotation to which a brief soteriology is joined. He does the same in Romans 1:3-6. A succinct theology of salvation is also found in the pre-Pauline Romans 3:25-26. The letter to Philippi just read from contains what looks like an Adam Christology, although some think not; in any case, not the Word made flesh Christology we are accustomed to from John. Christ Jesus is being celebrated "in the form of God" like the first human made in God's image and likeness (Gen. 1:26; cf. Phil. 2:7). This is an equality with God (not John's God and Word) that he forfeited for the form of a slave. He emptied himself of his former godlike condition but humbled himself *after* being found in human form. His humanity was not his humiliation; the death that came of his obedience was. Exaltation followed at every level and in every realm. All tongues proclaim openly that Jesus is Christ and Lord to the glory of the Father. Here Pascal's *misère* and *gloire* are joined in the one person. This hymn gives shape to our Holy Week worship as we proceed from contemplating death to resurrection.

Important for the homilist is the reason Paul gives in introducing the hymn. He is attracted by the way it joins Jesus' voluntary death and vindicating glory, but the first member of the two is his reason for inserting the hymn: "Let each of you look not to your own interests, but to the interests of others. Let the same mind be in you that was in Christ Jesus, who, though he was in the form of God . . ." (vv. 4-5). Unless we are impelled by this Week of the church's prayer to open ourselves to the Spirit acting in us, we do better to omit these acts of religion. The whole purpose of our life in Christ is to acquire his *phronēsis,* mind (wisdom, insight). We must let ourselves be made like him by these holy mysteries.

MONDAY IN HOLY WEEK

APRIL 17, 2000

REVISED COMMON	EPISCOPAL (BCP)	ROMAN CATHOLIC
Isa. 42:1-9	Isa. 42:1-9	Isa. 42:1-7
Ps. 36:5-11	Ps. 36:5-10	
Heb. 9:11-15	Heb. 11:39—12:3	
John 12:1-11 or Mark 14:3-9	John 12:1-11	John 12:1-11

FIRST READING

ISAIAH 42:1-9

The commentary here will be brief, not because the weekday worshipers are fewer but because the tone has been set by the readings of Passion/Palm Sunday. Isaiah 42:1-9 so closely resembles the portions from chapters 50 and 45 attended to in yesterday's proper and 52:13—53:12 on Good Friday that little need be said about today's lection. The synoptic Gospels will appropriate verse 1, "my chosen, in whom my soul delights," for the baptism and transfiguration narratives. Matthew will employ the first three of these nine verses as a fulfillment quotation after Jesus has healed the man with the withered hand (12:18-21). Applied to Jesus, "a bruised reed he will not break, and a dimly burning wick he will not quench; he will faithfully bring forth justice" (v. 3; cf. Matt. 12:20). Jesus' silence before Pilate (Matt. 27:14; John 19:9-10; Mark 15:5) is an echo of Psalm 42:2a. The suffering servant here is almost certainly the Jewish people whose role is to be "a covenant to the people [Israel]" and "a light to the nations" (v. 6c, cf. Luke 2:32) for whom he will bring forth justice (v. 1b) as "a covenant to the people."

RESPONSIVE READING

PSALM 36:5-11

In this psalm the congregation sings the praises of God's steadfast love. The foot of the arrogant, the hand of the wicked are never far from the upright of heart, who say, as was said by and of the much later Jesus, "in your light we see light (v. 9; see John 8:12; 12:46). This is basically a psalm of the justice of God (vv. 5-6) who will prevail over the plotter of mischief and deceit (see Mark 3:6).

SECOND READING

HEBREWS 9:11-15

Hebrews 9:11-15 places the high priest Jesus in the tent not of this creation, in the Holy Place which he entered with his own blood, thus obtaining for us eternal redemption. Jesus offered himself without blemish to God through the eternal Spirit (v. 14). We know we are redeemed by this mediator of a new covenant (a renewed covenant; for God "cannot deny himself" [2 Tim. 2:13]). We join our priesthood to that of the great High Priest throughout this Week in our sacramental celebration of his death and resurrection.

HEBREWS 11:39—12:3 (BCP)

Hebrews 11:39—12:3 goes in a different direction. The author has spent a chapter reviewing the faith of the saints of old but says, with St. Paul, that "God has provided something better" (v. 40). Jesus endured the cross, disregarding its shame, "for the sake of the joy that was set before him" and from his "seat at the right hand of the throne of God." He awaits us persevering runners in the race (v. 2, then 1). If he could endure such hostility from sinners we should not lose heart. Jesus redeems us as our exemplar, among other ways.

> JESUS ENDURED THE CROSS, DISREGARDING ITS SHAME, "FOR THE SAKE OF THE JOY THAT WAS SET BEFORE HIM" AND FROM HIS "SEAT AT THE RIGHT HAND OF THE THRONE OF GOD." IF HE COULD ENDURE SUCH HOSTILITY FROM SINNERS WE SHOULD NOT LOSE HEART.

JOHN 12:1-11 and MARK 14:3-9

Today's Gospel passage is a preparation for the paschal three days. John 12:1-11 and Mark 14:3-9 tell the same story but it must have reached them from different sources. Mary of Bethany in her own house or a woman guest of Simon the leper are details that make no difference. Neither does a pound or 300 days wages' worth of perfumed ointment of pure (*pistikos,* "scented?") nard. John's calling Judas a thief is proper to this Gospel. The true import of the account comes at the end. Both evangelists quote Deuteronomy 15:11, "For ye have the poor with you always" (KJV), and stop there not going on to, "I therefore command you, 'Open your hand to the poor and needy neighbor in your land.' " This use of the half-verse can give the hearer the impression of callousness on Jesus' part and a deplorable self-centeredness. In fact, it is the two evangelists and not Jesus who wish to highlight the fittingness of the woman's action because he will shortly die. Mark, but not John, is followed by Matthew in having Jesus prefix an *amen* to his statement, "Wherever the good news is proclaimed in the whole world, what she has done will be told in remembrance of her" (Mark 14:9, Matt. 26:13). The word "remembrance" is different from the one Jesus used over the bread in Luke 22:19 and 1 Corinthians 11:25, but both mean a memorial act. Elizabeth Schüssler Fiorenza's *In Memory of Her* is a book-length treatment of the difference in what the church has done or not done to keep the two memories of Jesus' equally worded *words* alive.

TUESDAY IN HOLY WEEK

APRIL 18, 2000

REVISED COMMON	EPISCOPAL (BCP)	ROMAN CATHOLIC
Isa. 49:1-7	Isa. 49:1-6	Isa. 49:1-6
Ps. 71:1-14	Ps. 71:1-12	Ps. 71:1-6, 15, 17
1 Cor. 1:18-31	1 Cor. 1:18-31	
John 12:20-36	John 12:37-38, 42-50	John 13:21-33, 36-38
	or Mark 11:15-19	

GOSPEL

JOHN 12:20-36

The verses from John continue from the reading from the day before. Jesus' setting in this Gospel is exclusively Palestinian Jewish with the exception of this mention of Greeks and the ethnically Jewish Samaritans of chapter 4, reckoned non-Jews religiously. As usual, characters in this Gospel are named, all but Mary (called simply "his mother") and John (never "the Baptist"). At John 2:4 Jesus has told his mother that his hour has not yet come. Now it has come (12:23) and with it the necessity in parabolic utterance of his being sown in the earth like a grain of wheat. Dying he will bear much fruit. The "where I am" of verse 26 is with the Father, as consistently in this Gospel. Verses 27-30 have been called the Johannine Gethsemane. A difference is that Jesus is not strengthened by the presence of an angel as in Luke (where the text seems to be a later addition), but by a confirming word from his Father, much as in the synoptic transfiguration accounts. John does not contain exorcism stories, but here Jesus' glorification achieves the ultimate driving-out of "this world's ruler" (v. 31). Such is God's judgment on evil. The believer has nothing to fear from diabolic influence.

The light-overcoming-darkness theme recurs (vv. 35-36) but in a new context, namely of the doubly significant verb, "being lifted up." This has occurred previously in 3:14-15, the figure of the elevation of the bronze serpent, and again at 8:28. The repetition of it as Jesus' death approaches makes clear that his being heaved up onto the cross and his upraising from the dead are the two elevations intended. Much of John's Gospel similarly features the real and the symbolic which is always the more real (*alēthinos,* "real," "true," used nine times to connote "of God"). John 12:42-43 records the silent believers in Jesus out of fear, like Nicodemus and the parents of the man blind from birth. These are references to the persons in the evangelist's community well after Jesus' day who are experiencing ostracism for their belief in him as Israel's messiah. The community continues to proclaim to fellow Jews their concern for belief in God's word and commandment, the key to which is faith in the Son God has sent (vv. 44-50).

FIRST READING
ISAIAH 49:1-7

The RCL employed a servant song from Isaiah 50 on the previous Sunday. On successive days of Holy Week, its first reading on Monday is a similar portion from chapter 42—today Isaiah 49:1-7, tomorrow a repetition of Passion/Palm Sunday's 50:4-9a, and on Good Friday 52:13—53:12. In all, the humiliation of the servant willingly borne is the main feature, with future vindication at God's hands a certainty. Prepared for his role before his birth like Jeremiah, John the Baptist, and Jesus (1b), the servant is trained to speak sharply but is for a long while hidden, his labors unrewarded. Yet his calling to bring the southern and northern kingdoms back to the LORD (v. 5) and to be a light to the gentiles (v. 6b) continues undiminished. The long verse 7 discloses the servant's identity. It is the Jewish people itself, deeply despised and abhorred by the nations; but the LORD who is faithful, the Redeemer of Israel and its Holy One, will bring kings and princes prostrate before it. It is no wonder that the earliest Christian interpreters of these Scriptures saw in them a perfect figure of the humiliated and triumphant Jesus, the *Christus Victor* of Anders Nygren's book title.

RESPONSIVE READING
PSALM 71:1-14

The responsorial Psalm is a prayer that asks God's protection against enemies and accusers. God is a rock and a fortress who, at the same time, will prove a rescuer from the unjust and the cruel. The typological application to Jesus is evident. RC's verses 15 and 17 proclaim that God alone is righteous, one whose deeds of salvation are forever to be praised.

The weekday worshipers are served rich fare, notably in 1 Corinthians 1:18-31 which they hear on only one Sunday every third year (A, Epiphany 4[4]). It prepares them for the commemoration of Jesus' sufferings and death on Good Friday. St. Paul chides some in Corinth for their folly in boasting about who baptized them. Their claim of wisdom ("We sit, after all, on the shoulders of the great philosophers") is a greater folly still. The only true wisdom is God's wisdom, the cross. The world calls it foolishness but true foolishness is what the world calls wisdom. Tucked in this long exercise of penetrating irony is Paul's reminder that many in the Corinthian church are neither high born nor of any great influence. In their social lowliness and uninfluential condition, however—some even "low and despised"—God has chosen them for life in Christ, God's wisdom.

No homilist is wise to demean a congregation, but there is such a thing as the regularly attended assembly of the church comfortable. In other parts of the city or county, there is the church marginal. All are brought to the one level of God's wisdom, the cross. The God of Israel says: "I bring low the high tree, I make high the low tree, I dry up the green tree and make the dry tree flourish" (Ezek. 17:24b). St. Paul did that with a difficult congregation. The Holy Spirit stands ready to do it in the Easter mysteries for whoever appears. What is their Easter finery if not a declaration: "I am of the baptized. I belong in this house this day!"? They need to be reminded of that.

WEDNESDAY IN HOLY WEEK

APRIL 19, 2000

REVISED COMMON	EPISCOPAL (BCP)	ROMAN CATHOLIC
Isa. 50:5-9a	Isa. 50:4-9a	Isa. 50:4-9
Ps. 70	Ps. 69:7-15, 22-23	Ps. 69:9-11, 20-21, 34-35
Heb. 12:1-3	Heb. 9:11-15, 24-28	
John 13:21-32	John 13:21-35	Matt. 26:14-25
	or Matt. 26:1-5, 14-25	

FIRST AND RESPONSIVE READINGS

ISAIAH 50:4-9a and PSALMS 69, 70

Isaiah 50:4-9a was proclaimed publicly on Sunday last, which we saw. Two psalms are indicated in response to it, the first being the shorter Psalm 70 (RCL). Verse 1 will be familiar to those who recite or sing the day hours: "O God, come to my assistance, O LORD, make haste to help me." Overall, this poem is an outcry for help against enemies who desire to hurt the psalmist, even to seek his life (Ps. 70:2; cf. Isa. 50:2). Verse 3 is reflected in the mocking of Jesus on the cross in Mark 15:29. More phrases of Psalm 69 than 70 have been employed by the Gospels or in Holy Week liturgies: thus, "my throat is parched" (69:3; John 19:28); "Zeal for your house has consumed me (69:9; John 2:17); "They gave me poison for [put gall in] my food, and for my thirst they gave me vinegar to drink" (69:21; John 19:29). The three lectionaries had no problem in finding psalms of anguish or lament by an innocent one amidst the shameful treatment visited on him, much of it figurative. In the passion narrative, the tortures are real.

SECOND READING

HEBREWS 12:1-3

Hebrews 12:1-3 could be seen flowing from chapter 11 before there were chapter divisions. There the faith of the ancients was praised, having been defined as "the assurance of things hoped for, the conviction of things not seen" (11:1). Methodically the author traces the trust in God shown by Noah, then Abraham, Isaac, Jacob, and Esau; Joseph followed by Moses, Rahab, and some minor figures down to David; Samuel; and the prophets. The tortures they endured for their witness to God are catalogued. All died in faith without having received the fruit of the promise. This cloud of witnesses surrounded the early believers and motivated them to rid themselves of sin and persevere in the race they were running. But their chief concentration, says Hebrews, should be on Jesus who "endured the cross, disregarding its shame." He could do this "for the sake of the joy that was set before him," which was no less than being seated "at the right hand of the throne of God" (v. 2). Today's weekday worshipers, like those early Christians, are challenged not to grow weary or lose heart. Contemplating all that Jesus suffered at the hands of sinners should do this. ("Gentile sinners" was one word for the Jews of the time, like "damn'Yankees.") Jesus is "the perfection of our faith," its pioneer in the sense of trailblazer. He leads the way having suffered before us on his way to joy.

HEBREWS 9:11-15, 24-28 (BCP)

For a comment on Hebrews 9:11-15 see Monday in Holy Week. Verses 24-28 have Jesus entering the true, heavenly sanctuary, not an earthly copy (the sacred author, probably an Alexandrian, favors Platonic categories). There Jesus who can die no more appears in the presence of God on our behalf. He appeared once on earth and "will appear a second time" to save those who wait for him. This is the source of the non-biblical phrase "the second coming." "Coming" or "appearance" (*parousía*) is the term consistently used.

GOSPEL

JOHN 13:21-35

Here is Jesus' prediction of his betrayal and the consternation that follows, as in Mark 14:18-19. Simon Peter's inquiry of the anonymous "disciple whom Jesus loved" as to whom Jesus speaks of, unique to John, is relayed to Jesus. He responds with the sign of the morsel dipped in the dish (vv. 21-26; cf. Mark 14:20). The disciple is "reclining next to Jesus" (v. 23, NRSV), a paraphrase of the literal rendering, "leaning on Jesus' bosom" (v. 23, KJV). Modern translators know the Jewish custom of eating

TODAY'S WEEKDAY WORSHIPERS LIKE THOSE EARLY CHRISTIANS ARE CHALLENGED NOT TO GROW WEARY OR LOSE HEART. CONTEMPLATING ALL THAT JESUS SUFFERED AT THE HANDS OF SINNERS SHOULD DO THIS.

the Passover meal while lying on their sides, Graeco-Roman style. Research has not disclosed the origins of the practice but its discovery has saved a new generation of artists from seating thirteen men at a table, one of them with head bent unnaturally to lean on Jesus' breast. The teacher says to the Satan-driven Judas: "Do quickly what you are going to do" (v. 27b). He departs having first eaten his morsel of bread, for John the symbol of his treachery. "And it was night" (v. 30b) is equally symbolic in a Gospel where darkness and light mean much in the realm of faith. This evangelist has earlier identified theft from the common purse as Judas's vice (12:6). Mention of the purse (13:29) may hint at a possible motive for his handing Jesus over. We shall never know what went on in the man's heart, only that his deed was remembered by the others as an act of betrayal.

For centuries in the West, Luke 22–23 was read in the liturgy of Wednesday, as Mark 14–15 was on Tuesday and Matthew 26–27 on Sunday. Monday worshipers heard John's resuscitation of Lazarus (12:1-9). Because Luke's lengthy passion began with Judas's conferral with the Temple priests and police as to how he might hand Jesus over, this day has traditionally been known as Spy Wednesday.

MATTHEW 26:1-5, 14-25 (BCP)

Two lectionaries choose Matthew 26:14-25 (and 26:1-5 BCP) as their Gospel reading. The high priest Caiaphas and other people of power are named as the conspirators gathered in his palace (vv. 1-5). Mark at 3:6 plants a similar clue early in his narrative, attributing such a plot to Pharisees and Herodians (the royal hangers-on largely out of power in Judea). Jesus' earliest believers cannot have known whose plan it was, only what came of it. The arrangement Judas arrived at makes him a bargainer interested in money as in John but not in Mark (Matt. 26:15). Only this gospel names the price, derived from two places in the Bible, Zechariah 11:12-13 and the erroneous attribution of such a sum to Jeremiah in Matthew 27:9. For the meal preparation Matthew replaces Mark's story of how the supper room was arrived at by a simple, "go to . . . a certain man" and gives the account at the identifying hand of Judas dipped in the dish. Jesus' statement that it would have been better for that man if he had never been born is a Semitic phrase deploring an act, not a judgment on his eternal fate.

MAUNDY THURSDAY
HOLY THURSDAY

APRIL 20, 2000

REVISED COMMON	EPISCOPAL (BCP)	ROMAN CATHOLIC
Exod. 12:1-4, (5-10), 11-14	Exod. 12:1-14a	Exod. 12:1-8, 11-14a
Ps. 116:1-2, 12-19	Ps. 78:14-20, 23-25	Ps. 116:10, 12-13, 15-18
1 Cor. 11:23-26	1 Cor. 11:12-26, (27-32)	1 Cor. 11:23-26
John 13:1-17, 31b-35	John 13:1-15 or Luke 22:14-30	John 13:1-15

THE TERM "MAUNDY" COMES FROM ANGLICAN and, before that, Catholic usage, being an Englishing of the Norman French for the opening word of Jesus in the Vulgate at John 13:34, *Mandatum novum do vobis,* "I give you a new commandment, that you love one another." The Latin service books called it "the Fifth Day [Thursday] of the Lord's Supper." It has come to be reckoned, after sundown, as the first of the "sacred three days," with Lent terminating just before the Supper rite. This goes back to the forty-day Lenten fast, Sundays not included, of which Holy Thursday was the last day. The modern three days are thus reckoned as Thursday night, Friday, and Saturday night through Sunday, Saturday being a day of no festal observance except as part of Jesus' forty-hour reposing in the tomb. Of old, however, St. Augustine wrote of the *triduum* as Jesus' three days of suffering, reposing in the sepulchre, and being raised up on the third day, obviously Friday, Saturday, and Sunday. Egeria reports on the Jerusalem practice of a morning and evening Eucharist on Thursday. When returning pilgrims reported this to Augustine a quarter-century later, he resisted the practice for North Africa. Rome by the year 500 evidently had three services on this day: a morning one for the reconciliation of penitents, a Eucharist at midday for the consecration of *chrisma,* the holy oil, and another in the evening to commemorate the Last Supper.

Gallo-Frankish reformers of the Roman Rite, like the scholarly bishop Theodulf of Orléans (d. 821), are responsible for the ceremony of footwashing in churches of the West on this evening. Parenthetically, he was the composer of the hymn "All Glory, Laud and Honor," which became the processional hymn of Palm Sunday. Some other features of Holy Week introduced to the West from the East include the Palm Sunday procession, the Good Friday veneration of the cross, the blessing of the new fire, and the hymn *Exsultet* ("Let the Angelic Host of Heaven Rejoice") sung to Christ in the symbol of the Easter candle at the Easter Vigil. The more than millennium-old practice of acting out the footwashing on this night with the proclamation of the appropriate Gospel pericope can be traced even further back to a Synod of Toledo in 694. Some U.S. Brethren Churches that have their roots in Germany early in the eighteenth century engage in the practice more frequently, some among these making it central to the Sunday service.

GOSPEL

JOHN 13:1-17, 31b-35

RCL chooses John 13:1-17, 31b-35 for this evening's gospel while the RC and BCP do the same, stopping at verse 15. St. John's Gospel has indicated that, well before the Passover festival, Jesus came first to Ephraim (11:54f), then to Bethany six days before the feast for a meal at the home of Lazarus, Martha, and Mary (12:2). It brings him in triumphal pilgrimage procession into Jerusalem (12:12-15) where the evangelist has him speak about his impending death (vv. 27-36). John further summarizes Jesus' teaching on the commandment given him by his Father which is eternal life (vv. 44-50). There follows none of the setting for the supper provided by the synoptics, possibly because for John it is not a Passover meal as with them. All four have him crucified on a Friday, the preparation day for the Sabbath. Passover begins for the synoptic three after sundown on the previous day, but for John the supper and Jesus' lengthy discourse and arrest all occur before and after a meal "before the festival" (13:1).

The introduction is abrupt. After mention of Jesus' awareness that his "hour" has come (predicted at Cana in 2:4 and spoken of again in 12:23 and 17:1), and the devil's entering into Judas's heart to hand him over (13:2), he leaves the table "during" supper and proceeds to wash and dry the disciples' feet. It was a normal act of hospitality to welcome dusty-sandaled travelers but one more usually performed by a serving person in hostelries and great homes (see vv. 3-5). Simon Peter's demurrer is the familiar misunderstanding or challenge raised by others in John's narrative technique to bring on an exposition by Jesus. Simon addresses Jesus as "Lord" as he has done in 6:68, a term not only of respect but of awe. He presses his discomfort at the gesture for its lack of fittingness, namely, Jesus in the role of servant. The first response Simon receives is one that is often found in this gospel: his understanding of Jesus' act will come not now but later (v. 7). Simon Peter's remonstration grows stronger but Jesus insists. At that point the disciple makes the puzzling demand that if there is to be any washing it is to be of his hands and head as well (vv. 8–9). This difficulty, obviously created by the evange-list, elicits Jesus' response that one who has bathed has no need to wash but is entirely clean (see v. 10). Interestingly, while the phrase "except for the feet" is found in most manuscripts it is missing from some early ones. It appears to have been inserted in order to clarify by distinguishing the feet from all other parts. But the verse conveys quite well without it that Jesus' one symbolic act is suffi-cient. Peter's demand for a thorough washing is characteristic of his "all or noth-ing" approach. The answer Jesus gives him is the point John wishes to make. All the disciples are already clean in figure except Judas who, Jesus knows, is about to hand him over (v. 11). Every sort of baptismal reference has been read into this passage including a polemic against the need to receive the sacramental bath a second time, but the meaning is simpler than that, as just proposed.

> PETER'S DEMAND FOR A THOROUGH WASH-ING IS CHARACTERISTIC OF HIS "ALL OR NOTHING" APPROACH. THE ANSWER JESUS GIVES HIM IS THE POINT JOHN WISHES TO MAKE. ALL THE DISCIPLES ARE ALREADY CLEAN IN FIGURE EXCEPT JUDAS WHO, JESUS KNOWS, IS ABOUT TO HAND HIM OVER.

Submission to a cleansing at Jesus' hands—with total purification as the intent—is proper disposition for partaking in the sacrificial drama to follow. Being bathed by Jesus means being symbolically taken into the event of the cross.[17]

Many modern congregations have lately adopted the custom of footwashing in the Maundy Thursday service. This goes back to the early practice in the church of Rome in which its bishop washed the feet of twelve beggars recruited from the city streets. Nowadays a dozen people of both sexes are widely taken to represent the disciples—their feet so clean upon arrival at the church that the washing is totally symbolic. Other more inventive congregations do a hand-to-hand washing in pairs until all, even in a large con-gregation, have been included in the rite. This adaptation can prove meaningful to Maundy Thursday worshipers, more so than a distant rite in the chancel between presider and a chosen twelve. Impressive as it is, however done, the ges-ture should not be let pass in a homily as the main point of the Gospel. To be sure Jesus proposed his action as an example (v. 15). But it was mutual service that he required in emulation of *his* service. That service was no less than the giving of his life for others, the event of the cross: "As I have done for you." The cleansing of feet in a posture of abasement was the symbol of a far greater reality, his tor-tured death on Calvary. He could have got out of it, could have slipped the bonds of his captors as he did many times before (see 7:46). He went ahead, letting it happen, for he saw in it the Father's will for him. This is the service that needs to be stressed in a homily, Christ as servant of the whole human race (see Phil. 2:7f). If we are to obey Jesus' command by loving one another—and the proof of love is in serving others, even those we heartily dislike—we must first master the les-son, "as I have loved you" (15:12). He loved us even unto death. Few are called to reciprocate Jesus' love with martyrdom but all who claim him as Teacher and Lord (v. 13) are to do a harder thing: to repay with love, expressed in service to all who slight us, injure us, despise us, in a word, those for whom he died. They are we ourselves and all who are like us.

Once Judas had departed, the glorification of the Son by the Father was imminent (v. 31). His disciples, addressed as "little children" only here (21:5 employs another word), cannot at the moment come after him (v. 33). He leaves them behind to obey a "new commandment" (v. 34f). It has long been asked what is new about it since all in Israel were under command to "love your neighbor as yourself" (Lev. 19:18). The answer has to be, with the love that Jesus displayed by his servant life and death. That is the example that was new in human existence, not any death in sacrifice but the love that prompted *his* death.

LUKE 22:14-30 (BCP)

The lectionary in the revised BCP provides Luke 22:14-30 as tonight's Gospel pericope, an alternative for congregations puzzled by the absence of a Gospel account of Jesus' words at the supper table. Here this is the liturgical formula used in the Lukan churches, just as we have three other wordings in the formula of the Matthean, Markan, and the Pauline churches, the last-named the second reading in this service. Only Luke provides the sequence cup, bread, cup (vv. 17, 19, 20 in 22:14-30). That sequence is textually authentic. The critics who thought the order or the repetition a dittograph have largely fallen silent.

Surely the early Christians of both Palestine and the diaspora would have encased these words in lengthier prayers and bodily movements since, being Jews accustomed to Temple pilgrimage feasts, they would have had a lively sense of ritual. Regrettably, we do not have the settings. Luke follows Mark, as does Matthew, in reporting Jesus' vow at table "not to eat [this Passover] until it is fulfilled in the kingdom of God" (22:16, repeated over the wine in v. 18). If taken literally these words would make him a ghost at the feast. More likely this is the gospel writers' way of conveying Jesus' progress toward the messianic banquet in the kingdom of God. Jesus' vow of abstention is seemingly their way of speculating on what Jesus might have looked forward to since they knew the outcome of his ordeal. The Lord's injunction, "Do this as my memorial," (v. 19c) is one that Luke either possesses as a reminiscence or has found in a source he has in common with Paul (cf. 1 Cor. 11:24b). Catholic and Orthodox eucharistic rites tend to contain a new composition derived from early liturgies, the conflated wording of various Gospels. The Reformation tradition more usually employs Jesus' actual words from one or the other Gospel. In any case, all eat his body and drink his blood sacramentally as commanded.

FIRST READING

EXODUS 12:1-4, (5-10), 11-14

Exodus 12:1-4, (5-10), 11-14 is clearly a cult legend developed to explain the origins of the Passover ritual. Two spring harvest festivals had come together at some time in the distant past and been given the religious meaning of gratitude for deliverance from Egypt. One feast was the *Pesah,* the Hebrew word for "passing over" (the blood-smeared Israelite doorposts, that is; v. 13) or perhaps originally an Egyptian word meaning "blow," the tenth plague that brought death to Egyptian first-borns (11:5). The other feast was *Massah,* the "unleavened bread," specified for offering along with other sacrifices in Leviticus 2:4, 11. Exodus 12:15 and 23:15 prescribe eating such bread for seven days beginning on the fourteenth day of Abib, called Nisan in the Babylonian calendar when the year began with the spring equinox. Why no yeast? This is unknown but it may be the required absence of any substance along with the grain offering, since honey is also proscribed. There is also the tradition of yeast as a corrupting element, because it is a ferment, echoed in 1 Corinthians 5:6-7 where it is a figure of boasting, malice and evil. The roasted lamb (v. 9) was the centerpiece of the meal, not the unleavened bread. The haste of the people's departure from Egypt is given as the reason there was no time for yeast (vv. 33-34). Eating by families or groups (vv. 3-4) on the first day of this pilgrimage feast accounts for the Last Supper as described in the synoptics, which call the gathering a Pascha. John dates it before the festival of the Passover (13:1) but like the others has Jesus die on the day of preparation a Friday preceding any Sabbath (14:19). For him this was not the first day of Passover, possibly because he wished to employ the symbolism of Jesus' dying on the afternoon animals were sacrificed in preparation for the meal.

The slaughter of the Egyptians is repulsive to modern venerators of the Bible but it must be understood as a detail in full color so to say, to highlight God's protection of Israel from a cruel oppressor. It resembles all the bloodshed in the holy books, including the total destruction commanded in the "ban" (see Deut. 13:13-16). Most of Israel's wars in ancient days were undoubtedly defensive small engagements against Canaanite tribes and the more formidable Philistines. They doubtless grew in magnitude with David's conquests but the earlier skirmishes are remembered as a total carnage visited on the enemy. Such is the nature of saga. Tragically, the high body count that began with the invention of firearms and culminated in the hydrogen bomb of Hiroshima is real. Ancient warfare was nothing like World War I and II and the arms sales ever since, in which this country is so deeply engaged.

Jews have placed a shank bone on the plate at some point since the destruction of the Temple, adding numerous other details in the Middle Ages to yield the modern *seder* ("order, sequence"). Modern Christians are unwise to hold such a simulated meal on Maundy Thursday, both because it is disrespectful to Jews to employ their rite but more importantly because the Christians' own rite commemorating deliverance is the Lord's Supper. They do not engage in the same offense, however, by baking cakes in the shape of a lamb or serving lamb at a Thursday or Sunday dinner. From earliest days they have not been aping Jewish practice but have seen in Jesus the Lamb of God self-offered in sacrifice. Learning all that they can about the Passover observance is entirely praiseworthy. Christians do it best when invited by Jewish families to participate, for Jews are delighted to reduce Christian ignorance of their observances.

There could be no celebration of the Great Eucharist in the spring without the Passover. Just as the cruel treatment of the Israelites in Egypt led to their deliverance, a symbol of the hoped-for liberation of Jews everywhere, so the Last Supper anticipated a redemptive death that led to life. Christians should remember the Jewish origins of their faith in gratitude this and every year, and not only when the reckoning of the paschal moon makes the two feasts coincide. The feasts mean liberty for both peoples. A *seder* is a joyous occasion for Jews. So are Maundy Thursday and Easter Day for Christians. While Good Friday is serious and solemn, it may not be lugubrious, as it has mistakenly been over many centuries.

> CHRISTIANS SHOULD REMEMBER THE JEWISH ORIGINS OF THEIR FAITH IN GRATITUDE THIS AND EVERY YEAR, AND NOT ONLY WHEN THE RECKONING OF THE PASCHAL MOON MAKES THE TWO FEASTS COINCIDE. THE FEASTS MEAN LIBERTY FOR BOTH PEOPLES.

RESPONSIVE READING

PSALM 116:1-2, 12-19 (RCL), 116:10, 12-13, 15-18 (RC), and PSALM 78:14-20, 23-25 (BCP)

Portions of Psalm 116 are sung in response to the Passover narrative of Exodus 12, first expressing love for God because the psalmist's petitions have been heard (vv. 1-2) but then responding to the divine bounty by "lifting up the cup of salvation" (v. 13). Surely a Last Supper reference is indicated by the church's choice, as is the phrase, "I will offer to you a thanksgiving sacrifice" (v. 17). All Christian prayer "calls on the name of the Lord" (vv. 13, 17) but the context of this evening's feast makes the call specific. The selection of Psalm 78 made by the BCP is equally specific with its mention of a "spread table" in verse 19, water gushing out of the rock (v. 20), and manna rained down as the "bread of angels" (v. 25)—a phrase long applied to the eucharistic food. Homilists should make a point of the text of the psalm in their respective churches because choirs and congregations are so often concentrated on the music that the hymn text escapes them. The refrain proposed in the RC *Lectionary for Mass* is "Our cup of blessing is a communion with the blood of Christ."

SECOND READING

1 CORINTHIANS 11:23-26 (RCL/RC), 11:12-26 (27-32) (BCP)

All three lectionaries fittingly choose 1 Corinthians 11:23-26 (27-32, BCP) as their second lection. St. Paul uses a familiar rabbinic formula for an item of tradition: "I received," in this case "from the Lord" meaning the church, the rite of the body and blood of the Lord and "I also handed [it] on to you" (v. 23; similarly 15:1 and in part 11:2). The apostle finds he has to remind the Corinthians strongly of the tradition he had first brought to them. The meal being commemorated took place on the eve of Jesus' being handed over. It was a heavily laden board but among its foods were bread—the "loaf" a pocket bread that modern Greek calls pita—and, of course, wine described as the "cup" (vv. 23, 25). The word of command of Jesus to repeat his action (v. 24; Luke 22:19) is better translated "memorial" than "remembrance," for a ritual act is being enjoined, not a mere calling to mind. The "new covenant in my blood" is new in the sense of a renewal of all former covenants, for as Paul says in another place "the gifts and the calling of God are irrevocable" (Rom. 11:29). Nothing of Israel's past is canceled for Christians, only completed. An exception is the observance of the "special laws" of the Mosaic code as a necessary complement to faith in the cross and resurrection, but then Jews have let many observances lapse. The newness of the covenant is the new deed of God done in Christ. In that sense only is it a fresh beginning like the various covenantal renewals that preceded it. It is unlike them because of the absolute newness of the redemptive act.

The eating and drinking of the body and blood that goes on over the ages is a proclamation of "the Lord's death until he come" (v. 26). For Paul, "death" or "cross" always means "and resurrection," just as "resurrection" always means "death" or "and the cross." He never uses both nouns together but his intent is clear each time. It is only he who speaks of the Lord's Supper as a rite in which believers "proclaim his death until he come." Such is the end-expectation of every Eucharist. Celebrated in the present, it never looks to the past alone. A Latin hymn, *O Sacrum Convivium,* puts it well: "O holy banquet in which Christ is consumed, the memorial of his passion celebrated, the spirit filled with grace, and a pledge of future glory given to us." That last phrase surely derives from Paul's phrase, "until he come"—the Lord's Supper as our assurance of being raised up on the Last Day. The "pledge" is the word translated as the "seal" of God's Spirit given in our hearts (2 Cor. 1:22).

Maundy Thursday is a bipolar feast for the many churches that commemorate the memorials of footwashing and the body and blood of Christ. It is also significant for the churches that bless the oils used in baptism, confirmation, and ordination symbolic of the universal priesthood of believers. It is everywhere celebrated joyously despite the knowledge of Jesus' upcoming passion and death. On this night worshipers receive the gifts of Jesus as servant of all (*doulos* in Jeremiah 13:16 is actually "slave") and the bread of life and cup of salvation as food for life's journey. They are required to discern the body—their relation to fellow believers—lest they eat and drink in an unworthy manner (1 Cor. 11:27-28). They may proceed to table and altar only if they know of no unreconciled difference with others (Matt. 5:23). In other words, a good conscience in the matter of justice to all is the sole qualification for celebrating the mystery of faith. On the previous Sunday and the one upcoming there may be some present who are there out of family tradition or social convention. Of their motives for celebrating so infrequently only God can say. No one is to be despised. All are to be praised for the measure of faith that brought them there. But the churches will be crowded. Praise God! The Maundy worshipers are fewer. They have had a hard day at work, some in school, a number uneventfully at home waiting for the evening. All deserve the finest ritual celebration and the best preaching a congregation is capable of.

GOOD FRIDAY

APRIL 21, 2000

REVISED COMMON	EPISCOPAL (BCP)	ROMAN CATHOLIC
Isa. 52:13—53:12	Isa. 52:13—53:12	Isa. 52:13—53:12
	or Gen. 22:1-8	
	or Wisd. 2:1, 12-24	
Ps. 22	Ps. 22:1-21 or 22:1-11	Ps. 31:2, 6, 12-13,
	or 40:1-14 or 69:1-23	15-17, 25
Heb. 10:16-25	Heb. 10:1-25	Heb. 4:14-16; 5:7-9
or Heb. 4:14-16; 5:7-9		
John 18:1—19:42	John 18:(1-40); 19:1-37	John 18:1—19:42

FROM EARLY DAYS, BELIEVERS SAW JESUS CHRIST on every page of the Bible. It would have been the Greek Bible, not the Hebrew. For the evangelist John, who set about writing what became Christian Scripture, that would have been the case. Paul and the evangelist Matthew would have known the Bible in Hebrew and Palestinian hearers the paraphrases in the Aramaic vernacular known as Targums. But know the Bible all did, and so, starting with the twenty-seven canonical books and through to the seventh century, the preachers and the teachers known as Church Fathers explored the First Testament in Greek. Some also had the Syriac or Coptic as their native tongue, later Latin and some gentiles Aramaic. In every case they found there the person of Christ in each word and story, precept and psalm.

FIRST READING

ISAIAH 52:13—53:12

Isaiah 52:13—53:12 is identified as the fourth Servant of the Lord Song. It was a special favorite among early Christians. Surprisingly, it is not quoted or paraphrased in the places we might expect it to be, the four passion narratives. 1 Peter 2:22 quotes Isaiah 53:9 and goes on to give the substance of verses 4-6 and 12 in the verses that follow, 23-25. St. Paul quotes 53:1, "Lord, who has believed our message?" in Romans at 10:16 and John 12:38 does the same. Matthew 8:17 is one of that Gospel's fulfillment quotations: "He took our infirmities and bore our diseases" (Isa. 53:4a). Another like it quotes Isaiah 42:1-14 as fulfilled in Matthew 12:17-21, while Matthew 27:30 may echo Isaiah 50:6. The widespread supposition is that when Paul wrote that "Christ died for our sins in accordance with the Scriptures" (1 Cor. 15:3), he had Isaiah 53:5-6 in mind. It speaks of an anonymous victim who was "crushed for our iniquities . . . [upon whom] was the punishment that made us whole and by [whose] bruises we were healed. . . . The Lord has laid on him the iniquities of us all." The Ethiopian eunuch of Acts 8:32-33 wondered who was being spoken of in Isaiah 53:7-8 but this is the author Luke's doing.

WISDOM 2:1, 12-24 (BCP)

Wisdom 2:1, 12-24, proposed by the BCP as another possible first lection is a passage Paul could have known just as well. It does not speak of a vicarious sufferer but of a righteous man who "professes to have knowledge of God and calls himself a servant/child of God" (2:13). "Let us test him with insult and torture," it goes on " . . . and make trial of his forbearance. Let us condemn him to a shameful death, for, according to what he says, he will be protected" (vv. 19-20). This is almost certainly a generic picture of the righteous Jew who has suffered obloquy at Jewish hands, even perhaps death at the hands of the pagans in the Maccabean uprising. Interestingly, the Dead Sea Scrolls cite the Isaiah passage almost not at all.

Can the Servant of the fourth and longest poem also be a generic figure? Or is it again the people Israel who are evidently the subject of the first three laments (see Isaiah 42:1-9; 49:1-7; 50:4-11)? Is he as some think the second Isaiah himself, the prophetic author of Isaiah 40–55? It does not matter whether the whole people or one representative figure is the speaker. A torture and death that is turned to the profit of the whole people is clearly the theme. It is no wonder that the New Testament writers sparingly and the Fathers copiously saw the sufferings of Jesus in the Servant Songs.

GENESIS 22:1-8 (BCP)

The BCP proposes another option for the first reading besides the one from Isaiah, namely, the "binding of Isaac" story of Genesis 22:1-8. The heartlessness of God's command is tempered somewhat by the story's outcome. We should remember that while it is a story, it is not only a story. It makes at least three points important to Israel: Abraham's obedience to a shocking divine command; his willingness to kill his only chance of an heir if God demands it; and, in light of the ram in the thicket (v. 13), the abhorrence in which God holds human sacrifice. Admittedly the brief tale, not proposed to be read in full, has many levels of understanding, none of them crystal clear. A point important to Christians derived from it is that God did, in fact, "put forward Christ Jesus as a sacrifice of atonement by his blood, effective through faith" (Rom. 3:24-25). The single Greek word for "a sacrifice of atonement" is *hilastērion*. In the Septuagint at Leviticus 16:14 it is translated the "mercy seat" (in Hebrew, *kipporeth*), the beaten gold cover of the ark on which Aaron sprinkled the blood of a goat in the rite that came to mark Yom Kippur. A further significance of the Isaac story to Christians is that Jesus is portrayed as the lamb that God provided (Gen. 22:8), first through the Baptist's pointing him out as such (John 2:29, 36) and then in Revelation 5:12; 6:1, and throughout as the Lamb who was slain. A secondary prefiguration is the son's carrying the wood for the sacrifice on his shoulder (Gen. 22:6), which patristic exegesis saw as a type of Jesus carrying his cross in obedience to his Father.

Homilists whose worship service is leisurely paced—it will be lengthy in any case if the cross is venerated and the two chapters of John are read—are well advised to speak briefly beforehand about the indignities heaped on the innocent, whether it be the servant or Jesus. They need to make clear that the human race is not redeemed by the psychological or physical sufferings of the Savior, intense though they were. Our faith is that we are ransomed from sin and death by Jesus' death and resurrection. The biblical code word for it is his "blood." That means his life obediently offered as a sacrifice on our behalf. The medieval West and all later Western piety made the mistake of concentrating on the torture he was subjected to, the terrible sufferings he endured. These were bad enough, but it was not they by which the world was saved. They were the outward symbol—real to be sure—of an inward reality. That reality was the life and death of the one human being who lived as all humans ought, namely, open to God's will for him at every moment of his life.

A misconceived theology of the redemption has taught that it was divinely decreed that Jesus should die in this shameful manner for our sakes. Another position equally hard to sustain is that he died in our place, understood to mean that the cruel indignities visited upon him should rightly have been ours for our sins. Jesus did die on our behalf but not in the substitutionary sense. God accepted his going to his death without a murmur except for his challenge to the blow on his face unjustly delivered (see John 18:21-23). Jesus' allowance of the inexorable chain of events was interpreted soon after his resurrection as obedience to the divine will. Had God and Jesus not permitted it, the cruel execution could not have happened. The homilist must take time to say in carefully prepared words, preferably before the Gospel reading, that humanity was saved not by hammer blows or a helmet of thorns beaten into his skull but by the spirit in which he endured it all. Revelation puts it well: "To him who loves us and freed us from our sins by his blood, and made us to be a kingdom of priests serving his God and Father, to him be glory and dominion forever and ever. Amen" (Rev. 1:5).

RESPONSIVE READING

PSALM 22 and PSALM 31

Psalm 22, in its entirety for RCL and in part for BCP, is a fitting sung response to the Isaian reading. The cry of forsakenness placed on Jesus' lips by Mark at 15:34a (paralleled in Matthew 27:46 but not found in Luke or John) begins the psalm. Several of its phrases turn up in the passion accounts. Thus, the mocking, jeering, and head-shaking of the psalmist's enemies in verse 7 is echoed by the passersby as Jesus hangs on the cross (Mark 15:29a followed by Matthew and Luke). The challenge of verse 8b, "let [the LORD] rescue the one in whom he delights," is quoted in Matthew 27:43. Verse 18 of the psalm about casting lots for the writer's garments becomes Matthew 27:35. The responsorial psalm in RC is 31:1-5, 11-12, 14-16, 24, and although it highlights the scorn of adversaries, it expresses unswerving trust in God. The refrain is "Father, I put my life in your hands" (cf. Psalm 31:6, 15; Luke 23:46).

> HUMANITY WAS SAVED NOT BY HAMMER BLOWS OR A HELMET OF THORNS BEATEN INTO HIS SKULL BUT BY THE SPIRIT IN WHICH HE ENDURED IT ALL.

SECOND READING

HEBREWS 4:14-16; 5:7-9 (RC)

Hebrews 4:14-16; 5:7-9 might better be read than the complete exchange between Jesus and Pilate in John's Gospel. Or, as will be suggested below, John 19:16-30 should be read as the gospel. It will convey the reality of Jesus' death more than adequately and not raise questions that would require great length to resolve. Hebrews proposes a satisfaction theology of salvation, a soteriology, by developing the idea of Jesus as our high priest. It declares him to be without sin but perfectly able to sympathize with our weakness because he has been tested in every way (14:15). The image of his passage through the heavens to the throne of grace situates him there making intercession for us. It also does more. It places us before that throne, boldly asking grace and mercy in our need. If Good Friday is to be "good" for us, as the catechisms say in answer to the question of what was good about a day in which Jesus died so cruel a death, it will be because we realize the power in our lives it led to.

Each of the Gospels contents itself with a phrase or two conveying his anguished cry from the cross. Hebrews is much more graphic in 5:7-9. There you have a description of the response of a sensitive human to the exquisite torture of execution. It elicited from Jesus loud cries, tears, prayers, supplications. In his dying he was remembered as a person weak as any human creature, not stoic, not expecting deliverance at God's hands as so often before, but begging relief from the eventuality of death. The prayer of this obedient man was made in total submission (*'islām* in Arabic), and for that reason was answered by God as so many of our prayers are, quite oppositely to the way he framed it. What came instead was the death that Jesus asked to avoid. But his obedience on that tree brought him perfection in God's sight. He was what God would have all of us be, a good son or daughter of a Father who wishes only what is good for us. Jesus' disposition in the midst of that chaotic scene with its shouts of the executioners, the wailing of women in the crowd, the stunned silence of the diaspora pilgrims who could not know who these three were or what the Romans had against them: all this horror and confusion the divine alchemy turned into "the source of eternal salvation for all who obey him" (v. 9).

Gospel
JOHN 18:1—19:42

Pilate, said John, let the title he had ordered placed over Jesus' head stand: "Jesus of Nazareth, King of Judea" (19:19). His refusal to change the wording entered into the literature, the preaching, and the language of the West: "What I have written I have written" (v. 22). The author of Hebrews knew in faith, indeed might have been born into an Alexandrian family that already believed it, that since the Temple was down and the priesthood dispersed, God had constituted a Jewish layman as high priest for all humanity. Made perfect through suffering, he offers prayers and intercessions for us in the heavenly sanctuary over all the ages. Our baptism has enabled us to join with him in this priestly liturgy for we, like Israel, are "a chosen race, a royal priesthood, a holy nation, God's own people" (1 Pet. 2:9; see Exod. 19:6).

The Germanic language calls this day *Karfreitag,* perhaps from an old Germanic root meaning "hard." Jesus did indeed die hard to win for us the softest, gentlest treasure: life through him and with him and in him. We said above that a complete reading of John 18:1—19:42 was pastorally unwise unless a homilist has long been schooling a congregation in the Gospel's mode of argument and symbolic phrasing. "King of Judea" is as good a rendering of the Greek and probably better than "King of the Jews," just as the Greek language would say "land of the Hellenes" for Hellas (the Roman Graecia) and so on for other peoples and their lands. John's Gospel almost always has two meanings for everything it says. Jesus was summoned before the Roman prefect at the urging of the Temple priesthood, it reports. It then speculates, correctly it would seem, on the mentality that foresaw the possibility of the Romans coming to "destroy both our holy place and our nation" unless Jesus is eliminated (11:48-50). After all, he consistently predicted the Temple's utter destruction (2:19; Mark 14:58; 15:29). John has Pilate order a placard made declaring Jesus, with a sneer, "King of Judea." The province had not had one since Herod Archelaus was deposed some twenty-five years before. The evangelist's faith understands the phrase to mean king over all Jews, including the Jews at whose hands his Jews were suffering. In this Gospel, "the Jews" usually mean "the Jews opposed to the Jews of John's community." Since the phrase is too long to say each time the word occurs, and when "the Jews" does not mean simply the Jews of Judea, the normal Good Friday congregation may well suppose as Christians have for centuries that Jews were primarily responsible for Jesus' death. In fact, most in the crowd at Calvary were undoubtedly sympathetic to these three new victims of Roman oppression. Many were Galilean followers of Jesus in particular who had heard his words and witnessed his deeds. This makes nonsense of a theme beloved of preachers that the crowds who welcomed him as he entered the city turned on him five days later. The idea is the bitter fruit of centuries of Christian anti-Judaism. Its sole basis is the mob outcry that accompanied this public execution, "Crucify him." Witness the vengeful faces on television of the crowd waiting to cheer the needle's plunge into the condemned man's arm. The Texans? The Louisianans? Scarcely.

John does in these two chapters what he has done throughout. He frames an exchange based on his knowledge of the outcome. All the rest is of his invention. It is thoroughly unlikely that any partisans of Jesus could have been present at the trial and sentencing. Pilate here stands for the "world" of previous discourses placed on Jesus' lips (see 1:10; 7:7; 8:23; 14:22; 15:18; 16:8; 17:14), a world hostile to the Jesus represented by John's community. When Pilate asks scornfully, "What is truth?" (18:38), this is not the jest of Lord Bacon's remembered phrase. It is the summit of Johannine irony. Truth itself (14:6) is standing before him and he does not recognize him. The dialogue is an exposition of the kingship of Jesus constituted by his testimony to the truth (18:47). The functionary of empire (19:12) has no part in this rule, only coercive political power. Pilate's weak capitulation ("he handed him over to them to be crucified," 19:16) and the reasonableness of the questioning that leads up to it are part of the Gospel tradition which exculpates this cruel man. His character is well known to history from Josephus' *Antiquities*. The tradition on Pilate that reaches the Gospels probably derives from the horror of Jesus' followers that the holiest officials in Israel, the temple priests, could be so perverted in their advocacy. Not even the hated pagan power could have acted as Caiaphas and his associates did, they thought. It is all a construct and a powerful one but it has left an unfortunate impress on the Christian centuries: Pilate the protagonist of Jesus, the priests and elders his enemies. The evangelist's greater success, however, is his portrayal of Jesus who puts Pilate on trial. The claim, "We have no king but Caesar" ("the emperor" in the weaker RSV rendering) has provided a watchword for all who would choose expediency over truth, political power over justice. The "world" is clearly no match for the power of Jesus' person and his word.

The remainder of chapter 19 is a series of memorable vignettes: the soldiers dicing for Jesus' seamless tunic, a garment made symbolic by the evangelist's art; Jesus' mother standing near; his committing his mother—the symbolic "Woman" of the Cana colloquy—to the care of the equally symbolic disciple of his special love; the breaking of Jesus' legs to hasten a victim's death seen as the fulfillment of Psalm 34:20, but even more, the injunction that no bone of the Passover lamb be broken (Exod. 12:46); the spear-thrust reminiscent of the similar treatment of a victim in Zechariah 12:10, but here seen as bringing forth blood and water, symbolic of exactly what is unclear (baptismal water and eucharistic blood?); and the rehabilitation of the once fearful and obtuse Nicodemus.

The pastoral wisdom of reading or singing only 19:16-42 in the Good Friday service, mentioned above, eliminates the possibility of creating in the minds of worshipers a wrong idea of the factuality of Pilate's speech and conduct and the behavior of the crowd. Neither is likely to have occurred quite as described. John possesses certain reminiscences in written form which he reworks. They are doubtless already embellishments, as we know from the other Gospels. He theologizes them further in his uniquely clever way. Few homilists have the time to spell out John's literary technique nor is today's prayer the time to do it. The latter half of chapter 19 in its stark succinctness conveys the manner of Jesus' death and the supposition of those who mourned him most that his entombment spelled the end of their hopes. It by no means spells the end of our hopes. His body's repose in "a new tomb in which no one had ever been laid" (19:41) was required to establish that he was really dead, not such in appearance. And, in fact, the Saturday that followed has a long history as a day on which there was no liturgical observance, not even the Communion service that was celebrated on Friday with its consecrated breads from Thursday's eucharistic celebration carried in procession. On that day the accompanying medieval hymn was *Pange Lingua* ("Sing, My Tongue, the Savior's Glory"), on Friday *Vexilla Regis Prodeunt* ("The Royal Banners Forward Go"). Certain customs have sprung up in Europe and been brought to churches in the Americas to mark the day of the dead, Jesus' burial. They respond to the fact that even though liturgically nothing is done, something must be done. And so an image of Jesus' body in the sleep of death is laid before an altar stripped bare of linens, the nearby tabernacle door open and the sacred vessels containing the Holy Bread elsewhere in an "altar of repose." This cry for realism by peoples whose sense of symbol has been weakened by centuries of pulpit silence on the nature of Christian symbolism is understandable.

This writer pulled open the curtain of a side chapel in the church in Palma, Mallorca, that has the body of native son Fray Junípero Serra and discovered a life-sized image of a mechanical foal of an ass with an image of Jesus astride it, for use once a year in procession. We do ill to deplore the practice of planting kisses on or touching the image of a human corpse. That may be because death, and their death, means so much less to us than to the people who do it.

THE GREAT VIGIL
OF EASTER
HOLY SATURDAY

APRIL 22, 2000

REVISED COMMON	EPISCOPAL (BCP)	ROMAN CATHOLIC
Gen. 1:1—2:4a	Gen. 1:1—2:2	Gen. 1:1—2:2 or 1:1, 26-31

Gen. 7:1-5, 11-18;
  8:6-18; 9:8-13
	Gen. 7:1-5, 11-18;
	  8:6-18; 9:8-13	

Gen. 22:1-18	Gen. 22:1-18	Gen. 22:1-18 or 22:1-2, 9-13, 15-18
Exod. 14:10-31; 15:20-21	Exod. 14:10—15:1	Exod. 14:15—15:1
	Isa. 4:2-6	Isa. 54:5-14
Isa. 55:1-11	Isa. 55:1-11	Isa. 55:1-11

Bar. 3:9-15, 32—4:4
  or Prov. 8:1-8, 19-21;
  9:4b-6
	Bar. 3:9-15, 32—4:4	Bar. 3:9-15; 32—4:4

Ezek. 36:24-28	Ezek. 36:24-28	Ezek. 36:16-28
Ezek. 37:1-14	Ezek. 37:1-14	
Zeph. 3:14-20	Zeph. 3:12-20	
Ps. 114	Ps. 114	Pss. 118:1-2, 16-17, 22-23
Rom. 6:3-11	Rom. 6:3-11	Rom. 6:3-11
Mark 16:1-8	Matt. 28:1-10	Mark 16:1-8

IT IS ESPECIALLY IMPORTANT THAT THESE READINGS be done well, whether out of doors around the blazing New Fire of Easter, within the church vestibule, or in the church itself. A brief introduction should suffice, not words between each reading. But the church's intent in proposing these selections must be made clear. Their original setting was prayer through the night in which people were kept awake by listening to the Bible and singing psalms. The Roman Rite had twelve such readings up until 1951/1955 while the previous Greek and Syriac liturgies employed many more. As can be seen above, they are reduced to ten and seven, respectively. The BCP departs from RC more usually than does RCL, for example, in its choice of Matthew for this night. The theme that runs through all three is God's concern for the people Israel in the world that came from God's creative word. The concern takes the form of rescue or deliverance, often through or by water. Traditionally, this was the night when candidates, long and well prepared, received the bath of baptism and chrismation and proceeded to the Lord's Supper for the first time. It is the same in congregations throughout the world today. They and the whole assembly are open to hearing again the stories of God's providential care of the Jewish people that will culminate in the reminder of the Jew Paul to the Church in Rome of what it means to Jew and gentile alike to be alive to God in Christ Jesus. Faith and baptism are what accomplish it, a rising from a former life to a new life with the Risen One.

The poetic triumph which is the creation story comes first (Gen. 1:1—2:2 [RCL to 4a]). God effortlessly creates the earth as we know it where a formless void and darkness had been. The winds that had swept over the face of the waters is stilled and they are separated into those above and beneath. Like any observant Jew, God rests on the Sabbath, the very reason the framework of a week was chosen. God sees the work as good and very good. The *Roman Missal* of 1570 had as its second reading all of Genesis 6 and edited versions of 7 and 8. RCL and BCP opt for retaining the story of the flood and adding the Noachide covenant with the rainbow as its sign. The Hebrews could not imagine the rest of the human race without a covenant like theirs which God gave to Abraham, so they provided the gentiles ("all flesh") with one. The rescue of Noah and his family of seven was achieved by the receding of the waters (Gen. 8:6-14), a point made by 1 Peter 3:20-22 with respect to baptism. But God makes a solemn promise to Noah that he will be reminded of the covenant by the rainbow and that the waters shall never again destroy all flesh (Gen. 9:15-17). This night's rites of baptism and eucharist are a celebrating of covenant renewal. RC goes from the creation narrative to the account of Abraham's not sparing his only first-born son in obedience to the terrifying divine command. It ends with a blessing delivered by an angel and the promise of covenant renewal via Abraham's offspring. St. Paul will understand this collective noun "seed" to be singular by identifying Christ as the offspring (Gal. 3:16). God's faithfulness to a promise earlier made when Abraham and Sarah were without hope of a child is what is important here. Every reading is a story of the divine fidelity.

RCL and BCP go next to deliverance (Exod. 14:13) from the waters of the sea which is not here identified. God's total unconcern for the fate of Pharaoh's charioteers, like the Egyptians in their houses a little earlier, is the stuff of saga—and saga understood literally is misunderstood. Rescue as from water is what matters here in contrast to destruction by water. BCP's next choice is Isaiah 4:2-6, a cryptic poem about the Lord's glory as shelter and protection for the survivors of

Israel who remain in Zion, probably after the judgment represented by the incursion of Assyria. The "Branch of the Lord" (v. 2) is that Davidic descendant who will be described by the word "branch" in Jeremiah 23:5 and Zechariah 3:8; 6:12. RC for its part has Isaiah 54:5-14 for the fifth reading, no doubt because the Lord is called Israel's redeemer on this night that celebrates human redemption. In later Jewish marriage practice a cast-off wife may never be reclaimed as one's spouse (see Deut. 24:4), whereas here and elsewhere in the books of the prophets a compassionate God as husband (Isa. 54:5) will take back the briefly abandoned Israel. The three lectionaries read Isaiah 55:1-11 this night because of its invitation to eat rich food: "Come, buy wine and milk without money and without price." It is a figure for the Lord's word which shall not return to the heavens empty. Like the rain and snow it gives seed to the sower and bread to the eater. Not only bread but wine and milk mixed with honey was given to the newly baptized in some early liturgies.

A reading from the deuterocanonical Baruch may come as an emotional stumbling block for pastors and people who know that it isn't in their Bible, but the beauty of this hymn in praise of Wisdom may help them overcome their scruple. This substitution of Wisdom for Torah in the later books of the Bible prepares the newly baptized to embrace Christ, the Wisdom of God (Rom. 1:24; Luke 11:49). The RCL proposes the familiar Proverbs 8–9 as an alternative to the wordier reading in praise of wisdom (prudence, good sense) and has in common with Isaiah 55:1 the invitation; "Come, eat of my food and drink of the wine I have mixed" (Prov. 9:5).

The Ezekiel reading promises the exiled Judah a new heart and a new spirit (36:26; cf. Jer. 31:33). This passage has been chosen perhaps primarily because of the baptism that will occur at the Easter Vigil: "I will sprinkle clean water upon you, and you shall be clean from all your uncleannesses" (Ezek. 36:25). The longer and better known passage on the many dry bones lying in the middle of a valley (Ezek. 37:1-14), which the LORD God told the prophet to address, is a prophecy in parable for a people in exile. Ezekiel was there in Babylon when he wrote it. Just as Judah will be restored to life by God's power despite its temporary loss of hope, so the adult candidates for baptism and those called to resume baptismal life in a Christian communion will hear on this night: "I will put my spirit within you and you shall live" (v. 14a). Zephaniah 3:14-20 (12-20, BCP) is the conclusion of a book written by Jeremiah's predecessor who predicted a day of judgment for Jerusalem because of its return to idolatrous practice. The remnant he praised—a people in whose mouths no deceit is found, "nor shall they do any wrong" (v. 13)—describes both the neophytes of tonight's Vigil and the long baptized who are the reconciled sinners of Easter's joyous feast (v. 14). The LORD has brought them home (v. 20a).

RCL and BCP sing Psalm 114 as a transition from the rite of baptism (and chrismation if it is administered) to the readings from Paul and Mark and the paschal Eucharist. It is a fitting song of Easter joy even if no new members enter the church via its local congregation. Still, the reason for its selection is clear: "The sea looked and fled" when Israel went out from Egypt; "Jordan turned back." Why do the mountains skip like rams? The earth is "in the presence of the God of Jacob who turns the rock into a pool of water, the flint into a spring." The baptismal font may be of metal or ceramic, not stone, but that is the rock from which the water flows this night. RC quarries six verses out of Psalm 118's twenty hymning the victory of life over death, a deed of the Lord's doing. "This [Easter] is the day the Lord has made."[18]

The baptism into the Lord's death that St. Paul features in Romans 6:3-11, a baptism that he himself received (v. 3), indicates immersion in the waters. Otherwise, the figure of burial in them and rising from them to new life would not make sense. Walking in that newness looks to a future resurrection with Christ (vv. 4-5). The "body of sin" is the old self crucified with him to bring an end to sin's grip, here called enslavement. The death Jesus died was a death not to his own sin but to an era of sin he had left behind as a member of a sinful race. That death to sin was final and so is it meant to be for believers in him. But Paul is a realist. He knows the tragic possibility of a fall subsequent to baptism. He therefore speaks, if sparingly, of "repentance" (Rom. 2:4; 2 Cor. 7:9). It is the proper stance for full and complete participation in the mystery of the sacred Pasch. The original conclusion to the Gospel of Mark has been commented on under Passion/Palm Sunday. "He is raised; he is not here" (16:6) is the reason for "all this juice, all this joy." Chicks pecking out of their rock shell! Rabbits proliferating madly! Everywhere new life! Proclaim it. Do not fear to do so.

> THE DEATH JESUS DIED WAS A DEATH NOT TO HIS OWN SIN BUT TO AN ERA OF SIN HE HAD LEFT BEHIND AS A MEMBER OF A SINFUL RACE. THAT DEATH TO SIN WAS FINAL AND SO IS IT MEANT TO BE FOR BELIEVERS IN HIM.

Is a homily in order after all this ritual behavior and many words? Yes, if it is brief—five to seven minutes—and makes a single point. That point must be the joy of having risen with Christ to a new life in baptism. Some churches baptize in full view within the eucharistic rite. That can take a while if the adult candidates are many or, if not they, then the numbers resuming active faith, whatever had been the church of their infant or adolescent baptism. These same churches tend to put to all the worshipers the threefold question about faith in God, Father, Son, and Holy Spirit—the Apostles' Creed in its early interrogative form.

The assembled worshipers are fittingly asked to reaffirm the Easter faith by which they are justified, made right in God's sight through union with Christ crucified and risen.

NOTES

1. John Walter Tyrer, *Historical Survey of Holy Week: Its Services and Ceremonial* (London: Oxford Univ. Press, 1932).

2. Cyril C. Richardson, ed., "Letters of Ignatius: Magnesians, 9.1-2" in *Early Christian Fathers* (New York: Macmillan, 1970), 96.

3. Ibid., 14.1, 178.

4. Ibid., 67, 287.

5. *The Apostolic Tradition of Hippolytus* I, 2, trans. Burton Scott Easton (New York: Archon, 1962), 33.

6. Ibid., VI, 1. Cited in Jean Daniélou, *The Bible and the Liturgy* (Notre Dame, Ind.: University of Notre Dame Press, 1956), 260.

7. Edgar Hennecke, "Epistula Apostolorum," in *New Testament Apocrypha*, ed. Wilhelm Schneemelcher (Philadelphia: Westminster, 1963), 1:199.

8. *Peri Pascha,* trans. S. G. Hall (Oxford: Oxford Early Christian Texts, 1979).

9. See Frank C. Senn, *Christian Liturgy, Catholic and Evangelical* (Minneapolis: Fortress, 1997), 90–91. On the Lord's Day, see pp. 86–89, 156–57.

10. *Corpus Christianorum, Series Latina* 175:17. The entire travel record is found on pp. 1–26.

11. *St. Cyril of Jerusalem's Lectures on the Christian Sacraments: The Protocatechesis and the Five Mystagogical Catecheses,* ed. F. L. Cross (London: S.P.C.K., 1951).

12. *Egeria's Travels,* ed. John Wilkinson (London: S.P.C.K., 1971).

13. *Le Codex Arménien Jérusalem 121,* ed. Athanase Renoux, *Patrologia Orientalis* 35:1; 36:2 (Turnhout: Brepols, 1969–71).

14. Ibid., 38.1-2.

15. Thomas Talley, *The Origins of the Liturgical Year* (New York: Pueblo, 1986), 182f.

16. Paul W. F. Harms, "When You Are Thinking Procession"; Gerard S. Sloyan, "A Plea for Unadulterated Joy"; Shawn Madigan, "Palm Sunday, Passion Sunday: Balancing the Readings"; Thomas H. Troeger, "The Dangers of Shouting 'Hosanna,'" in *Liturgy,* 12/4 (1995).

17. Gerard S. Sloyan, *The Crucifixion of Jesus: History, Myth, Faith* (Minneapolis: Fortress, 1995), 169.

18. S. Marian Bohen, O.S.U., "Studying the Lectionary" in *Homily Service,* 32/1 (April, 1999): 30, a publication of the Liturgical Conference (n. 16 above).